Spiritualist Healers In Mexico

Successes and Failures of Alternative Therapeutics

Kaja Finkler

University of North Carolina

Foreword by Arthur Kleinman

Sheffield Publishing Company

Salem, Wisconsin

For information about this book, write or call:
Sheffield Publishing Company
P.O. Box 359
Salem, Wisconsin 53168
(414) 843-2281

In Memory of My Mother

ISBN 1-879215-24-1

Printed in the United States of America

7 6 5 4 3 2

CONTENTS

List of Tables and Figures   iv

Foreword by Arthur Kleinman   v

1994 Preface   vii

Preface   xiii

1. Introduction   1

2. Spiritualism as a Religion   13

3. Ecological Considerations   35

4. Therapeutic Options   41

5. Illness Etiologies   48

6. Patients and Their Patterns of Resort   57

7. Spiritualist Healing Techniques   82

8. Spiritualist Therapeutic Outcomes   117

9. How Spiritualist Healers Heal   157

10. The Social Consequences of Wellness   184

11. Conclusion   193

Appendices

    A. Methodologies Used in the Study   200

    B. Regional Plants Used by Spiritualist Healers   205

    C. Miscellaneous Botanicals Used by Spiritualist Healers   218

    D. Principal Causes of Morbidity...State of Hidalgo   223

Notes   224

Bibliography   228

Glossary   243

Index   245

LIST OF TABLES

Table

4.1 Therapeutic Options 47

5.1 Traditional Categories of Illness Attribution 55–56

6.1 Pattern of Resort by Habitual Temple Users 75–76

6.2 Complaints Cited by Patients at the Temple 77

6.3 Personal Problems Presented to Spiritualist Healers 77

6.4 Patients' Complaints Presented to a Physician as Diagnosed by the Physician and Self-Diagnosed by Patients............. 78

6.5 CMI Score Results for Temple (First Comers and Habitual Temple Users) and Doctor Groups 78

6.6 Years of Schooling—Temple and Doctor Patients 79

6.7 Treatment Seeking Decisions in Male Headed Households . 79

8.1 Outcomes of Treatment at Spiritualist Temples Based Upon Follow-up Interviews 139

8.2 Successfully Treated Cases in a Spiritualist Temple 140–144

8.3 Comparison of CMI Scores for Patients Reporting Successful Treatment Outcomes and Patients Reporting Unsuccessful Treatment Outcomes 145

8.4 Regulars Treated at Spiritualist Temple 146–151

8.5 Mean CMI Scores of Regulars, Non-Regulars and Controls Along Sex Lines 152

8.6 Mean CMI Scores of Spiritualists and Professed Orthodox Catholics Along Sex Lines 152

LIST OF FIGURES

Figure

6.1 CMI Scores Male-Doctor-Non-Regular Groups 80
6.2 CMI Scores Female-Doctor-Non-Regular Groups 81
8.1 CMI Scores Male-Non-Regular-Regular-Controls 153
8.2 CMI Scores Female-Non-Regular-Regular-Controls 154
8.3 CMI Scores Male-Regular and Doctor Groups 155
8.4 CMI Scores Female Regular and Doctor Groups 156

FOREWORD

Kaja Finkler offers one of the more detailed medical anthropological accounts of a traditional healing system; one of the few that seeks to systematically assess outcome. This is what I take to be the book's core contribution: an intensive investigation of the successes and failures of Spiritualist healing in a rural Mexican setting.

To achieve this end, Finkler provides the reader with requisite knowledge concerning Spiritualism in Mexico, the Spiritualist center she studied, and much of medical anthropology that is pertinent to understand healing. The last includes an impressively wide array of issues, from the health ecology of the valley she studied, to the physiological, psychological and social problems of different patient groups and including material, interpersonal and symbolic dimensions of this Spiritualist center's healing techniques.

The reader is drawn deeper and deeper into the nexus of healing, beginning with the types of problems brought to Spiritualist healers and ending both with interpretations of how spiritualists heal and, quite originally, with an account of the social consequences of wellness. Finkler's methodology combines qualitative ethnographic techniques with more quantitative measurements of symptom levels and perceived change in illness. Her theoretical framework is equally as broad, emphasizing biopsychocultural interactions in illness and care.

Finkler's familiarity with the relevant literatures in biomedicine, psychiatry and other medical social sciences is one of the great strengths of the new body of clinically applied studies in medical anthropology. Like other of these studies she situates her analyses in several distinctive academic discourses and illustrates the utility of cross–disciplinary problem frameworks and solution frameworks. She aims to reach several audiences, not least of which are health care planners who are struggling to work out ways of relating traditional healers to biomedicine.

The World Health Organization has set this as the agenda for health care systems in developing societies, but unlike most WHO programs it has not set out guidelines based on empirical studies indicating the more useful and the more problematic ways of organizing such relationships. Finkler's study is important precisely because it provides empirical evidence of the types of problems traditional healers seem to deal with more effectively—somatization, limited psychiatric disorder, relatively mild medical problems; and those conditions—severe psychiatric and medical disorders—for which they seem much less effective. Finkler's findings are significant because they document that it is possible to predict which kinds of conditions are more and which less likely to improve in traditional healing. She debunks the romantic myth of the omnicompetent and always effective folk healer, by demonstrating that many patients fail to improve, and by exploring the physiological and psychosocial barriers to effective outcome. Her picture of the traditional healing system she studied as complementary to biomedicine fits in with a long tradition of studies that demonstrate such functional complementarity, but its evidence is more convincing than many other accounts.

All in all this is a valuable contribution to medical anthropology that deserves close attention from scholars interested in cross–cultural comparisons of the healing process. In a relatively short space it covers most of the major questions, offers new information against which some of the leading hypotheses can be evaluated, and encourages a synthesis of anthropological, psychiatric and public health, analyses of outcome. The interdisciplinary analysis of symbolic healing is especially innovative and will provoke responses from many categories of readers. The bibliography itself is a testament to this anthropologist's marvelous grasp of the many literatures that are relevant to the cultural discourse on healing. This is a real anthropological contribution to international health.

Arthur Kleinman
Professor of Medical Anthropology
and Psychiatry, Harvard

1994 PREFACE

There has been a surge of interest in alternative healing in the United States, as evidenced by the National Institutes of Health's opening the Office of Alternative Medicine in 1993 to promote studies of alternative medical practices and their efficacy.

Seventeen years have passed since I studied Spiritualist healing, one of many viable alternative healing regimens, and analyzed their successes and failures. At the time of my study, empirical research of this type was rare in the social sciences, and it continues to be so, although theorizing is common about the phenomenology of religious healing.

At the time of its publication, the book was innovative on several grounds. It combined a positivist analysis of how Spiritualist cures heal with the experiential aspects of the healing process. This was done by providing patients' perceptions and narratives of their sickness and its alleviation. Thus, the book provided "thick description" as well as a scientific analysis of Spiritualist beliefs and practices. By so doing I attempted to translate Spiritualist understandings into our Western comprehensions of the healing process, using physiological, psychological, cultural and sociological paradigms. The two types of analyses remain, however, clearly separated.

The work was innovative also because it identified not only the culture-bound syndromes that are usually regarded as the domain of traditional healers, but also the specific symptomatologies for which patients seek treatment from the healers. Moreover, we learn about different kinds of patients seeking treatment from traditional healers, disclosing the often overlooked fact that traditional healers do not treat an undifferentiated mass of the "folk."

While my concern at the time was with issues relating to the healing process and efficacy of traditional healing, the book reveals the important role women play in alternative healing.

Prior to its publication, the book was disconcerting to scholars who tended to idealize alternative healing of the spiritualist kind as faultless and flawless. For example, I had been taken to task by an anonymous reviewer, who felt that the book was doing a disservice to anthropologists working in developing nations, on the grounds that anthropologists would not be permitted to carry out research in developing nations if they presented the healers' failures. In short, traditional healers were to be presented in an ideal light, as anthropologists were wont to do.

I return to the Spiritualist temple in Juarez almost annually. During the past seventeen years Mexico has undergone an economic crisis and it has become part of the globalized Western economy. But Spiritualism has proliferated, as I predicted it would, and I watch it grow from year to year. The number of healers has increased in the Juarez temple alone from 8, at the time of the study, to 24 women working two shifts, on my last visit in the summer of 1993. The physical size of the temple tripled during a decade. The people I described in the book continue to do their work in the temple, including the head of the temple. They continue to fulfill their Spiritualist tasks: to heal others and thereby to heal themselves.

The book generated myriad research proposals, papers and dissertations. In fact, one economist[1], using this work, analyzed the data presented from an economic perspective, and wrote her dissertation on the economic aspects of Spiritualist healing. While the book stimulated research by others, it also informed my subsequent studies of biomedicine and of gender and health.

The findings that patients seeking treatment from Spiritualist healers usually did so after having been treated unsuccessfully by physicians led me subsequently to carry out a two-year investigation of biomedical practice in Mexico. I questioned why biomedical treatment failed to alleviate patients' non-life-threatening symptomatologies of the type that are also presented to Spiritualist healers.

The study of biomedical practice and patients' response[2] deepened my understanding of both Spiritualist healing and biomedicine. My comparison of both systems[3] revealed new dimensions of Spiritualist healing.

Even a synoptic view of Spiritualist healing reveals that Spiritualism and biomedicine diverge along many dimensions. Spiritualism is embedded in a sacred world while biomedicine is sanctioned by secular science. Biomedicine is a professional system staffed by professionals with years of formal training and legitimated by the state, whereas

Spiritualist healers are folk practitioners, lacking formal academies, academic preparation and state legitimation. The two systems are rooted in disparate realities and distinct epistemologies. Notwithstanding these differences, the two healing regimens become unified in day to day life by the people who resort to them. Unlike academicians, who regard the two healing systems as diametrically opposed and in competition, the people who seek treatment do not distinguish the profound epistemological differences between sacred healing, such as Spiritualism, and biomedicine. In their search for the alleviation of pain, pragmatism prevails; people judge the treatments they are given by their effects. They look toward those who provide them with the best medicine for a given sickness episode.

My comparison of Spiritualist healing with biomedicine brought into bold relief several dimensions of Spiritualist practices in addition to the importance of healing symbols for the therapeutic process that I emphasize in the book. Spiritualist healers, unlike physicians, confer coherent, parsimonious and unchanging etiological explanations. Spiritualist etiological understandings are reduced to a few explanations, whereas physicians' complex disease attributions are confusing and inaccessible to patients' understandings.

From the standpoint of good biomedical practice, a physician is required to test hypotheses and revise diagnoses according to empirical observations and the patient's response to the prescribed treatment, but from the patient's perspective, diagnostic revisions are puzzling and distressing. Unlike physicians, Spiritualist healers draw on a limited diagnostic repertoire and eschew multiple diagnoses for the same symptoms.

Most important, while a physician's clinical judgment entails uncertainty and is grounded in a process of exclusion, the Spiritualist healers' spirits treat patients with great *certainty*. Spiritualist healers are as sure of their diagnoses and course of cure as patients are certain of their pain. Spiritualist healers do not doubt that the spirits possessing their bodies in "the service of mankind" are omniscient, that the spirits know the person's pain and the required cure.

Spiritualist healing techniques require patients' participation in his or her cure, including the fact that patients are required to have faith in their ministrations, unlike physicians who take credit for successful treatment.

Significantly, too, while the physician must cast the patient's sickness in a temporal frame and localize the pain in a specific part of the body to make an accurate diagnosis, the omniscient and omnipotent spirits transcend time and space in the same way that the patient's sickness transcends temporal and spatial dimensions. The patient's major concern is that the healer or physician know his or her pain. When the patient confronts a Spiritualist healer, he or she need not tell the healer very much for the healer to know everything, because the healer's spirit protectors are omniscient.

But perhaps most important for those who become adherents and regulars, Spiritualist healing, unlike biomedicine, opens avenues for people to transform their lives by incorporating them into a community of persons who have suffered pain. As members of this community they experience the sacred that assists them to transcend their symptomatologies and minimize their suffering. The biomedical tool kit lacks channels that potentially can divert the patient into a similar transformation that will minimize non-life-threatening symptomatologies.

In this book I emphasize the power of symbols in the healing process and it has been shown that biomedicine too relies on healing symbols. However, my subsequent research has persuaded me that to effect patients' perceived recovery healers need to use appropriate symbols, but people's lives must also be transformed. Spiritualists accomplish this transformation when they incorporate individuals into their temples as functionaries and healers. And the transformative process in and of itself is as powerful an aspect of healing as are symbols associated with it.

The study of Spiritualist healers disclosed that women predominate both as patients and as healers. This finding led me to focus on issues pertaining to gender and health. The fact that the majority of the healers are recruited as a consequence of an affliction and that they are also women led me to raise the important question of why so many more women than men sought treatment from the healers. During the past decade I have devoted my attention to studying the relationship between gender and health, resulting in my most recent work, *Women in Pain.*[4]

During the past decade I have rethought the concept of somatization that I discuss in the book and I have become dissatisfied with it for at least two important reasons. First because the concept of somatization is a biomedically defined one. By this I mean that a patient is assessed as a somatizer when biomedicine cannot find any physiological dysfunction. It carries a "blame the victim" load.

Second, I eschew the notion of somatization because it is rooted in a mind-body dualism that I wish to avoid. Somatization suggests that psychological difficulties become converted into somatic dysfunction, that somehow they lack a reality. In my later work I have introduced the notion of *life's lesions* by which I mean the perceived adversities of existence, including inimical social relationships, and unresolved contradictions in which a person is entrenched and which gnaw at his or her being. Life's lesions can be as virulent as any virus. They become inscribed on the body and manifested in anguish, in generalized pain experienced in the entire body, and in non-life-threatening symptomatologies of the type brought to Spiritualist healers and which physicians often fail to heal. The people seeking treatment from Spiritualist healers have experienced life's lesions, unlike those in the control group who are discussed in the book. The biomedical script fails to incorporate life's lesions in making clinical judgments.

The research and analysis presented in the book led me then to conclude that quantitative methodologies are inadequate for the study of the healing process. In subsequent studies I combined both quantitative and qualitative methodologies but I became convinced more than ever that to comprehend the experience of pain and its alleviation, we must attend to the patient's personal narratives and understandings. As anthropologists we have admonished biomedicine and its practitioners for reifying the patient, but we frequently forget that our theorizing often results in similar reifications.

Kaja Finkler
Chapel Hill, NC

1. See Lenihan, Bonnie J. "The Economic Development Implications of Informal Sector Health Care." A dissertation presented for the Ph.D. The University of Tennessee, Knoxville, 1990.
2. See Finkler, K. *Physicians at Work, Patients in Pain*. Westview Press, 1991.
3. See Finkler, K. "Sacred and Biomedical Healing Compared" in *Medical Anthropological Quarterly* 8(2), 1994.
4. See Finkler, K. *Women in Pain*. University of Pennsylvania Press, 1994.

PREFACE

I became interested in Mexican Spiritualism through occasional visits to Spiritualist temples in rural Mexico. My friends and neighbors would ask me to drive them to a Spiritualist temple, and I still recall my astonishment upon first entering such an establishment. I was confronted by a sea of people of all ages, sitting patiently waiting to be received by one of several healers, and I watched the healers from a distance in turn attending to them. The healers were dressed in white robes, and were sitting side by side in trance in a small windowless alcove that smelled of incense. I wondered that so many people were there, and whether the ministrations would successfully deal with the litany of symptoms they presented.

During encounters with local physicians I mentioned these visits to the healers. Their uniform response was that "those quacks" interfered with good medical practice. The doctors lamented the ignorance of "those people" who consult nonbiomedical practitioners. Invariably, they claimed that by the time these patients sought their advice they were too sick to be helped. "Those people" referred to the relatively poor wage–laboring and peasant members of Mexican society that I lived with during various field trips beginning in 1970. They accepted me and made me feel at home in their communities, and I considered them to be anything but ignorant. To an anthropologist who sets out to learn an alien culture, the people among whom he or she lives are knowledgeable because they know what the anthropologist must often painstakingly learn. But allowing for this "anthropological effect" these people had an astute understanding of their harsh life circumstances. Yet, I was nagged by the question of why they went to nonbiomedical practitioners when many physicians were readily available to them within the same distance from the village.

While traveling in the car, my passengers recounted how they were cured by Spiritualist therapy. One *comadre* (ritual relative) testified that healers had cured a tumor the size of a handball that developed on her neck and an infant was successfully healed when a doctor had failed. This kind of retrospective account is suspect but it provoked my interest. Also, a good friend became a Spiritualist healer and invited me to her temple to meet her friends and the temple head. I attended the religious ceremonies that were part of a healer's weekly routine and they left me mystified and weary. Nevertheless, I continued to attend them from time to time chiefly because I found the participants friendly and eager to talk about their beliefs.

My interest in Spiritualist practitioners may not, however, have justified a scientific inquiry into Spiritualist healing were it not a propitious subject for exploring problems regarding outcomes of nonbiomedical healing techniques as viewed by the patients themselves, or the role of patient-healer interaction in influencing treatment outcomes. These concerns are important for biomedicine as well, so that my work would be relevant both to theory and to planning efforts to improve health care delivery.

I was well familiar with a large body of information on traditional healing practices but further perusal of that literature convinced me that few researchers had systematically studied the outcomes of traditional therapies. Most investigators simply assumed that such therapies are efficacious.

Confronted with anthropological exoneration on the one hand, and medical practitioners' condemnation on the other, I decided to assess systematically what precisely nonbiomedical healers of the Spiritualist kind do for their patients, why they are considered to be efficacious, and if indeed they are. When I initiated this inquiry in the field in 1975 (Finkler 1977), I discovered that Spiritualist healers and temples existed throughout Mexico, that they represent a religious movement with branches in the border towns and in cities such as Houston and San Francisco as well. Mexican Spiritualism merited investigation, then, not only from a medical perspective but also as an aspect of the Mexican and Mexican-American culture. I therefore undertook a two year field study in 1977–79 upon which this book is based.

Of several temples in the southern region of Hidalgo state, I selected two towns situated ten miles apart. Both had Spiritualist temples. The temple in the town I call Juarez, where I spent the greater amount of time is the best known in the entire area and has the largest patient clientele and membership. Other considerations for choosing Juarez was that it was one of the very few localities where with some luck, I could find a house for rent and it was centrally located for access to other towns and villages in the region.

This research created personal and ethical dilemmas which I had not previously encountered in field work. I had lived in villages and participated in the daily round of activities before, but that work had not required that I become immersed in beliefs and ideologies to the degree that temple participants demanded. A limited involvement in religious rituals sufficed in my earlier studies, whereas the present study necessitated active participation in religious ceremonies to the extent that I was urged to enter training to become a healer.

While I explained to people the character of my work, they nevertheless insisted that I should participate fully in their rituals. Initially the experience was mentally taxing, but I was grateful for the opportunity to understand the psychic struggles that a person must undergo in preparing to become a Spiritualist healer, and for the total immersion in the group's beliefs and practices I was encouraged to achieve. I became involved in training sessions reluctantly, hesitating because I did not know how I would respond in such situations, especially to the trancing activity. I was unaware of my capacities to enter a trance state, or what my reactions would be if I attained an altered state of consciousness. I was afraid, and I learned later that most participants were frightened when they were initially ordered to enter "development," as such sessions are called. Aside from the advantage for my research of being exposed to this experience, I benefited from it personally. It taught me a relaxation technique that I had not previously experienced and I found the process pleasing. Thus, an initially exhausting procedure gradually became gratifying, and an activity that I looked forward to.

In addition to participating in development sessions, I prepared to become a healer by working as an apprentice to healers in trance by assisting them as they administered to patients. My tasks included responding to their requests, interpreting their orders to patients, instructing new patients in the proper way to address them, and recording on a piece of paper what they prescribed to each patient. This work brought me into contact with numerous patients and led me to appreciate the fact that in spite of the strenuous physical activity of healers as they treated as many as 35 patients in a few hours, they emerged from trance looking cheerful and refreshed.

Ethical dilemmas of a type I had not previously encountered presented themselves. To give but one example, my *comadre,* a Spiritualist healer, brought her dying newborn infant for treatment to the temple. This was an unusual situation because life-threatening cases are rarely, if ever, brought to temple healers without prior treatment by a physician. I thought that the case was beyond the expertise of Spiritualist healers, and it turned out to be even beyond the competence of biomedicine. I felt the child required immediate biomedical treatment, preferably in a Mexico City hospital. My dilemma was compounded by knowing about the mother's extraordinarily complex family circumstances, including the fact that this was an undesired pregnancy and birth. Two other situations of less severity occurred during my field stay. They would have been much less problematic for me had I not been a participant in the temple, or had I been dealing with less deeply felt phenomena than illness and questions of healing efficacy.

To what extent my presence in the temple affected temple patients and participants can only be conjectured. I do know that at first I was received with caution but as people became accustomed to my presence my occasional absence was noted and questioned. In the final analysis, despite the ethical quandaries, the research experience was extremely satisfying. My one personal disappointment is that the investigation fails to support some of the enthusiastic claims of healing made by Spiritualist friends whom I deeply respect and cherish.

The study could not have been done without the assistance of many people, most of all those in the temple where I spent so much of my time during the research period. I am grateful for the warm acceptance I received. I owe special thanks to Dr. Laberto Melero for assisting my investigation in every possible way. I am most grateful to Maria Porras, my assistant, for her intelligent and dedicated help in every step of the research. The computer generated results could not have been done without the able computer programming of Chicaco Usui, and in consultation with Bruce Warren and Ira Wasserman. The scientific names of plants that I collected in the region and that are presented in Appendix B were identified by Michael Angeles Martinez and his team at the Autonomous University of Mexico. I very much appreciate too the assistance of Bernardo Ortiz de Montellano with the identification of some of the plants in Appendices B and C. I very gratefully acknowledge the support from the National Science Foundation (Grant #BNS77/13980 and #BNS8013077) for making this research and analysis possible.

1. Introduction

At half past nine on a warm October morning I arrived for my first day as an apprentice in a Spiritualist temple in rural Central Mexico. As I entered the courtyard, dominated by a big huisache tree and surrounded by the temple head's house, outhouse, and a water tub and faucet, seven men and thirteen women were quietly waiting for the temple to open. Inside I found Mariana, the temple head, dressed in the worn dress I had seen her wear on previous occasions, sweeping the floor. Three women carrying paper shopping bags followed me in, set their parcels down, and proceeded with their customary tasks. One assisted Mariana by sprinkling water on the floor to keep the dust down, another began to sweep the healing room adjacent to the temple's anteroom, and the third moved benches from the main hall into the anteroom, converting it into a waiting room for patients.

Mariana finished sweeping and began to prepare the aromatic water that healers use to treat patients. She combined ammonia, a cheap eau de cologne, and water and poured the mixture into three plastic bottles, which she placed on a small table in the nearly empty healing room. The healing room had a broken window, and wooden chairs were placed in the corners. Having mixed the liquids, Mariana fetched a bucket of cold water to pour into a barrel for holy water. She covered the barrel with a tray holding plastic cups, with which to dispense the water to patients as they left the temple.

After Mariana, age 60, completed these activities, which were routine on healing days, she put on her long, spotless white robe. The other three women, ranging in age from 30 to 60, removed their white robes from the shopping bags and followed Mariana's example. As they were putting them on, I saw ordinary-looking women being transformed into repositories of power, capable of summoning spirits,

1

and into experts for whose ministrations many people waited to entrust themselves.

The temple doors were formally opened at 10:30 A.M. By this time many more patients had gathered in the courtyard. The patients marched in and seated themselves on the benches in the order that they had arrived. Except for one--an elderly-looking man dressed in a business suit holding in his hands a brazier with coals and rosemary branches--the men and women were dressed much the same way as rural Mexican peasants and wage laborers. Many of the women wore rebozos, and some of them also carried their infants, wrapped in the rebozos as well, hanging down from their chests. The benches were quickly occupied with patients sitting quietly waiting to be seen by a healer. Men and women occupied separate benches.

As the three healers stood quietly listening at the altar, Mariana initiated the usual day's proceedings with an invocation. Once she finished, they moved to the healing room, an area of approximately 10 by 15 feet. A fourth healer arrived, and all of them sat down on the wooden chairs, tucked their feet under them, backs straight, hands on their laps, and closed their eyes, while Mariana stood motionless, watching. After about a minute, the healers breathed deeply, shook the upper half of their bodies as if shuddering, and one by one pronounced a different name to announce the arrival of a spirit who, in their words, came to dispense charity to mankind. At this point all four healers were in trance. Four assistants, including myself, sat next to the healers to attend to their requests.

During the first day I was overpowered by new sights, sounds, and smells: I observed patients and listened to their exchanges, including the screaming babies who were held on a healer's lap, and smelled the aromatic waters and the incense from the brazier and rosemary branches. The last patient, who was attended at 3:20 P.M., ended a day of tumultuous activity. More than ninety people had been seen by the healers, and I had written prescriptions dictated by the healers for more than twenty patients.

This book analyzes the vigorous and growing Spiritualist health-care delivery system. But, although the research materials are based upon Spiritualist healers and their patients, encompassing a cross-section of the population in one region of Mexico, the book addresses theoretical and clinical issues within the healing context that have not as yet been thoroughly explored in the literature. These issues bear on nonbiomedical therapeutic regimes cross-culturally as well as on biomedicine.

Granted that we can learn about important human problems in this context, a layman, a physician, a nurse, or other practitioner might nevertheless ask why anyone would wish to know anything about obscure rural Mexican women, mostly housewives, who by resorting to trance transform themselves into healers. What can these healers, women from the lower strata of Mexican society, with little education, teach either lay or professional medical practitioners with years of study behind them? A priori, the nonanthropologist may assume that this is a wasted exercise in academic scholarship with little practical clinical application. Yet scholars from different disciplines have recognized the necessity of studying different types of medical systems. For example, Engel (1973) states that the study of other cultures provides a royal road to the "universals that regulate the behavior of the sick as well as of the healer, be he physician, priest, or witch-doctor" (p. 185). Engel continues as follows:

> Such knowledge may be embedded in those attributes of medicine which have endured over the ages in different cultures and at different times, and is essential not only for the modern physician who aspires to provide the best care for his patients but also for the planner who would design more effective systems for the delivery of health care. The answers are to be sought in rural America, and in the Chiapas Highlands of Mexico, in the ghettos and boulevards of our big cities, in the practices of faith healers, acupuncturists, and root workers, and in the pages of history, folklore and demonology. Western medicine is superior in one noteworthy respect, its commitment to the application of the scientific method to the solution of health problems. But only when it effectively applies the scientific method to the elucidation of the universals underlying patient and physician behavior will it advance beyond its present stage of biologic maturity but behavioral infancy. (ibid.)

Thus, aside from its theoretical importance, it is essential to gain knowledge of other systems in order that we may maximize biomedicine's benefits. By looking at what makes patients well in different cultural settings, we gain a better understanding of universal underpinnings of the healing process. Hence, while the focus is on Mexican Spiritualists, the discussion is structured within a comparative framework in order that we might obtain a better understanding of our own medical system as well.

As a nonbiomedical, folk-produced, therapeutic regime, Spiritualism shares epistemologies, premises, and techniques with other traditional therapeutic interventions. Unlike modern therapeutics, which is distinguished "not by its superior rationality (all therapeutic systems are rational) but its scientific epistemology" (Pellegrino 1979:256); nonbiomedical therapeutic systems as a whole are not dependent on complex technologies and share a theory of disease that incorporates natural and supernatural phenomena. Although Mexican Spiritualists display some unique features, they also share certain basic characteristics with other nonbiomedical modalities, thus opening the way for broader generalization and wider application.

There is, of course, a plethora of cross-cultural materials dealing with a variety of important medical and related concerns, including etiological beliefs, healing techniques, cultural syndromes, therapeutic choices, vis-a-vis medical practitioners, and patient-healer interactions.[1] These salient problems will be dealt with here as we explore Spiritualist healing. My major concern is with two fundamental issues, however. First, patient-perceived nonbiomedical therapeutic outcomes and the ways in which favorable outcomes are achieved by folk practitioners, and second the ways in which historical, social and economic forces foster a therapeutic system. These concerns, both theoretical and empirical form the purpose of the book.

THE NEED FOR THERAPEUTIC OUTCOME STUDIES

Therapeutic benefits of folk practitioners have been discussed at length in the literature, but with few exceptions[2], studies of treatment outcomes have not been carried out with follow-ups and continuous interaction with individual patients over an extensive period of time, as has been noted by various scholars (Fiske et al. 1970; Foster & Anderson 1978; Kleinman 1980) and as this study has done. Yet, as Kleinman (1977) correctly observes, little is known about how therapeutic effects are achieved, and we cannot learn much more about them until biological and behavioral outcomes are more precisely measured.

No doubt an important reason for the dearth of investigations relating to therapeutic outcomes of nonbiomedical practitioners is the fact that studies of outcomes and efficacy of both biomedical and nonbiomedical therapeutics pose numerous difficulties, difficulties that have been considered by many scholars (Bergin 1971; Fabrega 1974; Kleinman 1980; Marshall 1980a; McAuliffe 1979). These include the most obvious fact that diseases are self-limiting; in large measure the body heals itself with or without ministration. But additionally, there are problems of definition, measurement, and evidence of efficacy, problems that I consider and explore in detail. To anticipate the later discussion, I assess therapeutic outcomes based upon subjectively perceived symptom relief and alleviation or behavioral incapacities (i.e., target complaints (Battle et al. 1966), the latter being a universal patient concern (Kleinman 1980). Focus on patients' subjective evaluation of treatment outcomes illuminates therapeutic options and patients' desired effects, or "consumer satisfaction," which some consider the ultimate criterion for measuring a given health-care delivery system (Foster & Anderson 1978). While these criteria are appropriate outcome measures, they are not without problems because some patients seeking temple treatment tend to sustain their self-perceived symptoms, yet avow, and also demonstrate, that they have been restored to functioning and health. Despite the difficulties in executing outcome studies, an attempt nevertheless had to be made in order to shed light on the requisites of the healing process, and on the beneficial components of a health-care delivery system.

To determine therapeutic outcomes requires us to turn in several allied directions. We must follow some definitions of illness and health that have been established as culturally constituted (Fabrega & Silver 1973; Kleinman 1980). In fact, a useful distinction between disease and illness has been furnished by Kleinman for analytical purposes. Accordingly, disease is defined as a biological and biochemical malfunction (Kleinman 1980), and illness as impaired functioning as perceived by the patient within the cultural context.[3]

Whereas scholars usually concur that illness is the subjective and cultural manifestation of disease, there has been less agreement on what is meant by health (Antonovsky 1980). The now widely quoted World Health Organization definition of health as a state of complete physical, mental, and social well-being has been criticized as too broad (Antonovsky 1980), and because certain types of diseases (including, for example, hypertension) are frequently asymptomatic. Thus, individuals may enjoy a state of well-being yet suffer from disease, if not illness. In keeping with a patient-perceived perspective, restoration to health occurs with patients' reports of symptom removal and absence of pain and when behavioral incapacities are restored irrespective of physiological underpinnings.[4]

In this manner, outcome assessment explicates questions such as these: What constituent elements of curing procedures are most beneficial to patients? and, concomitantly, to what do patients attribute successful treatment? and how successful is a given local health-care system in coping with different types of disorders? It is not sufficient to say, as some have done, that all therapeutic systems can be judged analytically effective because they are rational and produce affective involvement (Fabrega 1974). Indeed, therapeutic systems may successfully treat some dysfunctions but fail to resolve others.

Moreover, a systematic analysis of treatment outcomes permits an exogenous evaluation of the extent to which a nonbiomedical health-care delivery system succeeds or fails, thereby yielding a better understanding of the reason for the tenacity of alternate systems of health care. In this context, various scholars have posed the question of the "dual use" (Press 1969) of physicians and local curers.[5] However, none of these studies examines the question of "dual use" based upon empirical observation of treatment outcomes. Moreover, while some scholars (Garrison 1977; Press 1969) identify several patterns of resort among dual users, the existing literature usually suggests that the population seeking the services of nonbiomedical practitioners comprises an undifferentiated mass, all practicing similar patterns of hierarchical resort. Here, then, come into view patterns of intra-cultural variability sometimes ignored by anthropologists.

Such studies presuppose that all members of a given sociocultural group or socioeconomic segment of a complex society (e.g., the poor, as in Freidson 1970; Suchman 1965, 1966, 1972) share the same nonbiomedical orientation. The discussions usually revolve around how a given group responds to biomedicine; regarded as a "foreign imposition" (Press 1978) within the context of sociocultural change (Lieban 1973). But while it cannot be assumed that all persons avail themselves similarly of competing systems of health care, little attention has been devoted by anthropologists to the diversity of health-seeking behavior and especially to those who are disposed only to physicians when alternative therapies are available.

These questions are not only academic but also practical. In this book I explore issues of concern to anthropologists and to health practitioners with a cross-cultural orientation, but at the same time my findings demystify nonbiomedical therapeutic regimes. Many people romanticize folk practitioners and associate them with a holistic healing perspective, while others regard their practices as claptrap and the curers themselves as charlatans. The literature, in fact, is replete with statements regarding the effectiveness of folk healing systems which lack ample supporting empirical evidence. Spiritualist healers are neither charlatans nor workers of miraculous cures; they successfully deal with some dysfunctions and unsuccessfully with others, in much the same way as the physicians and psychiatrists with whom I briefly compare them.

In fact, the study of Spiritualist healers and their healing techniques dispels several suppositions advanced in the literature on folk practitioners. Some scholars have noted that personal relations with health practitioners are necessary for healing to take place (Clark 1959; Fabrega & Manning 1973; Fabrega & Silver 1973; Madsen 1974; Mechanic 1968); others have observed that traditional healers seek to provide meaningful explanations for illness (Kleinman et al. 1978), or that folk medicine places special emphasis on the cooperation of the patient (Nash 1967), or that patient and healer share similar world views (Kearney 1978a; Landy 1977), and that nonbiomedical healers tend to sustain the sick role by treating the patient for folk illnesses (Uzzell 1974). Indeed, initial brief investigation (Finkler 1977) tended to support these assumptions by other scholars. However, extensive field investigation reveals that Spiritualist healers' interaction with their patients is impersonal and that they tend to expedite patients rapidly, similar to urban *curanderos* (Press 1971). Spiritualist healers generally fail to explain the etiology of the illness for which the patient is being treated, fail to share similar etiological beliefs with their patients, and frequently they fail to uphold the patient's claim to the sick role.

From a practical perspective, outcome assessment and demystification of nonbiomedical therapeutics allow a more realistic appraisal of the degree to which folk practitioners ought to be incorporated into medical practice as has sometimes been advo-cated. There are also economic considerations; witness, for example, the debates regarding the efficacy of chiropractic (Holden 1973) and whether public funds ought to be earmarked for such types of therapeutics. Judicious exploration of these questions respecting other nonbiomedical modalities can lead to a more rational use of funds designated for health care.

Appraisal of therapeutic outcomes leads us to question which aspects of a therapeutic encounter are most beneficial to patients in resolving an illness episode. For analytical purposes I have divided the therapeutic encounter into three components: the doctor-patient relationship, standard procedures associated with a given therapeutic regime, and the patient himself along with his syndrome. Each component has received attention in the anthropological and medical literature, especially the doctor-patient relationships which is widely considered central to the healing process. In addition, many researchers assert that "the success of the doctor-patient relationship is in large part attributable to the extent the doctor and patient share common frames of reference" (Mechanic 1968:164). My findings indicate that healing techniques and procedures have greater significance in influencing beneficial outcomes than the healer-patient relationship, and this suggests that when therapeutics are underwritten by religious ideology, as Spiritualist healing is, ritual aspects of healing are crucial to the therapeutic process above and beyond the patient-curer relationship.

Because therapeutic techniques assume an important role in Spiritualist healing, they are given close scrutiny. Examination of the ways in which therapeutic techniques influence positive outcomes requires utilization of physiological, sociological, psychological, and cultural paradigms. For one thing, trancing and tactile communication, intrinsic to Spiritualist healing techniques, are considered by some health practitioners and scholars to have physiological underpinnings and potentially beneficial effects. I have thus cut across traditional disciplinary boundaries, as I believe anthropologists must do when dealing with medical phenomena, in order to demonstrate the many different ways healing takes place. This requires us to draw upon researches in disciplines outside of anthropology. All too often we resort to a single type of explanation. For example, when dealing with medical phenomena it is necessary to attempt to show the ways in which symbolic healing may become transformed on a physiological level. Traditional anthropological holism is well suited for this type of synthesis as I have undertaken here.

Therapeutic outcomes also feed back on yet broader cultural issues. In fact, my analysis of the requisites for recovery from illness reveals cognitive models affecting the deepest level of experience. They constitute the symbolic requirements of health restoration. Of course, not all afflictions require symbolic mediation. Biomedicine, which treats human disease by technical management, also has a wide array of symbolic and cultural components, but they are not meaningful to nonindustrial or marginally industrial populations. In fact, the efficacy of scientific medicine depends on healing symbols that emerge from technologically oriented sociocultural settings. This is so especially when biomedical intervention fails to achieve a speedy recovery and biomedicine's symbols are applied to prolonged illness. When biomedicine lacks a real cure and only provides symbolic remedies, people turn to nonmedical therapeutics that furnish healing symbols produced by their own culture. Unlike biomedicine, nonbiomedical therapeutic systems use symbols that emerge from the depths of their cultural experience and that reach the bearers of that culture at the most profound levels of their existence.

My argument is that biomedicine's symbolic cures are frequently rejected by patients with syndromes not readily amenable to speedy recovery in favor of culturally specific recovery symbols. Symbolic requisites for removing the sick role become imperative when patients experience prolonged illness. Biomedical symbols lack efficacy outside Western industrial society because illness not subject to speedy recovery is resolved not only by biomedical symbolic manipulation but by culturally meaningful symbols. Empirical consideration must thus be given to the contextual (i.e., the culturally specific) aspect of healing symbols. In Mexico, Spiritualist healers utilize purification procedures that symbolically terminate the sick role.

In the region of Mexico here studied, prolonged illness is perpetuated to a great extent by exogenous circumstances, including adverse ecological conditions. The environment fosters parasitosis, with which the population is incessantly burdened; parasitosis perpetuates an illness state. Along with this problem, modern medical technology contributes to prolonged illness by keeping persons alive and functioning without curing them (Pellegrino 1979). Paradoxically, the expansion of scientific medical technology serves to promote folk therapeutics, which, even if only temporarily, at least symbolically curtail the sick role and thus provide periods of respite for people who suffer from chronic disease and illness.

In a very broad sense symbolic healing can be related to the placebo effect (Brody 1977). Establishing patients' positive response to a particular set of symbols illuminates the ways in which placebo effects are achieved, and provides us with new insights into illness resolution. Additionally, recent biochemical investigations suggest that the placebo effect has physiological correlates. As the physiological substrate of the placebo effect becomes better understood, it will open the way for elucidating direct linkages between cultural and biological phenomena.

Spiritualist therapeutics also influence patients' perception of pain without having their symptoms totally removed. Here, we encounter symbolic techniques that effect a restructuring of perceptions without changing the underlying conditions. Significantly, not all patients, however, respond similarly to symbolic interventions of this type.

This leads to another important consideration. It is a well established fact that the placebo effect has its limits. Analogously, so does symbolic manipulation in effecting positive therapeutic outcomes. In fact, we must examine whether all patients are indeed equally susceptible to symbolic healing and whether all members in a given culture respond equally to the same therapeutic symbols. The present analysis of Spiritualist treatment outcomes throws into bold relief categories of syndromes that fail to respond to temple therapeutic interventions and patients who fail to be reached by symbolic manipulation or fail to restructure their perceptions of their afflictions. I contend that successful outcomes of certain syndromes are linked to symbolic manipulation with recovery being dependent on the healer providing the proper symbols, but, concomitantly, the patient must also be capable of responding to these symbols. Thus, for the majority of patients to perceive themselves healed it is more important for them to respond to symbolic manipulation than, for example, to enjoy a personalistic relationship with the curer.

Consideration of therapeutic outcomes within a symbolic framework leads us to ask whether all persons within a given sociocultural segment share the same healing symbols. The evidence demonstrates that they do not. There are, in fact, those who fail to recognize Spiritualism as a viable therapeutic option. Analysis of these findings, however, suggests an important hypothesis regarding the ways in which symbols become shared. I postulate that each cultural enclave has a symbolic fund of recovery requisites, which individual members may or may not tap given their life circumstances, and that these requisites are tapped under a specific set of existential conditions. In this manner, persons sharing corresponding existential dilemmas, including similar impairments, come to share the same recovery symbols.

Patients' subjective perceptions of their condition must therefore be ascertained. To focus on illness and its resolution, then, is to learn about cultural phenomena that tap human beings' very basic cognitive and emotional resources and that also reflect on social and behavioral phenomena. In fact, knowledge of therapeutic regimes in general allows access to other cultural beliefs and practices, including religion and world view (Fabrega & Silver 1973).

The research uses both quantitative and qualitative methodologies aimed at elucidating these various points. Quantitative techniques including direct observations of large numbers of persons seeking treatment from healers illuminates the diversity of treatment seeking behaviors, as well as, a new, and less romantisized, perspective on healing techniques and healer-patient interactions. However, after having employed both these methodologies, I must also emphasize that illness and health must be explored by face-to-face interaction using traditional anthropological techniques, including life and illness histories to attain a genuine understanding of experiences leading to illness, illness resolution and choice of health care.

THE SIGNIFICANCE OF MEXICAN SPIRITUALISM

Mexican Spiritualism is interesting in its own right. There is a wide variety of healers in Mexico, including *curanderos,* bone-setters, medicine hucksters, and of course, physicians. But, for several reasons, Mexican Spiritualists merit special attention as Mexican and Mexican-American cultural phenomena.

Spiritualist healers cut across geographic and ethnic boundaries and in some measure across class lines. While it is not known exactly how many Spiritualist temples there are in the entire country and in the United States affiliated with the movement in Mexico, temples exist in the United States border towns and are said to exist in the large cities of the West and Southwest.[6]

These temples provide health care for a large number of Mexicans. Unlike Spiritism (Garrison 1977; Harwood 1977a; Macklin 1974a, 1974b), which is a form of folk Catholocism (Macklin 1974a), Mexican Spiritualism is both a dissident religious movement, vehemently anti-Catholic, and a nonbiomedical health-care delivery system. Spiritualist temples are usually headed by women (Finkler 1981b) and are unified under the banner of a head temple located in Mexico City. As a sectarian movement Spiritualism possesses its separate rituals and doctrines, which stand in opposition to those of the Catholic Church (Finkler 1981a). The movement has grown in Mexico since the mid-1920s, and, with the exception of a few descriptive studies (Kelly 1965; Lagarriga 1975; Madsen 1968), little is known about the group. The reasons for its growth as a sectarian movement and for its proliferation as a provider of health care are relevant to the present discussion.

Spiritualism has commonly been considered an urban phenomenon (e.g., Kearney 1978b; Willems 1974); however, as will be seen, it provides health-care services to a large segment of the rural population. The expansion of Spiritualist temples in the rural zones in recent decades is related to a constellation of factors. First, the extension of roads and public transportation serves to facilitate access to a customary referral network to Spiritualist temples, which consists of word-of-mouth recommendation. Spiritualist temples are not readily accessible otherwise. Second, with the advent of scientific medicine and the availability of doctors in the rural areas, local secular *curanderas* have lost their legitimacy, and their credibility has been eroded. In fact, as they die out, traditional *curanderas* are not being replaced by a younger generation of secular healers.

Third, the growth and popularity of Spiritualist healers may be related to their advocacy of ideological change compatible with the gradual sociostructural changes that have been taking place in Mexico. Specifically, whereas traditional ideology frequently attributes illness etiology to witchcraft, which serves to reinforce suspicion of one's friends, relatives, and neighbors, Mexican Spiritualists deny the existence of witchcraft. When Spiritualist curers succeed in removing a patient's suspicion of his neighbor, friend, or relative, they are not only healing the patient of the specific complaint but they are also promoting a more harmonious social environment for the patient to function within; thereby they reduce possible future tensions and may eliminate future illness episodes. Many patients consciously recognize the advantages of an ideology of this type. To the extent that Spiritualist healers succeed in eradicating belief in witchcraft among their adherents and patients they also become agents of cultural change by altering patients' ideologies. Ironically, the contrast in ideological beliefs between patient and healer leads to an interesting dialectic resulting, in some instances, in the patient's intensifying his or her belief in witchcraft. For example, many believe that an illness not curable by medical doctors must surely have been caused by malfeasance. Paradoxically, then, the very ideology Spiritualists seek to obliterate in their patients may in some instances become reinforced as a result of medical fallibility and the Spiritualists' successful therapy.

Mexican Spiritualism furnishes us with an excellent example of the intricate interlocking relationship between historical forces, socioeconomic structure, religion, and health. To illustrate, for its adherents Spiritualism is first and foremost a religion and only secondly a health-care delivery establishment. Consequently, Spiritualist temples exist because they constitute a dissident religious movement. Because Spiritualism as a therapeutic regime is contingent upon its existence as a sectarian movement, it is necessary to examine the reasons why it came into being in the first place. As we shall see, it arose in the nineteenth century, when Mexico was in the process of becoming industrialized and increasingly differentiated along social class lines, and the movement responds specifically to cognitive demands for social equality and order.

Thus, my view is that Spiritualist therapy, like all other health-care delivery systems, must also be considered from the perspective of the social aggregate. Generally speaking, I explore Spiritualist therapeutics from the individual participant's perspective, meaning that my focus is on the ways in which Spiritualist procedures affect individuals; but, in fact, there are compelling linkages between the individual and social levels. For instance, while Spiritualism as a therapeutic mode may be viewed as adaptive from the individual's point of view, it is maladaptive when examined from the vantage point of the society as a whole. This contention is developed in the following chapters.

This book will be of special interest to scholars of Mexican and Mexican-American culture in general, and particularly to those whose special concerns are health care and minority religions in Mexico.

By way of background, Chapter 2 examines Spiritualism, its attendant beliefs, and the historical period in which it emerged as a religious system, and Chapter 3 furnishes the ecological and socioeconomic settings of the region. Chapter 4 turns to the various therapeutic options available to rural Mexicans, including biomedical and Spiritualist facilities.

The remaining chapters address various issues of medical anthropology from the vantage point of Spiritualism and are relevant to scholars of cross-cultural health-care delivery systems. Each chapter is introduced by a short discussion of some of the broader theoretical concerns that Spiritualist materials illuminate. Quantitative and qualitative materials, including case vignettes, are interwoven in the discussion.

Chapter 5 explores etiological beliefs in rural Mexico and compares them with Spiritualist illness attributions. Chapters 4 and 5 set the stage for Chapter 6, which focuses on sociological and health profiles of patients seeking treatment in Spiritualist temples and in a physician's office. Additionally, in this chapter I identify several categories of temple patients and examine the different patterns of resort practiced by these various groups.

Chapter 7 describes in some detail Spiritualist healing techniques and their special significance within the Spiritualist healing context. In Chapter 8 I present my findings of Spiritualist therapeutic successes and failures among the various categories of patients seeking Spiritualist treatment.

In Chapter 9, we turn to theoretical considerations regarding the ways in which Spiritualist healers accomplish their aims. Paradigms derived from several different disciplines are used.

Chapter 10 looks at the social effects of Spiritualist therapy on Mexican society and examines the healers and adherents along sociological and health dimensions.

The methodologies used are briefly described in Appendix A; this will be of special interest to students desirous of combining qualitative and quantitative approaches in medical anthropology. Appendixes B and C display the native flora used by Spiritualist healers. I have identified 152 plants that were prescribed by Spiritualist healers and have tabulated them in two broad categories: those native to the region (Appendix B), those that must be purchased, and homegrown varieties (Appendix C). Whenever available, the scientific nomenclature as well as the English and Spanish names and the chemical compositions of the materia medica have been provided.

2. SPIRITUALISM AS A RELIGION

Although our major interest in Mexican Spiritualism concerns its role as a health-care delivery system; the focus of this chapter is the history, organization, and beliefs of Spiritualism. Our attention turns to the structural and ideological aspects of the religion because from the perspective of the Spiritualists, unlike that of their patients, Spiritualism is a religion first and a health-care establishment second. Moreover, viewed analytically, the reasons for the movement's very existence are intimately linked with its rituals, which are also associated with Spiritualist healing practices and with social changes that have taken place in Mexico in the last century.

Mexican Spiritualists, unlike Spiritists (Harwood 1977a; Macklin 1974a) regard their religion as distinct from Catholicism rather than as its variant. In the words of the head of all Spiritualist temples, "We are an *obra completa* 'total religion'; we have our symbols, our laws, and our liturgy." Indeed, Spiritualism provides its followers with a clearly defined cosmology, ethics, and liturgical order. It defines the relationship of human beings with God, with the Spirit word, and with fellow human beings; and, when one travels from temple to temple, the temples' interior design, the liturgical order, and the adherents' expressed beliefs are easily recognizable. Only physical size and the size of temple membership vary.

PHYSICAL LAYOUT OF SPIRITUALIST TEMPLES

Mexican Spiritualist temples are clearly distinguishable from groups such as Spiritists, whose establishments are adorned with statues of Catholic saints and with other Catholic paraphernalia reflecting their folk Catholic cast (Macklin 1974a, 1974b). Spiritualist temples are devoid of images, except for a photograph of

13

the founder and a picture of an eye encased in a triangle, which hangs on the wall above the altar. The altar stands on a marble podium usually consisting of a terraced pyramidal structure of seven steps (symbolizing Jacob's Ladder). The altar is always decorated with vases of fresh flowers[1] and three perpetually burning lights for the congregants to contemplate. From the base of the altar rise three large paraffin candles, which are lit only during rituals. In one corner of the podium is an armchair, reminiscent of a throne and occupied only when a medium irradiates God's message. The throne is flanked by two chairs, the one on the left reserved for the head of the temple. Many temples exhibit the Mexican flag and also the temple banner in one corner. The congregation is seated on benches facing the podium. A prescribed seating arrangement, which reflects the Mexican Spiritualists hierarchical structure, must be followed not only on the podium but also in the hall of the temple. Benches closest to the podium are reserved for developed mediums, who are also the temple functionaries. Behind them sit novices in training for functionary roles, followed by persons who have been designated by God to serve Him but who have not yet entered training. The congregants are seated behind this group in the order they arrive, with males and females seated on separate benches. Those sitting nearest to the podium benefit most from God's radiating light; therefore, the earlier one arrives, the closer one is to the podium and to God's light. Special functionaries attend to the seating of the congregation and see to it that one bench is filled before another is occupied. Thus, worshipers may not sit down on any vacant bench but must be seated on the next available seat. Upon being seated, the congregant is expected to contemplate the altar, sit in absolute silence, and pay attention throughout the ritual. If one dozes off, moves one's body, or chews gum at any time during a ritual, an attendant arrives immediately and gently nudges the person to full attention.

SOCIAL ORGANIZATION OF SPIRITUAL TEMPLES

Several variants of Spiritualism exist in Mexico today, each tracing its origins to the same founder (Ortiz 1977). The Spiritualists discussed here embody both communitas and structure (Turner 1969), representing concurrently two models of human interaction. On the local level, each branch temple's congregation forms a communitas where individuals interact informally and relatively freely; however, on the national level Spiritualist temples are ranked and rigidly organized (personnel is predominantly female).

When the movement arose in the nineteenth century, it formed a community of dissidents, but as it gained momentum around 1923 with the establishment of the head temple in Mexico City, it developed a hierarchical organization. Many temples are formally affiliated with at least one other Spiritualist temple of a higher rank in the hierarchy and possibly with three.

First in importance is the head temple in Mexico City which is referred to as the "womb" and which has founded branch temples throughout Mexico and the United States.

The second most important temple is situated several blocks from the head temple, and the third-ranking temple is located in the city of Puebla. Heads of branch temples are expected to come once a month both to the head temple and to the second Mexico City temple for instruction. Visits to the Puebla temple need be made only once a year.

According to Spiritualist rules set down by the head temple, each Spiritualist temple must have a head, who is frequently but not always a woman. In addition, temple officials include the office of overseer, usually held by a male or by a male spirit. While this office symbolizes the temple's foundation, the overseer's duties are mainly limited to substituting for the head in the head's absence. Third in importance is the post of guardian, usually filled by a woman. The guardian is required to see that the temple is always clean, to attend to various errands, and to stand guard at the temple doors during services. There are several pillars whose job it is to keep close watch over the congregants during services, as was described earlier in this chapter. There are at least two clairvoyants, who testify during rituals. The pen of gold functionary is charged with transcribing verbatim God's teachings as they are uttered during irradiation rituals. In recent years, the wealthier temples have acquired tape recorders; in such cases the pen of gold functionary is responsible for taping the speeches. Finally, there are the healers, who possess curing powers, which they exercise by lending their bodies to spirits capable of healing the sick. As a general rule, the other functionaries may also possess healing powers.

Although interactions among the various functionaries within each temple are informal, interactions between branch temple heads and the head of the Mexico City temple are formal and relatively structured. Functionaries at the head temple keep records of the monthly attendance of heads of branch temples, who also contribute financially to the head temple on an irregular basis. The head temple also sets down the ritual and healing procedures that branch temples are expected to follow. Lastly, the Mexico City temple also sends out "spiritual food," irradiations, to feed the flocks in local temples. For this purpose, it maintains a corps of specially designated pairs who travel around the country and even across the border. These couples preside over irradiating services once a month, at which times are celebrated baptisms, weddings, and *quinzeañeras* (coming-out parties for 15-year old girls). Representatives from the Mexico City temple, and all the temple congregants are invited for a special service and feast. This anniversary of the founding of the temple is the most important day in any temple's calendar. It is also one of the few days when temple congregants socialize with one another.

Branch temples seek affiliation with the head temple in Mexico City because official affiliation confers societal legitimacy, which they otherwise lack. A temple head announces with pride that her temple belongs to a larger network of temples headed by the one in Mexico City, from whom she, like all others, receives her orders. The head temple and its affiliates are formally registered with one of the Mexican government ministries and thus have official and formal recognition as a minority religion, along with a variety of Protestant sects. Unlike Protestants and other minority religious groups in Mexico, Spiritualists are regarded by many as witches, however. This reputation no doubt stems from an implicit assumption that anyone who can control good spirits must possess the power to call upon evil spirits as well. The Spiritualists' reputation as witches is fostered by the Catholic Church, whose priests formally encourage the popular belief (as the church also does with Spiritists (Harwood 1977a).

Partly because of its formal structure, Spiritualism continues to be a vigorous movement, despite the fact that a branch temple may disintegrate with the death of its head, who was in most cases also its founder. In fact, a branch temple's existence is tied to its head's ability to maintain her flock, and to groom a successor, usually a member of her family as is done in the head temple in Mexico City.

Temple heads are well known curers who receive an order from God to establish a new temple that is sanctified by the head temple in Mexico City. The women who become temple heads are enterprising, energetic and sometimes even charismatic (Finkler 1981a) But as others have noted (Koss 1975; Macklin 1974a), dissention between temple heads and functionaries may lead to an adherent to sever his or her ties with the temple, as was the case of three functionaries during my stay. Inasmuch as the temple head's relationship with functionaries is usually intense, persons tend to be sensitive to every behavior nuance that may easily become perceived as an emotional hurt. Those who break their ties with one temple may join another or, of course, cease participation. The latter alternative is considered undesirable because of the adverse consequences. Spiritualists believe that failure to fulfill their obligations to God as He willed it results in physical impairments, such as headaches.

HISTORICAL CONTEXT OF MEXICAN SPIRITUALISM

The history of Mexican Spiritualists and the period during which they emerged merit consideration because they illuminate important reasons for the movement's rise and continual growth, thereby elucidating the reasons for its existence as an important health care provider in Mexico. The mid-nineteenth century in Mexico, during which the movement arose, was a turbulent era of political, economic, and social changes that affected many segments of Mexican society. It was a time marked by strife, banditry, and European occupation (Cosio Villegas 1956).

According to Spiritualists, the movement was founded by a recalcitrant priest in 1861 during the Liberal Reforms of 1855-1862, a period in which Mexico was undergoing its most profound crisis since its independence from Spain in 1821. Mexico's War of Independence, initiated and led by Father Miguel Hidalgo in 1810, was directed not only against Spain but also against Spanish clerics and the Catholic church (Villoro 1967). However, the war was supported by Catholic religious ideology (Ocampo 1969), and after the war the church continued to yield great power and maintain its vast holdings; the result was a war between conservative forces representing the church and liberal forces striving for a republican government based on the separation of church and state (Simpson 1967). The continuing internal dissension prompted a European invasion, which installed Maxmillian on the throne in Mexico City (1864-1867).

The Liberal Reform period, dominated by Benito Juarez (1855-1862 and 1867-1872), ushered in numerous social transformations with its reform laws and also promoted industrialization, laissez-faire capitalism, and a veneration for foreign goods (Cosio Villegas 1956). Prior to the War of Independence, Mexico's rudimentary industry was chiefly confined to mineral mining and textiles (Flores Caballero 1972), industries largely demolished by the war. These and other industries were restored during the Reform, with the textile industry growing especially rapidly because of the Civil War in the United States. Industrialization, combined with the preference for foreign goods, caused the displacement and proletarianization of the artisan class (Cosio Villegas 1956). And with industrialization, the personalistic employee-employer relationships that had characterized the colonial period shifted to increased division between employer and employee (Florescano & Lanzagarta 1972).

Social differentiation intensified with increased industrialization by the mid-nineteenth century, especially in Mexico City and the Federal District (Flores Caballero 1972; Di Tella 1973). The Reform Laws fostered formation of a new middle class in the capital by legally divesting the church of its properties. Church-owned individual houses situated in Mexico City were given over to persons of middle means, thereby expanding and fortifying the incipient middle class, which was comprised largely of government officials and professionals (Bazant 1972).

Although the Reform Laws were instrumental in implementing sociostructural changes in Mexico City, they were less effective in altering the extant social structure in Mexico's countryside.

Boundless church properties in the rural regions remained undivided and intact. These were simply transferred to secular proprietors, fifty percent of whom were foreign-owned corporations (Bazant 1972). Thus, while Mexico City became more socially fluid, social arrangements in the countryside remained largely unchanged (Zoraida Vasquez 1976) with gross inequalities prevailing (L. Gonzalez 1972) until the Mexican Revolution of 1910.

This revolution swept in social upheavals that in fact perdured for more than 25 years after the revolution and that continue to abide in the memories of the older generation. Even more important, after the revolution sociostructural changes occurred throughout the country because of accelerated industrialization (Glade 1968) and implementation of agrarian reforms (the *ejido* system) in the rural sector. Prior to the 1910 revolution, social-class differentiation took place mainly in the urban centers, whereas traditional Mexican rural communities emphasized social equality. After the Revolution, however, social-class differences proliferated throughout Mexico, including to village communities (Finkler 1980a, 1980b; Glade 1968; Goldkind 1965; Kunkel 1961; Wolf 1956). These were produced by intensified industrialization, nationwide penetration of market forces, and the land tenure system.

Industrialization tends to accelerate social-class differentiation and class fluidity (Goode 1963). But, ironically, *ejido* tenure, initially designed to breakup monopolistic control of land to create symmetrical social and economic relations among landholders, intensified socioeconomic differences as well (Finkler 1978, 1980a, 1980b; Glade 1968; Goldkin 1965; Kunkel 1961; Wolf 1956). In fact, as we shall see shortly, this is an important reason why Spiritualist temples have branched out into the rural sector.

In sum, to look back on the events in Mexico of the past century is to see that the country has experienced social transformations and social disorder going back to the cataclysmic effects of the conquest (Paz 1961; Wolf 1959), which ushered in a dictatorial presence and sociopolitical domination for a period of three centuries. Although this foreign presence was terminated by Mexico's War of Independence from Spain in 1810, it was followed by a century of political and social turmoil, culminating with the Mexican Revolution of 1910.

The social perturbations that continue to the present result from an intensification of industrialization in the country as a whole, including the rural region of this study. Industrialization causes major social transformations wherever it occurs (Berger et al. 1974), and, as is the case in other industrially developing nations, industrialization in Mexico is being grafted on to what is essentially an agrarian society adapted to agrarian rhythms and patterns of social organization (Adams 1967). Hence, although industrialization in Mexico has been proceeding at full speed since the nineteenth century, societal institutions have not as yet been sufficiently developed to correspond with the requirements of an industrialized society, including infrastructural supports for the individual.

This is important because, as I will show later, absence of supporting societal institutions generate cognitive models for behavior and symbolic meanings relevant to illness etiologies. To cite a contemporary example of the various support systems that are lacking, the legal structure is particularly pertinent to the present discussion. Legal mechanisms to which individuals from the lower social strata can resort to settle disputes are still insufficiently developed. Scholars have recognized that when legal institutions are weakly developed, witchcraft flourishes, since justice cannot be obtained by other mechanisms (Adams & Rubel 1967; Douglas 1966; Swanson 1974). Moreover, in the absence of conflict-mediating institutions, individuals will often correct perceived wrongs by resorting to homicide, as is the case in our region and elsewhere (Romanucci-Ross 1973; Selby 1974). Setting aside sociological consequences of homicide, the high frequency of murder is symbolically transformed into beliefs in spirits that produce illness. As we shall see in Chapter 4, the spirits of the persons who have died a violent death are significant illness-producing agents. Thus, Mexico's history, with its resulting sociostructural arrangements, take on special meaning because this history and its arrangements become cognitively linked with illness attribution. This important point will be elucidated further in Chapter 10.

SPIRITUALIST BELIEFS AND IDEOLOGY

Spiritualist epistemology has its roots in nineteenth-century ideological currents that had swept over the Western world. Historically, new ideologies were fostered during this period in Mexico. Foreign settlers were encouraged to open and settle new lands and to promote industrialization. To accommodate the new immigrants, religions other than Catholic were fomented and Protestant missionaries were encouraged to come from North America to minister to foreigners (Cosio Villegas 1956). In fact, the period is notable for unprecedented religious tolerance. but other ideological transformations were taking place as well. The Liberal Reform fostered an ideology of equality, which was initially promoted after independence from Spain was achieved (Gonzalez Navarro 1954), and in addition it emphasized positivism, with materialism as its ideological correlate. During the Reform, science and technology were enthusiastically promoted (Cosio Villegas 1956), with positivism, science, and rationalism becoming the formal creed (Romanell 1952; Zea 1968).

Concurrent with positivism, the intellectual *Zeitgeist* of the mid-nineteenth century throughout the Western world nurtured a belief in the existence of embodied spirits with whom human beings can communicate. Belief in spirits is ancient and universal (Firth 1967). It is embraced in Latin Catholic doctrines for example, in the belief that the spirits of the dead return on All Saints Day. However, the idea that human beings can communicate with spirits emerged with new force in Europe and Latin America in the last century when it was advanced by the Frenchman Allan Kardec in an attempt to deal with personally experienced phenomena in a scientific manner. The aim was to bring scientific knowledge to bear on paranormal events and to use the alleged manifestations of spirits as scientific evidence for such events (Moore 1977).

Spiritualism in America emerged separately from Kardec (Nelson 1969), but it was similarly regarded as scientific proof of the paranormal (Moore 1977). With Spiritualism planting its roots in America in 1848 (Macklin 1974a; Moore 1977; Nelson 1969) it diffused to Mexico and other points south. Unlike many Spiritist groups in Mexico (Macklin 1974a) and elsewhere in Latin America (Willems 1967) that do trace their teachings to Allan Kardec, the Mexican Spiritualists I studied are largely ignorant of Kardec. The Mexican Spiritualists under present consideration have drawn upon Christianity and Judaism for their beliefs and practices. Although their millenarian cast has its roots in Catholicism (cf Lafaye 1974), Spiritualists regard themselves as the Children of Israel, the Chosen People, and their pantheon consists of Jehovah, Moses, Jesus Christ, and the Virgin Mary. The Judeo-Christian ideology is merged with beliefs in disembodied spirits, but, according to Spiritualists, these beliefs were first proclaimed by their founder.[2]

According to Spiritualist teachings, their founder was the son of an Otomi Indian mother from Hidalgo State and a *mestizo* father of Spanish and Jewish descent. He proclaimed himself the incarnate of the Holy Ghost, and is called "Father Elias" by Spiritualists. Although there are only a few biographical sources referring to the founder (e.g., Ortiz 1977) other than an alleged autobiography published by Spiritualists, it can be deduced that some aspects of Father Elias's teachings derive from the writings of other clerics. For example, it is quite likely that parts of the founder's teachings were derived from the ideas of Joachim of Flor, a Calabrese monk of the twelfth century. Joachim's theories of history closely parallel those advanced by the founder and accepted as fact by Mexican Spiritualists of today (Finkler 1981a).

Like Joachim, Mexican Spiritualists believe in a threefold division of human history with the third stage in which we live today, having been ushered in by their founder. Joachim, who called for the abolishment of the carnal Church, predicted that after a series of tests, the faithful would see God face to face. Interestingly Joachim's prediction is made to come to pass at Spiritualist services, when God addresses the congregation directly. His word is spoken to the followers through a medium in trance who, according to Spiritualists, is but a radio transmitter for His message.

SPIRITUALIST RITUALS

Personages in the Spiritualist pantheon--Jehovah, Jesus Christ, the Virgin Mary, and Father Elias--irradiate their teachings orally thirteen times a month, each on appointed days. Official days for irradiations include the first, seventh, ninth, thirteenth, and twenty-first of every month,[3] as well as each Sunday morning and Thursday, but the most important irradiations are held on Sundays and on the first day of each month. Because of lack of attendance or lack of personnel to transmit the word, not all temples hold services on all designated days (except Sundays). In the Juarez temple, irradiations take place every Sunday, and on the first, the thirteenth, and the twenty-first. Excluding Thursdays and the seventh day of each month, which are designated for Father Elias and the Virgin Mary, respectively, Jesus Christ irradiates at all times. Additionally, there are four annual celebrations when all four Spiritualist deities irradiate jointly. During these rituals a dialogue takes place among Jehovah, Christ, Father Elias, and Mother Mary, with the latter three pleading with Jehovah to save His children, the Tribe of Israel, the Chosen People, who now stand before him. Jehovah agrees to forgive, protect, and watch over His followers, providing they obey His teachings and His laws, embodied in twenty-two commandments.

The twenty-two commandments proclaimed by the founder in 1866, incorporate the Ten Commandments and an additional twelve relating to Mexican life, e.g., injunctions against drinking alcoholic beverages, taking up arms against one's brother, participating in civil wars, abandoning one's children, and believing in idols and witches. The last noted commandment is especially interesting because it pertains to the Catholic saints and to beliefs in witchcraft, both of which Spiritualists oppose.

Each of the four Sunday mornings of the month, God addresses His teachings to a separate segment of His followers. The first Sunday of the month is dedicated to children. Baptisms and weddings may also take place on this day. It is also the only Sunday on which parents are permitted to bring infants and young children to the temple. The second Sunday is dedicated to the youth, the third to adults, and the fourth to temple functionaries.

Irradiations, delivered in rhythmic cadences, may last from a half-hour to three hours, with an average of a little over an hour. The content is patterned and repetitive and usually revolves around God's praise of His own greatness and His· beneficence to His people. He continually reminds His children of His demand for their absolute obedience. He reproves them for their disobedience and for failing to obey his twenty-two commandments; nevertheless, He promises to bestow His goodness upon them because they are His children. An important point is God's reminder to His children that He bestows on them few material benefits because if He provided them with wealth they would abandon Him. He encourages all to continue their struggle. This point will be developed in Chapter 10.

Irradiations invariably include references to Mexico as the New Jerusalem, the pearl and light of the world where all mankind will congregate one day. He also reminds the congregants that He does not expect them to absorb all His words, that each individual will take in those words that are most pertinent for him or her, suggesting that followers are free to project their own meaning onto the sermons and thereby allowing them interpretative flexibility. Significantly, when congregants are queried about what they understand of the irradiation, many are uncertain, and some refer to the passage just described, to the effect that each listener absorbs what pertains to him or her. Importantly too, the fact that teachings are transmitted orally allows each individual to project his or her own personal meanings onto the sermons; it also permits changes in dogma and in practices because during irradiations irradiating mediums may issue new orders to the followers[4].

Irradiations begin at an appointed time with the singing of hymns by the congregation under the leadership of a temple functionary. During this phase of the ritual, temple functionaries are seated on the podium, and the medium presenting God's words moves to the throne-like seat, closes his or her eyes, and gradually goes into a trance by breathing heavily. The hymns stop, and the temple head recites an invocation and the twenty-two commandments. As soon as she finishes her recitation, God begins His irradiation with a salutation to His people. The temple is overtaken by total silence. No one approaching the temple at this time is permitted to enter and be seated until some way into the presentation.

About two-thirds into the irradiation God addresses two clairvoyants, who are seated on the podium with eyes closed but not in trance, asking them to testify to His grandeur. Their responses, like the irradiations, are highly patterned, usually including some reference to visions of bright light and to great mansions somewhere in space, although occasionally a clairvoyant may inject more personal symbolism. God's voice responds to these testimonials by interpreting their meaning, which usually bears upon the great gifts He grants His followers. Significantly, every irradiation invariably terminates with a blessing for doctors, hospitals, and jails. The congregants are then asked whether they are satisfied with His words, to which they respond with a resounding, "Yes."

Until that moment, the congregants sit motionless, silent, transformed, and in a mild trance state. The proceedings are terminated with a hymn or two and a special hymn sung at the very end of each irradiation, which orders the congregants to march on. They must leave in the same orderly manner they entered, those seated in the last rows marching out first, one by one. No one is permitted to leave before his turn. Adherents drink a glass of holy water supplied by the temple and leave a contribution with a functionary standing at the door. People disperse quickly after each ritual, going their separate ways.

Spiritualist healers encourage those who seek their ministrations to attend all ritual activities but especially the irradiation sessions because, according to them, listening to His word forms a part of the cure. While most patients fail to follow the healers' urgings to attend irradiations, those who do, including adherents, indicate that after witnessing an irradiation ritual they feel somewhat disoriented, or far off in space, but very happy and invigorated. They note that what they like most about the irradiation ritual procedures is the enforced order imposed by the rituals. This point requires special consideration and I will examine it later in this chapter.

Regularity and order are evinced by Spiritualists not only during irradiation rituals but also during daily ritual activities. In fact, each day of the week is designated for a different religious activity. Mondays and Saturdays are designated for "development" of novices and "giving light" to spirits. Development trains novices to trance and to carry out their appointed roles. On Saturdays, special indoctrination sessions are held for children as well.

Development sessions begin with a rhythmic recitation by the temple head as novices sit motionless, with hands palms down on their knees and eyes closed. Once the recitation ends, the novices continue to sit in perfect silence, presumably in trance, for exactly forty-five minutes. The head of the temple terminates the trancing period with a customary salutation to which the novices respond by gradually opening and rubbing their eyes--in their words, "waking up." Following trancing, the temple head preaches to the novices for as little as a half an hour or as long as three hours, during which time she instructs them in Spiritualist symbolism, doctrine, and ideology, including the necessity for obedience and submission to the spirit world.

Giving light to spirits involves developed mediums who, sitting in trance, call out the names of dead persons, especially those who died a violent death resulting in perturbation to their souls. With this ritual, perturbed spirits are relieved of their miserable plight in space and set at peace. With this ritual and the Spiritualist mediums' mere mention of their names, troubled spirits cease to inflict illness on the living by attacking and occupying their bodies. This is important in view of the fact that, as I noted before, perturbed spirits produce illness. (This point is explored in Chapter 5.)

Tuesdays and Fridays are dedicated to healing the sick. On Wednesdays developed mediums take part in the giving of light ritual and in consultations between spirit protectors. All developed mediums have their own spirit protector, through which they also heal the sick. The spirit protectors are central to Spiritualist epistemology, which is discussed in the next section of this chapter.

At this juncture it is instructive to note that Spiritualist rituals, especially irradiations, may indeed have powerful influences on listeners for several reasons. First, the Spiritualist emphasis on direct, face-to-face communication with the deity is unique in the Mexican setting; no other religion in Mexico makes a similar claim. Second, while God may scold His children for their lack of obedience, He also reminds them that they are the Chosen People--adding a dignity to their self-image and a dignity to their social position by role reversal (Wilson 1963). Third, the strong emphasis on nationalism inculcates a pride in the listeners, who are aware that Mexico has been dominated by foreigners. The nationalistic cast becomes evident with God's reminder of Mexico as the new Jerusalem, with the Mexican flag displayed on the podiums, and with the fact that all religious rituals are canceled on September 16, Mexico's Independence Day. This day supersedes a day of service to God.

SPIRITUALIST EPISTEMOLOGY

The God of the Spiritualists, as He informs the congregants, is perfect in contrast to human beings, who are imperfect. When they, His children, recognize His perfection, generosity, and grandeur, they will have achieved similar perfection. The time has not as yet come, however. All He sees now is that they have failed to know Him; failed to love Him, and failed to obey His twenty-two laws. This failure is not because of any impediments placed in their way by others such as "scientists or other religionists," but only by "you yourself, you stop yourself from seeking me out." In essence, the assumptive world of Spiritualists and their God is that life on this earth is wretched, but society is not at fault for one's miserable condition on this earth. One is responsible for one's own destiny. Importantly, however, while conditions are bad and human beings themselves are bad, one can change oneself if not earthly conditions. In short, the world is an imperfect place, human beings are imperfect, but while the world may not change, human beings can change by being submissive and obedient to God's teachings; to His wishes, to the temple head, and to Spiritualist functionaries. In fact, as we have seen, submission and obedience are recurrent themes of all irradiations and of sermons by temple heads.

Paradoxically, while Spiritualist teachings recognize that humans exist in an imperfect world, they stress the perpetuation of the social status quo. This is reflected in the twenty-two commandments forbidding brother to take up arms against brother in a civil war and forbidding attempts to rectify social wrongs. Temple heads usually preach a philosophy of non involvement in social concerns. A glaring example of this philosophy came into view when the head of one temple publicly admonished one functionary because the latter had participated in organizing the workers in a sweat shop where she worked and where, because of abysmally poor working conditions, she had lost two fingers. We see also how Spiritualist teachings encourage the individual's status quo when we listen to God explain that He has failed to improve His children's lot because if He did they would abandon Him. Hence, I argue that Spiritualism, in contrast to other similar movements (Macklin 1974a, Roberts 1968; Willems 1967) fails to facilitate social mobility for its members by placing emphasis on sustaining the status quo (as also do some pentecostal groups [Butler Flora 1976]).

Spiritualism shares with countless other movements the belief that the world is divided into the spiritual and the material. The material world is transient, while the world of spirits perdures. In this respect, Mexican Spiritualists do not differ from Spiritist groups studied by other scholars (Garrison 1977; Harwood 1977a, 1977b; Macklin 1974a).

In fact, according to Spiritualists there are three broad categories of spirits: spirits of *alta luz, media luz,* and *seres obscuros.* Spirits of *alta luz* or *luz completa* ("high" or "complete" light) were once housed in the bodies of persons who lived exemplary lives on this earth, as, for example, obedient Spiritualists. These spirits occupy the bodies of highly developed mediums, such as those who irradiate God's teaching and give advice to other functionaries during consultations between spirits. Spirits of *alta luz* have completed their mission on earth and return to earth only during consultation rituals. Although they may previously have been reincarnated many times, their final reward has been nonreincarnation.

Spirits of *alta luz* were once spirits of *media luz* ("half light"). The latter failed to complete their appointed missions on this earth, and they may do so only by becoming spirit protectors to Spiritualist functionaries. After manifesting themselves at some point during development, spirit protectors guide and protect their bearer, throughout the latter's lifetime. In fact, once a spirit protector identifies himself or herself to the bearer, a medium's most important stage in development is completed. Spirit protectors, who are either male or female, were once important pre-Conquest personages, such as Aztec and other Indians possessing great knowledge of healing during their lifetime, known famous individuals from biblical times, or known doctors, scientists, or other gifted persons from the recent past. The spirit protector's name and the type of medication he or she prescribes suggest the period in which he or she had lived. Spirit protectors with Indian names obviously existed during pre-Columbian times. They prescribe herbal medicines exclusively, whereas those who had lived after the Conquest prescribe a mixture of herbal and pharmaceutical medicines, and their names are Spanish.

Normally mediums know very little about the spirit protectors who possess their bodies. Unlike Catholic saints, the protectors are impersonal beings. Protectors are talked about as if they were third-party strangers. Once a medium is awakened from a healing session, her spirit becomes removed from her, and she maintains no contact with the spirit during her waking state. Separation is, of course, necessary to give the spirit world its separate reality.

Seres obscuros ("dark spirits") were previously housed in the bodies of evil and contentious individuals, drunkards, murderers, the debouchers, etc. These are perturbed spirits who linger in the same spots where they had met their demise or in cemeteries, or who hover at night and attack living persons. According to Spiritualists these tormented spirits, never at peace, are sometimes reborn, their rebirth manifesting itself in badly behaved children, or they attach unsuspecting individuals causing them to become ill. According to Spiritualists, many human afflictions are brought about by these dark spirits.

Although dark spirits produce illness in humans, humans actually control the spirits by influencing their destinies. In fact, Spiritualists, who lack power on this earth, become powerful by controlling the spirits. The symbiosis between humans and the spirit world comes into view in various ways. Spiritualists say that Jehovah controls the number of times a spirit evolves until it reaches the final state of complete light, *alta luz,* but the spirit's status is also dependent upon the comportment of the person in whose body it is housed. In fact, whether a spirit becomes released from the reincarnation cycle depends on the exemplary life of the person on this earth. Furthermore, when a spirit is housed in the body of a curer, it is actually being given the opportunity to complete its task on this earth and thereby eventually become a spirit of complete light.

Heads of temples control the spirits by their instructions, which the spirits are expected to obey. To illustrate, when a spirit protector is overheard prescribing to a patient an herb unavailable in the region, the head of the temple quickly indicates to the protector to change the prescription to an herb that is readily obtainable in the vicinity. Or, when a temple head overhears a spirit protector agreeing with a patient that he or she was a victim of witchcraft, the spirit is immediately chastised for not working *limpio.*

The concept of *limpio* is important in Spiritualism. It signifies that things are being done as they should be; otherwise they are not *limpio* "clean". Functionaries or spirit protectors fail to work *limpio* when, for instance, they prescribe medical dosages in numbers other than the numbers symbolically significant to Spiritualism 1, 3, 7, 13, 21. Thus, a spirit protector who prescribes four and not three drops of a medication is not working *limpio.* In fact, if a spirit protector makes reference to witchcraft or uses numbers other than those cited, it immediately suggests that the medium is not in real trance, that is to say, not working *limpio*. A medium who is not thinking *limpio* may be having doubts about Spiritualist metaphysics, for example, the existence of spirits, or may be doubting that God addresses the congregants directly during irradiations. Other manifestations of not working *limpio* are failing to live by the twenty-two commandments and charging for Spiritualist therapy.

But in addition to controlling the spirits, Spiritualists also impose controls on themselves. This is particularly evident during irradiations and development sessions, when Spiritualists are required to maintain extraordinary physical control. Unlike other possession cults (see, e.g., Lewis 1971) that practice ecstatic trance, Spiritualists are admonished against any cathartic displays. Trance behavior is controlled at all times by the head of the temple or the person in charge of development sessions. Novices in training, like developed mediums and congregants, are expected to sit motionless when trancing. Sometimes a novice may cry out or gyrate his or her body. When this occurs, the trainer immediately stands before the person and indicates that such behavior is unacceptable and unbecoming a spirit. Such conduct is attributed to dark spirits who temporarily possess the novice's body, and the trainer tells the spirit to vacate the trainee's body instantly. It is, however, recognized that novices are especially vulnerable to possession by dark spirits because until they acquire their own spirit protector their heads-- specifically the backs of their heads, the *cerebro*--remain "open."

It must be stressed that not all Spiritualist adherents are equally aware of the millenium, the hierarchical order of spirits, and the meaing of Spiritualist symbolism. In fact, at this stage of its growth as a religious movement, Mexican Spiritualism has developed an elite of top functionaries, who alone are knowledgeable about the entire corpus of Spiritualist lore. In contrast, the majority of adherents-- and, of course, nonadherents who seek temple treatment--fail to understand the symbolic and contextual meanings of Spiritualism. Doubtless, one of the reasons why literate adherents have a poor understanding of Spiritualist metaphysics is that the Spiritualists prohibit the writing down of God's teaching (except, of course, those who serve as the "pen of gold"; and only temple heads have access to these materials). Adherents must learn the teachings by listening to irradiations, at which time they pick up a few stock phrases.

Paradoxically, then, although Spiritualism began as communitas, as an unstructured group of individuals united by comradeship and egalitarian ideals, it is developing into a rigidly structured and hierarchically organized religion headed by an elite comprised of temple functionaries, thus replicating the Catholic structure so vehemently opposed by their founder.

RECRUITMENT TO SPIRITUALISM

The functionary, the patient, and the healing role are intricately related in Mexican Spiritualism, as they are in other cultures (Lewis 1971). According to Spiritualist doctrine, all human beings have a capacity to heal; everyone is born with a spirit protector who, as we have seen, proclaims his existence during development. Addressing a group of novices during a development session, the head of one temple asked rhetorically, "How many of you have studied medicine? Of course, none. Yet we know how to cure; protectors give us power. In place of titles, you have intelligence." ("Intelligence" as used in this context is synonymous with "spirit protector").

Spiritualists do not proselytize. Since Spiritualism's period of growth in the early 1920s, three generations of Spiritualist offspring have been reared in Spiritualist temples without experiencing any other religion. However, those who are Spiritualists by birth comprise a minority of the membership. The majority of persons who become Spiritualists were born Catholics and became Spiritualists at some point in their life after the onset of an affliction. Even the Spiritualist God is cognizant of this fact, as during irradiations, he acknowledges that had it not been for their pain, His children would not have come to His doors. In our sample of regulars or adherents, 82 percent were recruited into the movement as a consequence of having entered an illness network during an illness episode unsuccessfully treated biomedically. Persons successfully healed in the temple usually also recruit their spouses, children, siblings, parents, and occasionally even neighbors.

Recruitment procedures follow a uniform course. Normally, when patients first arrive at the temple, they are given a customary treatment (described in Chapter 9) and are urged to attend irradiation rituals. If, after several temple treatments, the patient fails to respond to established procedures, the healer diagnoses the problem as "troubled spiritually" and informs the patient that the latter possesses a gift. With this diagnosis, the healer is in effect recruiting the patient into temple participation. The patient is then ordered to enter development and participate in all religious rituals as part of the Spiritualist therapy.

In effect, adherents are persons who tend to suffer from disorders not readily amenable to treatment either by the medical model or by standard Spiritualist treatment procedures. Not all patients ordered by healers to participate in rituals and in development do so, of course. Some attend only once or twice, but those who attend regularly become incorporated into the temple community, either as functionaries or simply as adherents to Spiritualism by attending irradiations regularly and by identifying their religion as Spiritualism.

Functionaries, who comprise the core membership in a temple, enter the hierarchy after being "marked" by God for a specific position during an irradiation. To be marked for the irradiation role in "three powers" (that is, to be given the role of transmitting the word of Jehovah, Jesus Christ, and Father Elias) is the highest designation and is usually accorded persons deemed "well prepared"--that is, intelligent.

Normally, novices marked for the curing role are eased into their tasks as soon as their spirit protectors have identified themselves, but a person designated to irradiate God's word requires lengthy preparation in development. Irradiators may also function as curers, but curers may not irradiate God's word. This is consistent with the notions that the curing role is secondary to the religious role in the Spiritualist hierarchy, and that Spiritualism regards itself as a religion first and a health-care delivery establishment second.

By way of illustration of the recruitment process, the four case vignettes presented next reveal the various modes of becoming a temple regular, along with the diverse circumstances that bring persons to the temple. Lupe's and Stephan's cases are perhaps most significant, because they are representative of the majority of regulars who initially arrived in the temple with an illness.

Lupe

Lupe the 48-year-old mother of eight living children, first came as a patient to a temple when she was fifteen years old, two years after her marriage. At that time she was experiencing "attacks": her tongue felt inflamed; she could not talk; and she suffered from severe diarrhea and vomiting. She was also very fearful of everything. Her vision was blurred, and she experienced mirages. She attributed her first attack to eating food and drinking *pulque* given to her by her mother-in-law. Later attacks she ascribed to nerves resulting from the difficult life she had with her husband and her mother-in-law. Her husband beat her incessantly. The first attack she experienced coincided with the death of her firstborn infant at 4 months of age. She held herself responsible for its death. Lupe first sought treatment with a physician who diagnosed her condition as a liver dysfunction; another doctor told her she had cerebral infarction due to an embolism. Lupe herself continued to ascribe her condition to nerves. In any event, her problems were not relieved by the physicians, and she was directed by a friend to a Spiritualist temple, where she was told that she must enter development because she possessed a gift. The Spiritualist healer's diagnosis was an open *cerebro* (referring to the occipital region of the skull), which rendered susceptible to attacks by perturbed spirits, who were, in fact, causing her attacks.

During one irradiation, God called Lupe up to stand before Him. He told her that the baby's death was not her fault but rather that it was His will, that she was being tested, and that it was her duty to serve Him in His house. He designated her to work as a curer and clairvoyant. Subsequently, she recovered from the attacks and ceased attending the temple because she lacked time. For much of her life she worked as a vegetable vendor, buying her merchandise in Mexico City, returning with it on her back, and selling it in the countryside. She visited various Spiritualist temples intermittently. At the time we met she had been working regularly as a curer and clairvoyant for about six months, and she was pregnant with a child that was not her husband's. Because of the pregnancy she had been banished from her home by her husband and sons. Lupe now laments her very difficult life, which, in her words, was spent in perpetual anger (*con puros corajes*) and unceasing conflicts with her husband. She lost two infants carried to term and three that aborted. Lupe's two grown daughters and 14-year-old granddaughter came regularly to temple rituals as well.

Stephan

Stephan, a 56-year-old peasant, is male temple head--one of a minority. His temple is situated next to his home on the farm where he has spent most of his life. Stephan was a very heavy drinker and fell ill twenty-nine years ago, at which time he experienced excruciating pain. Physicians told him he was suffering from liver dysfunction because he drank tap water and ate irregularly. During this illness he also dreamed ugly dreams about bulls and about his back being broken. Twelve years after the onset of this illness, Stephan learned about a Spiritualist temple. To his surprise, he was told that an evil dark spirit had attacked his intestine. Stephan had attributed his illness to an unexpected fright; he had been startled by a sudden brightly shining light, while irrigating his fields at night.

God marked Stephan to irradiate His word, and Stephan was in development for five years, during which time he recovered totally. He now sleeps without interruption and no longer feels angry or scolds everyone the way he did before. In his words, "I was bad and perverse, but I am no longer any of these things." Stephan had twelve children, four of whom died. Significantly, Stephan frequently refers to the Catholic church and the Spaniards as the exploiters of Mexico.

Juanita

Juanita, a women in her mid-40s in excellent health, joined the temple fifteen years ago because she disliked Catholic ritual and the church. She is married but has never had any children, which for a Mexican woman is a great tragedy, because in Mexico children are especially valued. Two years prior to the interview she miscarried, at which time she also entered development. Recently she has begun working as a curer. She is an only child and has been a fruit vendor since childhood. Unlike the husbands of other female adherents, Juanita's husband rarely accompanies her to temple rituals.

Luis

The fourth illustrative case is that of Luis, a 29-year-old electrician in excellent health who has a well-paid but temporary job. He became a participant in the temple because his maternal aunt is a healer there, and his parents also attend a temple in the town where they currently reside. Luis is married to a devout Catholic woman and has two children. Although he is a devoted father and husband, he spends much of his time at the temple, especially after working hours. Otherwise, he is forced to accompany his fellow workers to a bar. As Luis observed, there are extraordinary pressures on him to join other men in drinking. Luis said that by coming to the temple he avoids drinking, which he does not enjoy.

In fact, men drinking together is the *sine qua non* of conviviality and leads to alcohol abuse in the rural region. This is an important point, to which I will return shortly.

SPIRITUALISM VS CATHOLICISM

Mexican Spiritualism incorporated themes prevalent during the period of its birth by embodying an anticlerical and anti-Catholic stance. Contextually, Spiritualism negates or reverses Catholic beliefs and practices. Structurally, Spiritualism allocates ritual positions to women and militates against social-class differences, which, as we have seen, have increased since the mid-nineteenth century.

As for the diametric opposition of Spiritualist practices and traditional Mexican folk Catholicism, Spiritualists admit no images in their temples; they are vehemently opposed to the worship of saints, the very backbone of Mexican and Latin American folk Catholicism (Willems 1967; Wolf & Hansen 1972); and they do not believe in the many guises of the Virgin Mary. The Virgin of Guadalupe, who in Mexican folk Catholicism is the patron saint of Mexico, represents but a national symbol for Spiritualists (Finkler 1981a). Spiritualists refer to the Catholic worship of saints as idolatry; they celebrate but few Catholic holidays, and they characterize such practices as kneeling and crossing oneself as religious fanaticism. They oppose confession on the ground that only God can forgive human transgression, and they do not believe in making promises to God.

Spiritualists tend to make abstract certain religious practices that Catholicism concretizes. For example, whereas it is a common practice in Mexican folk Catholicism to light candles for the dead, presumably to illuminate the way for the soul, Spiritualists accomplish this by verbal recitations of the names of the dead during the giving of light ritual. Or, on All Saints Day, it is common Mexican Catholic practice to put out specially prepared bread for the dead, a custom Spiritualists joke about. For Spiritualists, All Saints

Day is a time when adherents communicate verbally with spirits of dead relatives summoned through a medium in trance.

Spiritualists evince an interesting paradox with respect to women, which also contrasts with Catholic practice in several ways. On the one hand, they, like the Catholic church, teach that women must adhere to their traditional obligations as wives and mothers. On the other hand, they, unlike the Catholic church, allocate formal positions to women in the temple and advocate equality between the sexes.

But viewed phenomenologically, when I asked adherents why they become Spiritualists, again and again the response was the same regardless of the degree of participation: that church services, unlike Spiritualist services, lack order; people in church are permitted to talk and look over their shoulders; and, what is worse, people in church always talk about others, always criticize their appearance, their clothes, how they walk, and move--in short their overall stance and presentation of self.

Respondents indicated that they could not tolerate being talked about, ridiculed, or criticized, especially when they were attending church services. This finding merits special consideration because, in the final analysis, it illuminates the reasons why Spiritualism continues to flourish as a religious movement and concomitantly as a health-care delivery system.

DISSIDENT RELIGIOUS MOVEMENTS AND SOCIAL CLASS

It has been frequently asserted that dissident religious groups emerge during periods of psychosocial stress, social change, and cultural dislocations (Eister 1974; LaBarre 1971; Willems 1967; Lanternari 1963; and many others). There is no doubt that social change plays a crucial role in the formation of new religious alignments and ideologies. In fact, as I have shown earlier, Mexican Spiritualism affords us an excellent example of the ways in which dissident religious movements reflect the historical period of social perturbation during which they emerged.

Yet few scholars have specifically identified the cognitive correlates of stresses produced by social transformations. That is, what specific aspects of social change is sufficiently stressful to impel individuals to become adherents of a new religion? Willems (1967), in his analysis of Protestant groups in Latin America, argues that these religions prevail as protests against the Catholic church, because, according to him, Catholicism is no longer adapted to the anomie that results from a breakdown of social controls and inflicts doubts on the validity of the underlying order. Willems suggests that Protestantism is a lower-class urban phenomenon. He implies that it attracts lower-class derelicts, dissipating their lives in alcohol and other vices. There is no doubt that Spiritualism, like Protestantism, is a protest against Catholicism. However, I postulate that participation in Spiritualist temples is a response to the increasing differentiation in social class that has been taking place in Mexico. I argue that by joining a Spiritualist temple the individual removes himself from psychosocial pressures generated by *face-to-face* encounters with class distinction. Thus, Spiritualism represents a protest not only against Catholic clerics and their beliefs and practices, but also against the church's tolerance of social differentiation, which Spiritualists recognize when they state, "In church we are criticized." Membership in Spiritualist temples, as in other millenarian movements, suggests a quest for dignity (cf. Burridge 1969), a declaration against social inequality wherein the individual removes himself from a perceived stressor that he or she associates with criticism and ridicule created by socioeconomic differentiation in face of an ideology of equality that has prevailed in rural Mexican villages for centuries and in the nation state since the revolution of 1910. And it is possible that when Spiritualists speak of the lack of order in the Catholic church, they may not only be referring to the actual disorder sometimes encountered in churches during rituals, but also employing a metaphor for the continuing process of social differentiation occurring in both the urban and rural sectors.

In elucidating the relationship between dissident sectarian movements such as Spiritualism and social class differentiation, Stavenhagen's (1967) distinction between social stratification and social class is useful. Stavenhagen distinguishes social strata of hierarchically ordered groups held together by common values from social classes or groups standing in conflict as a result of differential access to the same economic resources, the former having long existed in human societies, while the latter is a historical phenomenon. Stavenhagen observes that social class conflicts become exacerbated by socioeconomic development.

Using this model, we see that the social structure of Mexico prior to its war of independence is characterized by rigidly stratified divisions, which began breaking down with industrialization and economic development during the nineteenth century. Industrialization tends to accelerate formation of class divisions and class fluidity, as can be seen in Mexico. Rigid Mexican social divisions have been partially dismantled in the twentieth century, opening the way for socioeconomic mobility not only in urban centers but in village communities as well.

While social class differentiation was developing in the 19th century urban centers, traditional Mexican rural communities were still emphasizing social equality (Wolf 1959). Following the 1910 revolution, however, class differences spread throughout Mexico and into traditionally egalitarian communities as a consequence of several interrelated factors, which included intensified industrialization, penetration of market forces and the land reform program

(Finkler 1980a, 1980b; Glade 1968; Goldkind 1965; Kunkel 1961; Wolf 1956).

With increased class differences and class fluidity, individuals are brought face to face with various kinds of invidious distinctions not only during their daily routines but also in the sanctuary of the church, where social conflicts are formalized and expressed verbally. And while escape may not be possible in one's daily rounds, Spiritualist temples furnish at least a sacred place for escape from unpleasant encounters and potential social conflict. Persons are less likely to be exposed to social differences in a Spiritualist temple, where social interaction and gossip are inhibited by the very structure of the ritual. We have seen that Spiritualist rituals prohibit social interchanges both directly by their rigid rules of demeanor and indirectly by incorporating trancing into the rituals. Spiritualism, in fact, is not conducive to generation of social interaction of any kind, because the very nature of the rituals fosters the retreat of each individual into the self. Interaction is hence vertical between man and the supernatural rather than horizontal between man and man. Within the context of the Turner model, we may conclude that while Spiritualist temples create the underpinnings for *communitas,* paradoxically the Spiritualists fail to achieve it or its postulated social changes because of their emphasis on vertical relations with spirits through trance.

Because differences in social class become manifestly more apparent in cities, this hypothesis illuminates why movements such as Spiritualism initially arise in urban centers and are ordinarily regarded as urban phenomena (Willems 1967). It also sheds light on the reason why industrialization is frequently implicated as a stressor and associated with dissident religious movements. The stressors need not necessarily be the technological changes emanating from industrialization, as is commonly supposed, but rather changes in social-structural arrangement, which it generates and with which individuals may have difficulty coping.

Along this line of analysis, Wallace (1960) relates how the Iroquois nation moved from a cathartic healing strategy to one of control as Iroquois society moved from cohesion to disorganization and chaos. Analogously, the Spiritualists emphasis on control in both their religious and healing rituals confronts ongoing social differentiation, along with its behavioral correlates such as perceived disparagement by others. In fact, given the rapid social-structural changes that are currently taking place in Mexico, I anticipate that Spiritualism will continue to thrive there. With a continual increase of Spiritualist temples, Spiritualist therapy will persist as an important health-care delivery establishment as well, especially in view of the ecological and societal conditions briefly described in the next chapter.

3. ECOLOGICAL CONSIDERATIONS

In this chapter I examine the ecological, economic, and social settings in the region because they are relevant to the people's health status.

ECOLOGY

Mexico is a country of great geographical diversity, with a great assortment of ecological zones. These range from tropical areas on its two coasts to moderately temperate regions in the central plateau, where elevations reach 6000 or more feet above sea level. The region of this study, situated approximately eighty miles north of Mexico City in the semi-desert part of Hidalgo state, is set in one of several valleys comprising the zone of the temperate central plateau.

The valley, divided into an irrigated and an unirrigated sector, has the unique benefit of untreated sewage waters siphoned off from Mexico City for irrigation. Because these waters flow into the ubiquitous irrigation canals in the region where they also become stagnant, they are of special concern within the context of the present discussion. Although the use of untreated sewage waters for irrigation contributes to high agricultural yields for the peasants of the area (Finkler 1974; 1978; 1980a, 1980b), these waters also afford a conduit for transmission of enteropathogens by vectors.

Irrigation in the valley is not an artifact of modern technology. The population has been exposed to sewage waters for many years. Sewage waters came into use for irrigation because of drainage problems in the basin of Mexico that date back to pre-Columbian times. During that early period, unregulated rain waters produced sufficient flooding to necessitate the construction of the now-famous causeways, the remains of which can still be seen in Mexico City today.

After the conquest, the problem of drainage was further aggravated by the systematic destruction of the forests that had once surrounded the area where Mexico City now stands. Numerous solutions were sought for periodic floodings and occasional inundations. In 1888 a plan was finally devised to construct a canal to drain the sewage and rain waters from the capital. However, one canal was insufficient to accommodate the increased volumes of sewage waters that resulted from Mexico City's expanding population, and a second canal was built in 1937. Currently the two tunnels divert waters out of the basin of Mexico into the valley.

The tunnels conduct the waters into reservoirs where they are mixed with river and rain water and from whence a complex network of principal, secondary, and tertiary canals emanates. Since the early 1950s, when the Ministry of Hydraulic Resources took over the control of the region's irrigation system, there has been a continuous expansion of irrigation canals from the southern part of the valley to its northern reaches (Finkler 1974).

Sewage waters are formally defined as "waters of domestic and industrial liquid wastes that also include rain waters, runoff sewage waters, and subsurface drainage waters" (Heukelekian 1962:6; my translation). Thus, although their specific chemical composition varies with the seasonal rainfall, they are rich in organic materials as well as detergents. The sewage waters are known to carry an array of intestinal parasites, including, among others, vibrio, cholera, salmonella, shigella, endamoeba histolytica, and enterovirus (ibid.). Moreover, these waters absorb chemical wastes sloughed off by factories on their way from Mexico City to the region, but the effects of these wastes on crops and humans have not been ascertained. Although potable water flows through separate conduits, the degree to which the irrigation waters may contaminate the potable water supply is also uncertain (ibid.), but an ever-present danger of direct contamination exists.

Another environmental condition contributing to poor public health in the region is the unsanitary living environment prevalent in the Mexican countryside. Inasmuch as most village houses and many town houses lack indoor plumbing facilities, human wastes are left to be disposed of by domestic animals, including pigs and dogs. Other garbage is disposed of in municipal town dumps, and flies breed everywhere, particularly during rainy months.

As a result of these adverse ecological conditions, parasitosis is endemic to the region. Significantly, enteritis and diarrheas were the principal causes of morbidity in Hidalgo between 1973 and 1975, followed by respiratory malfunctions (Appendix D).[1] According to local doctors, there is a higher frequency of intestinal disease in the region, relative to Mexico as a whole. But although the region differs epidemiologically from the rest of Mexico, the disease patterns found in the area do not differ from other third-world countries. In fact, as in other parts of the developing world, we are dealing with a "malnourished, anemic, and parasite-burdened individual" (Brown 1966:272). These conditions, sometimes asymptomatic, clearly weaken and attenuate immune responses and the individual's resistance to other potential health hazards (cf. Scrimshaw et al. 1969; Solomons and Keusch 1981), diminish the beneficial effects of nutritional intake, and produce a perpetual sense of discomfort, including fatigue, intermittent bouts of diarrhea, stomach distension, constipation, and flatulence. This is extremely important to keep in mind, because as we shall see in Chapter 6, people in the region report numerous diverse symptoms that could be associated with the population's generally poor state of physiological health.

SOCIOECONOMIC CONDITIONS

The local socioeconomic situation compounds the harmful ecological conditions and further contributes to the people's poor state of health. As in many parts of Latin America, wealth is unequally distributed, with a small percentage of the population enjoying great wealth and the majority subsisting on meager land holdings, daily wage work, or petty commerce. The population in the valley is no exception. In fact, this region is often cited as one of the poorest of rural Mexico. The peasants and daily wage workers predominating in the area owe their poverty in large measure to the local socioeconomic structure and the land tenure system (Finkler 1974, 1978, 1980a, 1980b), as well as national economic trends.

Although an in-depth analysis of the region's economy and land tenure system is outside the scope of the present discussion, it is noteworthy that a large segment of the population holds *ejido* land, that is, land redistributed to the peasantry under Mexico's land reform program after Mexico's 1910 revolution. *Ejido* tenure adds a degree of uncertainty above and beyond that experienced normally by peasant cultivators and, as such, may be an additional economic stressor. *Ejido* tenure has, of course, opened access to the agricultural economy to a broad segment of a previously landless peasantry; however, this access is conditional. As stipulated by agrarian laws, *ejido* land is not owned outright and an *ejidatario (ejido* holder) is never certain of his land. Most important from our perspective, *ejido* tenure is a major source of both intracommunity and intercommunity conflict. In fact, according to many *ejidatarios,* the major source of dissension among villagers revolves around *ejidos.* With a constantly expanding population and a diminishing land supply, there has been less and less land available for distribution. In fact, in our region all the available nonirrigated land has already been redistributed. Hence, according to many villagers, everyone is trying to get a plot for his sons, leaving no *ejido* holder certain of his land. If it can be demonstrated that an *ejido* land parcel is not being worked, it can legally be taken away from the holder.[2] But even access to *ejido* land provides a family only a minimum income.

The average *ejido* land holding in the region is about three hectares (approximately 7.4 acres) of irrigated crop land. Many *ejidatarios* hold less than one hectare. Private land plots are, for the most part, no larger, except for those of a few wealthy individuals with extensive land holdings. Because of the lack of available new lands for redistribution, the younger generation of men has been thrust into the wage-labor cycle, seeking daily wage work in the region or in Mexico City.[3]

In the early 1970s, the irrigated zone experienced intensive industrialization with the building of a hydroelectric plant and a giant oil refinery. During the first part of the decade the construction of these large government works opened up opportunities for unskilled labor within the region, and many men were contracted to work on governmental works. By the end of the 1970s, however, both these projects were completed and work opportunities for unskilled labor ceased. By then having become accustomed to earning relatively high wages with weekends off, most young men found themselves suddenly and painfully unemployed. Now these men seek work in other industrializing sectors of the country, including Mexico City and in far-off economically booming areas in the states of Chiapas and Tabasco.

To accommodate the newly built government plants, new roads were built, creating a network of freshly paved highways in the region, which linked villages hitherto not connected by paved roads. Concomitantly, new bus routes were introduced. This furnished easily accessible public transportation to many new communities and connected them with small and larger towns, including Juarez and Mexico City. The new transportation networks are not only significant for industrial development but, as we shall see later, are also important for expanding people's therapeutic choices. These have included Spiritualist treatment.

Expanded government investments of this type and other benefits of industrialization have been offset by accompanying increased costs of manufactured products and by the resulting hardships generated in part by increased consumption needs and wants, of which education of children has gained priority. Aside from the fact that rural wage laborers, unlike peasant cultivators, must purchase their daily food, sold at high prices in the rural regions, the recently created educational requirements of a growing industrial nation have put great economic strains on rural households, adding to the day-to-day tension of the people. Whereas, previously compulsory sixth-grade education usually terminated a youngster's educational career, high-school education has become a *sine qua non* for both boys and girls, despite minimum direct government subsidies for education above the elementary school level. As a matter of fact, most households expend extraordinary efforts to send their children to high-school, but the newly created aspiration for schooling promotes economic and psychological stresses for parents who wish to meet their children's demands for an education.

Children's educational requirements resonate differentially on adult male and female members of the household and result in increased work loads for the women. Although both men and women are preoccupied with meeting increased financial commitments, the women are faced with dilemmas above and beyond those of the men, and this is of special interest because the majority of patients seeking temple treatment are women.

With both male and female children attending high school, the woman is left with less help at home, while her daily chores are not diminished commensurately. In rural households the women still prepare tortillas at home rather than purchase them for each meal. Few households have modern conveniences to lighten the women's household chores. Gas stoves have come into wide use in recent years, but few households possess refrigerators or washing machines, and the women must still prepare fresh meals and wash laundry daily, especially when there are infants in the house. In view of the traditional sexual division of labor, women continue to carry out their incessant daily household activities, but now lack the help they previously received from their daughters. Moreover, because of the expanding need for cash, many women attempt to supplement their spouse's income by petty commerce, or washing laundry for others. Such increased household burdens have become stressful for women.

Increased industrialization accompanied by wage labor tends also to alter family arrangements (Goode 1963), especially adversely affecting the women of the region. While extended family arrangements were once very common in the agricultural households, there has been a growing increase in nuclear families as a consequence of an expanding cash economy based upon wage labor. Presently, 57 percent of the total population sample in the region (N = 1140) resides in nuclear families. This change has evoked stresses that might otherwise have lain dormant. From the perspective of stress-producing social structures, nuclear families have important advantages, because they tend to eliminate the day-to-day tensions common in extended families between mother-in-law and daughter-in-law and between sisters-in-law. Moreover, nuclear families avoid recurrent tension among sisters-in-law over conflicts produced by the numerous children of different siblings residing in an extended family.

On the other hand, despite the intermittent tensions in extended families, the women assist one another in their daily chores, and this assistance diminishes individual household obligations. More important, however, nuclear families place greater emphasis on the male-female dyad, accentuating the tensions between the spouses which might have been attenuated or cushioned by the senior members of an extended family.[4]

Significantly, extreme tension between spouses are reflected in the numerous illnesses which are attributed by the women to anger and dissension between spouses. These tensions take on special importance in the rural Mexican setting, where illness is frequently attributed to emotional discharges of anger.

The stresses produced by male-female interaction no doubt reflect on the health of both males and females. While dissension between males and females is inherently stressful to both sexes, the men can more easily remove themselves from the situation by leaving the house and dissipating the emotional strains in the *cantina* (liquor-serving station) with their cohorts. Rural Mexican women lack such escapes and outlets. In fact, in this region, among the peasant and wage-laboring class, women remain relatively isolated and require permission from their spouses to leave their households. In nuclear-family households, women spend most of their days alone at home doing their chores with little outside daily interaction other than with their spouses.

Additional sociocultural factors contributing to the underlying health problems in the female popoulation include the high rate of alcohol consumption by males. In addition to the economic drain on household funds created by alcohol consumption and the resultant budgetary deficits that the women must solve, the women may also be subject to physical abuse contributing to physical and psychological distress and to an overall state of ill health.

One last important point must still be made. The ecology along with the overall socio-economic conditions and nutritional deficits create an overall setting for relatively high infant mortality (Alba 1982; Escudero 1980). In personal terms these statistics translate into mother's grief that may become expressed symptomatically in chronic pain underlaying affective disorders as we see in Chapter 6.

To summarize, it can be assumed that we are confronted by a population whose overall impoverished state of health is attributable to a constellation of factors, including adverse ecological, economic and sociocultural conditions. To what degree these stresses are instrumental in producing specific symptoms patients present to Spiritualist healers and physicians remains a research question. But it is safe to say, based upon what is currently known about stress, that inimical ecological, social and economic conditions contribute to symptom formation.

4. THERAPEUTIC OPTIONS

The predominant health providers in the region are physicians and Spiritualist healers. In fact, the latter furnish health care to a large segment of the population throughout Mexico today (Foster & Anderson 1978; Lagarriga 1978; Madsen 1967). The healing role is assumed by many different persons, however, and several therapeutic modalities merit consideration. The purpose of this chapter is to describe briefly the medical and nonbiomedical options for managing illness that are available to the rural population. Present-day Mexico lacks a great medical tradition of the kind encountered currently in China, India, and Japan (Kleinman 1980; Leslie 1976; Lock 1980; Obeyesekere 1976). Biomedicine, differentially accessible to various segments of Mexican society, is the dominant treatment regime in Mexico. It is well entrenched and might even be regarded as the formal state "religion," analogous to the position it occupies in the United States and other industrialized societies (Freidson 1970).

Additionally, there are various kinds of nonbiomedical or quasi-medical health providers comprising the little tradition of folk practices. The present Mexican folk tradition is an amalgam whose roots are in the pre-Conquest period, but chiefly in medical beliefs and procedures introduced to Mexico by the Spanish after the Conquest in 1519 (Fabrega & Manning 1973), beliefs and procedures that are also incorporated into Spiritualist healing.

To facilitate the discussion, I have separated biomedical from nonbiomedical practices and gratis from nongratis choices, as is displayed in Table 4.1.

Among nonbiomedical gratis options, first and foremost is self-diagnosis and self-treatment, a prevalent phenomenon the world over (Kleinman 1980). Self-treatment usually entails administrating some type of herbal tea, and an analgesic or an antidiarrheal agent easily purchased in the local grocery store. Related to the first option are self-treatments performed on the advice of relatives, neighbors, or even casual acquaintances. Generally speaking, the local population regards medicines of any type as suitable for an illness condition rather than for a specific person. As a result, medicines are regarded as interchangeable among people, as long as the people's symptoms are the same. Although this view prevails in most societies respecting some types of medicines (such as aspirin for headaches), in rural Mexico this perception is probably more widespread. An example will illustrate the point. A woman, feeling ill, recounted her distress to her cousin. The cousin immediately associated the woman's symptoms with the ones she (the cousin) had experienced recently, for which a physician had prescribed a seemingly effective medicine. The cousin recommended that the woman take the medicine the cousin had been prescribed, and the woman followed the cousin's advice and purchased the same medicine. (The woman, however, continued to experience the same symptoms.)

Free therapeutic counsel is also provided, as in much of the world today, by radio and television commercials. Every rural household possesses a radio, and a majority of town and city families also own television sets. There are gradually becoming more widespread, even in rural villages.[1] It is difficult to know to what degree the Mexican rural population is influenced by television and radio advertising, as compared with the populations in industrial societies, but it seems likely that radio and television commercials have great impact in rural Mexico, where a relatively unsophisticated consumer population tends to accept commercial propaganda as fact. And people everywhere take remedies because of their advertised appeal.

Technically, Spiritualist treatment must be regarded as a gratis therapeutic option because Spiritualists do not charge any fees for their services; however, voluntary contributions are expected.

Most other nonbiomedical options involve payment, with some nonbiomedical practitioners charging higher fees than private physicians. Included among these are homeopaths and several types of traditional healers. The homeopaths are not widely dispersed in the region. There is a well-known homeopath practicing twenty-five miles from Juarez, and people occasionally reported having received special pills from him. My experience suggests that homeopaths are popular among all segments of Mexican society throughout the country.

Many individuals who claim powers to summon spirits treat patients in their homes. Some are Spiritists (Macklin 1974b, 1978), who, as we saw earlier, are not affiliated with the Mexican Spiritualists discussed here. Others include persons who were once associated with a Spiritualist temple but who later defected to establish a private practice. Spiritualist temple healers are not permitted to treat patients privately at home unless granted special permission by the temple head. The Spiritualist-type healers that receive patients at home charge almost as high, and sometimes higher, fees as physicians, and they sell pharmaceuticals at higher costs than pharmacies.

In one instance, a woman treated patients at home prescribing medicines chosen by her daughter, a young woman with a less than sixth grade education. The daughter consulted a standard pharmaceutical directory published for physicians and pharmacists. Patients patronizing healers of this type may have known them previously from Spiritualist temples. Such entrepreneurial healers, in contrast to physicians, dispense their services and medicines on credit and are ready to attend patients day or night.

There are other men and women who deal with misfortunes of any kind, including illness. These individuals, well known in the anthropological literature as witches or sorcerers, attend individuals who suspect that their misfortune is due to witchcraft. These persons, unlike Spiritualist healers, claim supernatural powers without entering trance, and they address their ministrations not to the patient's problems but to the person who allegedly caused the problems. People sometimes travel outside the region to consult with such practitioners, who may charge prices running into thousands of pesos.[2]

Another category of traditional practitioners are persons who, in this region, normally lay no claim to supernatural powers including bone-setters and *curanderas.* The former specialize in resetting fractures and broken bones. The latter are ordinary *curanderas,* well described in the literature (Adams and Rubel 1967; Foster & Anderson 1978), who depend on traditional curing procedures and a wide variety of medicinal plants. Their fees vary but are usually not exorbitant. However, as noted earlier, these secular practitioners are losing their popularity and are not being replaced by a younger generation of secular healers. On the other hand, Spiritualist curers, who vehemently dissociate themselves from *curanderas,* are increasing. They derive their legitimacy through the control and sanction of supernatural figures including Jehovah, Jesus Christ, and, most significantly in the Mexican context, the Virgin Mary. Consequently, traditional curers are being replaced more and more by Spiritualist healers.

Spiritualist healers are also replacing yet another category of traditional curers: women specializing in children's diseases. Such women still exist, but are becoming less numerous. These practitioners treat diarrheal disorders attributed to the evil eye as well as *cuajo,* a common syndrome in children, associated with symptoms such as intestinal dysfunction and a loss of body symmetry, with one leg becoming elongated or one eye enlarged.

Finally, there is a miscellaneous category of medicine dispensers, such as traveling vendors, medicine hucksters, and herbalists. Vendors, who come to people's doors to peddle their tonics, frequently succeed in convincing persons that their concoctions, for which they charge unconscienable prices, will alleviate all ailments. One always encounters herbalists in the local weekly markets, where they display and sell a large pharmacopoeia (see Appendix C) for every conceivable type of dysfunction--including male impotence and female infertility--at relatively low prices. Persons may inquire for an herb appropriate to their self-diagnosed condition, or they may consult an anatomical chart displayed by herb vendors indicating the proper herb for each anatomical part. Generally speaking, herbal cures are very popular among all social sectors and are usually regarded as safer than pharmaceutical preparations. The weekly markets also attract medicine hucksters (Simoni & Ball 1978) who sell cure-alls at relatively steep prices and from whom people may occasionally seek advice for their ailments.

It is noteworthy that at no time do subjects of the study recognize a very basic epistemological disparity between the various folk health providers and physicians (cf. Rubel 1971; Waxler 1976). Health providers of any kind, be they hucksters or physicians, are usually judged on the basis of one criterion: "Do they give good medicines?" That is to say, How well does the prescribed medicine alleviate the patient's symptoms and restore him to a self-perceived health state?

There are many physicians in the region. In fact, because Juarez is geographically situated in the heartland of the region, it is a medical center of sorts. Juarez and its environs are densely populated (127 persons per square mile), with a population of 17,000.[3] The town itself supports at least 15 practicing physicians. Although there are doctors in nearby small towns, Juarez has the reputation for having good physicians, meaning, as it happens, that they prescribe "good medicine."

Although rural regions usually experience difficulties in attracting physicians (Lopez Acuña 1976), physicians have been continuously moving into this area. Because of the region's high population density, the town is attractive to medical practitioners despite its rural location. It is, in the words of one doctor, a "good market for physicians." No doubt the region's excellent climate, unpolluted air, and proximity to Mexico City by newly constructed roads add to its desirability as a place to establish a medical practice outside the capital. Moreover, according to some recent medical-school graduates (See also Lopez Acuña 1976), there is an abundance of physicians in the country as a whole, and many graduates, including Juarez natives, are unable to find positions in Mexico City, their first preference. Consequently, several recent graduates set up practice in their home town. Juarez physicians are general practitioners who also perform surgery irrespective of their medical training. Their specialties are advertised on plaques outside their offices. For example, the most successful surgeon advertises dermatology as his specialty.

Local physicians usually do not keep records or medical histories on their patients. A patient restates symptoms on every visit and presents any previous prescription still in his or her possession. A physician's fees vary, ranging from 50 to 100 pesos. Several doctors maintain clinics, where they accommodate postsurgical and obstetrical patients, and pharmacies adjacent to clinics, where patients purchase their prescriptions.

However, patients seek the advice of the pharmacy attendants who normally have a sixth-grade education before they consult with a physician. Pharmacy attendants dispense free advice in cases of self-diagnosis, but many of them also charge for simple services. A case in point: a woman came into a pharmacy to purchase medicine for a cold. The attendant, an 18-year old girl with about a year's experience as a pharmacy clerk, informed the client that the medication she had requested was not available, but the clerk could recommend a similar injectable medicine. The customer agreed that an injection acts faster than a pill, and the girl injected the medication for the client for a small fee.

Among gratis medical options, there are three types of government subsidized health services in Mexico. Government employees are furnished health care by the Health and Social Service system provided for all federal employees. Of the three national health-care programs, the federal employees' health service is regarded as the best in the country. Mexico's social security system serves the health-care needs of the country's labor force and is usually available to permanently employed factory workers. Only about 16 percent of the subject population in the region is covered by one of the three federally supported health plans (Finkler 1981b).

The majority of the rural population must seek medical care from private physicians or from government-run health centers, considered the poorest of the three government health care facilities (Lopez Acuña 1976). To serve the majority of Mexico's population--(over 70 percent in 1976 Lopez Acuña 1976)--not covered by the two previously mentioned health programs, the government established a network of health centers throughout Mexico. In the rural regions these centers are staffed mostly by *pasantes* or inexperienced physicians (Davis Tzu 1980). *Pasantes* are medical students who have completed all their requirements except a one-year mandatory social service. To meet this requirement *pasantes* are sent to rural health-care centers. These young physicians usually originate from economically well-situated homes in large cities for whom residing in an alien rural region is a hardship post. It is no wonder, then, that these facilities are under-utilized (Davis Tzu 1980), as my observations also reveal,[4] despite the fact that the Mexican government has made a great effort to extend medical services for the rural population (Meneses 1979). Mothers usually take their infants for mandatory inoculations, but except for the public-health campaigns, the government health centers had had little success in providing medical options at a minimal cost.

Finally, the relationship between medical doctors and Spiritualist healers is noteworthy. The formal relationship between the two therapeutic regimes is skewed. Whereas, on the one hand, as I noted in Chapter 2, every Spiritualist religious ritual terminates with a specific blessing for all doctors, physicians, on the other hand, usually brand Spiritualist healers as sorcerers *brujas,* who must be avoided at all times. From this it follows that although physicians are not likely to recommend a patient to a Spiritualist healer, some Spiritualist curers, as we will see, will counsel a patient to seek medical therapy.

In summary, biomedical services are readily accessible in Juarez and its environs. Government health centers are scattered throughout the region; however, these establishments are greatly underutilized. We have also seen the different types of folk practitioners supplying treatment and dispensing health-care advice. In Chapter 6 we will examine the patterns of resort of the patients, who may use Spiritualists, physicians, or both.

Table 4.1　Therapeutic Options

	Nonbiomedical	Biomedical
Gratis	Self-treatment Radio and TV commercials Spiritualist temples Pharmacy attendants	Government health centers Mexican health-insurance plans
Not gratis	Homeopaths Private Spiritualist healers; 　Spiritists; sorcerers Curanderas Traveling vendors Medicine hucksters Herbalists Pharmacy attendants Injection specialists Bonesetters	Private physicians

5. ILLNESS ETIOLOGIES

TRADITIONAL MEXICAN BELIEFS

Traditional Mexican attributions of illness are influenced by societal patterns and are also closely linked to therapeutic resorts that I explore in the next chapter. According to Foster (1976), to understand illness attributions is to know a therapeutic system and its attendant procedures. Moreover, like religion itself, a people's explanations of illness origins shape illness expression and illness behavior, and they reflect premises about the relation of human beings to the environment, to other human beings and society, and to themselves. Spiritualist illness ascriptions depart from traditional folk understandings in important ways, but, surprisingly, they share significant attributes of the medical model. Importantly, the parallelism between biomedical and Spiritualist paradigms even may facilitate in some measure the observed complementarity in patients' therapeutic choices, as comes into view in the next chapter.

Traditionally, illness is ascribed to natural and supernatural causes in Mexico as elsewhere (Foster 1976). Table 5.1 displays two prevailing explanatory models of illness etiologies. These fall into two groupings, those that are exogenous and those that are endogenous to the organism. As can be seen in Table 5.1, exogenous attributions of impairments reflect a cognitive model that posits an environment inimical to the organism, as, for example, in the belief that cold, wet, rainy weather causes organic distress.

Environmental and behavioral factors are sometimes interwoven to account for physical impairments. For instance, hard work in the hot sun is considered detrimental to health. Behavioral factors alone, including physical and mental exertions, may also produce illness.

Appropriate   nutrition   is   believed   to   mitigate   illness. Dysfunctions are imputed to irregularity of food intake, when meals are not taken on time or when too much or too little food is consumed. Importantly too, it is believed that nutritional deficits stimulate emotional reactions, especially anger, to which a wide array of illnesses are ascribed, as shown in Table 5.1.

Moving to endogenously produced impairments, the traditional model of illlness places little emphasis on person's relation to himself or herself in terms of imputing illness to internal psychological conflicts, as is done, for example, in psychoanalytic theory. The most important origins of illness are natural endogenous causes that refer to individual emotional states intentionally or inadvertently generated by   others,   reflecting   traditional   premises   respecting   human interpersonal relationships.

Fabrega and Manning (1979) observe that in the theory of disease of the Ladinos of Chiapas, emotional states occupy the logical analogue to germs in biomedical theory. Their findings are equally relevant to our region, where it is believed that emotions produce a variety of syndromes. Bereavement, for example, is regarded as a powerful emotional response to an external occurrence, outside the individual's control; it is frequently associated with an overall feeling of being sick. Another example of emotion-induced illness is the well-described phenomenon of *susto* (O'Nell & Selby 1968; Rubel 1964; Uzzell 1974), which is traced to an unexpected fright. It, too, is an affliction caused by a person's response to an astounding personal event, for instance, the unanticipated death of a loved one, the unexpected appearance of an animal, or an accidental brush with death. *Susto* is so powerful a cause of illness that physical symptoms may appear even after a year's delay.

Muina, coraje, and *bilis* represent differential intensities of anger. Anger of any type is instrumental in numerous impairments (as is shown in Table 5.1), including headaches (i.e., pain in the *cabeza*) and   pain   in   the   *cerebro*   (distinct   problems   in   the   Mexican categorization of illness). Pain in the *cabeza* is glossed as "headache" and pertains to the area around the temples and forehead. Pain in the *cerebro* is identified as pain in the occipital-medulla region down to the nuchal muscle. Although headache (pain in the *cabeza*) is most frequently attributed to natural causes in conjunction with a cold or grippe, pain in the *cerebro* is most assuredly caused by *muina, coraje,* or *bilis.*

Mexicans readily admit to feelings of anger and recognize it as an inevitable human emotion. People characterize themselves by saying. "I am an angry person." More pointedly, anger of varying intensity is an episodic response by a person to an upsetting interaction   with   a   spouse,   a   child,   or   a   neighbor.   In   such circumstances, the blame is imputed not to the sufferer but to the person who provoked the anger. Anger is so potent a cause of illness, it is believed, that a nursing mother who experiences rage most assuredly will transmit an illness to her offspring.

In view of the belief that anger produces illness, implicitly its inhibition promotes smooth social interaction. Thus, illness attribution is an important mechanism of social control and social interaction.

Feelings of anger are closely associated with nerves, a condition prevalent throughout Latin America (Low 1981). Nerves, or *nervios,* are regarded both as a cause of illness and an illness state. As an illness state, the condition refers to a general nervous state with aches in the entire body, quick temper, and the sense that nothing seems to go right. This syndrome is most frequently thought to originate with *susto,* anger, poor diet, or high blood pressure. Nerves, in turn, can also provoke a headache, pain in the *cerebro,* and other physiological states.

At this juncture it is instructive to emphasize that Mexican physicians, like physicians everywhere (Engel 1977; Thomas 1977) tend to minimize beliefs in emotionally produced illness states. By so doing, Mexican doctors run counter to a prevailing holistic model of sickness. In fact, whereas physicians dismiss somatized symptoms with, "Oh, it's nothing; it's just nerves," the traditional view is, "If it's nerves, it *is* something."

This leads to yet another important consideration. In the traditional system the imputation of illness to emotions is not based on mind/body dualism. Traditional Mexican beliefs emphasize an interactional view between mind and body, and in this respect the system closely corresponds to scientifically produced paradigms emphasizing the role of psychological stress in producing disease (e.g., Antonovsky 1980; Holmes and Masuda 1974; Pelletier 1979).

Consider, for example, Amkraut and Solomon's (1975) findings that stress and emotional distress may influence the functions of the immunological system, presumably through neuroendocrine mediation. Moreover, social factors and psychological depression have been linked to susceptibility to delayed recovery from infectious disease. Holmes and Masuda (1974) find a positive correlation between magnitude of life change in life crises and the gravity of chronic illness. Significantly, loss and bereavement are first and foremost on their list of life's tragedies leading to affliction (Engel 1977; Holmes and Masuda (1974), and even mortality (Jacobs & Ostfeld 1977; Lloyd 1980). Loss has been implicated in depressive disorders, as is revealed by recent investigations demonstrating that 95 percent of depressions are related to separation (Lloyd 1980). Aside from loss, Lloyd also discloses that depression is related to interpersonal conflict within the family and especially between spouses. As we will see in Chapter 6, emotional distresses concomitant with somatization of depression are common dysfunctions encountered among Spiritualist patients, reflecting the local explanatory model of illness as well as the role of emotional etiological factors in disease and illness.

In fact, I hypothesize that subjectively perceived stressful life events may play a crucial role in illness when they are culturally and collectively accepted to be stressful, as they are in Mexico. As culturally constituted etiological statements such events as bereavement, separation, and stressful emotions may indeed become instrumental in producing illness, especially depressive disorders.

The supernatural causes of affliction displayed in Table 5.1 are imputed to forces external to the individual. Supernatural illness etiologies, usually exogenous forces such as witchcraft or *aire*, are linked with illnesses that are not curable biomedically. It is commonly believed that when an illness is not curable by physicians, it must surely have been caused by witchcraft. The syllogism produced may be stated as follows: If doctors cannot cure the illness, it must be due to witchcraft; if it were not witchcraft, a doctor could cure it; therefore, it is due to witchcraft. A symbiosis is thus established between biomedicine's deficits and the imputation of illness to supernatural causes. Because biomedicine fails to cure or alleviate an array of dysfunctions, numerous illnesses fall under the category of "caused supernaturally." This includes psychotic episodes *(loco)* characterizing persons who "don't know what they are doing," who respond inappropriately to given situations, and who have lost "their five senses." Interestingly, although witchcraft could be performed in the victim's absence, in cases of psychosis the victim had invariably been fed an unspecified food; thus, the victim's presence would have been required.

Traditional beliefs in *aire* resemble Spiritualist concepts of "perturbed spirits." *Aire*, like nerves, is regarded both as a cause of illness and an illness state. In fact, in our region *aire* is rarely mentioned as an illness per se; however, it is frequently implicated in symptoms that, as shown in Table 5.1, range from diarrhea to body paralysis. In all cases of mandibular or maxillary contortions, or generalized body pain that is expressed in a feeling of numbness in one or both arms or feet, the cause is without hesitation attributed to *aire*.[1]

Aire, often cited in the literature as a Mesoamerican illness category (Adams & Rubel 1967; Foster 1953; Ingham 1970; W. Madsen 1955), is variously explained in different regions. Locally, *aire* is ascribed to the spirits of individuals who died a violent death or lived a violent life, such as persons who were murdered or who fell into irrigation canals, a particular danger in this region. These spirits, most always identified as male, linger in the same spots where they met their demise, or at the cemetery, and they attack living persons as they pass by.

Witchcraft and *aire* ideologies exemplify the point made earlier that illness attributions reflect the social order and interpersonal relations. Beliefs in witchcraft suggest intense social interactions among equals (Lewis 1971) and as I noted at the outset, they promote suspicion among neighbors, friends and relatives, and thereby also induce emotional responses that cause anger and sickness.

Witchcraft beliefs also reflect institutional deficits, as we have seen in Chapter 3, when mechanisms to mitigate disputes are lacking, and individuals must resort instead to either witchcraft or homicide. Homicide, as we have seen, is associated with *aire*, or malignant spirits that come into existence as a result of human beings having committed murder or other evil acts. Imputation of illness to malevolent spirits, such as beliefs in *aire*, mirror extant societal deficiencies that lead to homicide and to the release of perturbed spirits into the atmosphere to inflict illness on innocent victims.

SPIRITUALIST ILLNESS ATTRIBUTION

Spiritualists, like traditional Mexicans, believe in the same natural causes of illness; Spiritualists, however, diverge from the customary explanatory model by denying the existence of witchcraft and by emphasizing a mind/body dualism that lacks prominence in the traditional model. Spiritualists believe that all illnesses not curable by physicians are attributable to perturbed spirits. In a curious way, Spiritualist illness etiologies, like traditional explanations, are likewise contingent upon biomedicines's failures.

Nevertheless, while both traditional beliefs and Spiritualism impute illness to *aire*, Spiritualists have expanded the belief in *aire* to incorporate dysfunctions not included in the traditional explanatory model. Spiritualists claim that perturbed spirits are instrumental in producing all types of illness that refuse to yield to biomedical or routine Spiritual ministrations.

According to some Spiritualists, perturbed spirits are especially prone to cause chronic impairments of the type not cured biomedically, including kidney dysfunction, cancer, and schizophrenia. Thus, while traditional etiology frequently ascribes illness to witchcraft, Spiritualists, in contrast, deny the existence of witchcraft and attribute various afflictions to impersonal perturbed spirits. In distinction to the beliefs in other cultures, where perturbed spirits can cause all types of misfortunes (Foster 1976), the Spiritualists believe that perturbed spirits tend to cause only illnesses, misfortunes of other kinds being attributed to the will of God.

By imputing affliction solely to impersonal spirits, Spiritualists make an important statement about human interaction and the shaping of illness. For instance, the great importance Spiritualists attach to amiable social relations is evidenced by their shifting the onus of an illness from one's neighbors, friends, or relatives to impersonal spirits. By so doing, they eliminate emotional discharges aimed at individuals in close relationships, discharges that might otherwise be instrumental in producing future illness episodes. As I have already noted, many patients recognize the advantages of an ideology that stresses positive social interaction. Later we will encounter patients like Jaime, whose condition deteriorated after he visited one of the traditional *curanderas* who, unlike Spiritualist healers, confirm patients' beliefs in witchcraft. The reasons Spiritualist healing is attractive to patients are examined in Chapter 9, but at this juncture it is useful to call attention to the fact that Spiritualist healers' popularity may be related to their advocacy of ideological change of this type.

One other significant point remains to be made regarding the change in etiological explanations from witchcraft to spirit possession that Spiritualists have introduced. Lewis (1971) cogently argues that witchcraft strategems reflect egalitarian social interactions whereas possession by spirits suggests the prevalence of social inequality. In societies where social inequalities predominate spirit possession is launched as an attack by the subordinate on the superior. The practice of spirit possession is thus a symbolic recognition of extant inequalities in the social order. We have seen in Chapter 2 that Mexican society has undergone a change on a local level from egalitarian to unequal social relations. The etiological explanations Spiritualists promote are thus consonant with the social trans-formations that had occurred in the country within the past century. The change in etiological explanation also demonstrates an important theoretical consideration that such explanations are linked with social and cultural forces in the society at large.

In contrast to the traditional holistic concept of human illness, mind/body dualism is prominent in Spiritualism. As a matter of fact, Spiritualists largely recruit their membership from that pool of patients seeking their ministrations whom they consider to be suffering from "spiritual" as opposed to "material" or physical dysfunctions. Spiritualists hold the view that those afflicted spiritually are possessed by dark spirits, as described in Chapter 2, who stubbornly refuse to vacate the bodies of the persons they occupy. In later chapters I will deal with the variety of symptoms included in this category of dysfunctions; but within the present context Spiritualist dualism is interesting because it differs from the traditional Mexican view and corresponds more closely to the Cartesian mind/body dichotomy.

What is interesting about comparing the Spiritualist and biomedical models of illness is that they paradoxically resemble each other structurally more than the traditional Mexican and Spiritualist models do, both by imputing illness to impersonal rather than personal agents and by their emphasis on mind/body dualism.

Much has been written about the biomedical model of disease, and it need not be elaborated upon in detail here. Suffice it to say that it is reductionist and dualistic, attributing disease to attacks on the organism by pathogens, to endogenously produced malfunction, or to attenuated endogenous defenses. This view is best summarized by Engel (1977:130); who notes of biomedicine:

> It leaves no room within its framework for the social, psychological, and behavioral dimensions of illness. The biomedical model not only requires that disease be dealt with as an entity independent of social behavior, it also demands that behavioral aberrations be explained on the basis of disordered somatic (biochemical) or neuro-physiological processes. Thus the biomedical model embraces both reductionism, the philosophic view that complex phenomena are ultimately derived from a single primary principle, and mind/body dualism, the doctrine that separates the mental from the somatic.

Biomedicine removes the responsibility for physiological insults from the patient and places it on impersonal mechanistic forces in much the same way as Spiritualism transforms etiological beliefs from witchcraft to perturbed spirits at large in the universe. Neither Spiritualism nor biomedicine holds patients liable for their illnesses. Like medical and behavioral models of mental disorders (cf. Eisenberg 1977), Spiritualism regards illness of the spirit as caused by forces apart from the patient as a thinking and feeling person.

The mind/body duality we witness in Spiritualism is instructive in yet another respect. It has frequently been asserted that, unlike medical practitioners, folk healers share with their patients the same etiological premises and vision of the universes (e.g. Fabrega and Silver 1973; Foster and Anderson 1978; Kearney 1978a). It is assumed that the sharing of common understandings fosters the interaction between the two parties and forms a basis for a people's choice of folk practitioners in place of physicians. Spiritualist healers however fail to share etiological premises with the majority of the patients whom they treat suggesting that patients and healers need not always share common etiological assumptions for the encounter to take place.

The foregoing discussion brings into perspective the complementarity between biomedicine and Spiritualism as a health-care delivery system. This complementarity between the two regimes is brought into sharper focus behaviorally when patients' resort patterns are explored, in Chapter 6. It will be seen that the two therapeutic systems are not in competition with one another, contrary to the belief of even some Mexican physicians.

Table 5.1   Traditional Categories of Illness Attribution

NATURAL CAUSES

Cause	Exogenous Illness	Cause	Endogenous Illness
Environmental		**Emotional**	
Inclement Weather	Rheumatism; cold; grippe; bronchitis; pulmonary condition; vaginal secretions; fever/chills	Bereavement	Unspecified illness state
Behavioral		Susto (fright)	Tuberculosis/pulmonary impairment; diabetes; abdominal distress; lack of appetite; listlessness; cerebro/headaches; nerves; skin disorders; depigmentation
Heavy mental concentration; too much thinking	Headache		
Hard work Lifting heavy loads	Cintura* Hernia; kidney condition ovarian pain	Muinas/coraje; bilis (anger)	Gallbladder problems; cerebro; convulsion; diarrhea; tumor; rheumatism; liver impairment; pneumonia; nerves
Sitting in one spot for a long time (e.g., driving) Sitting on hot stones or hot ground	Hemorrhoids	Nerves	Tonsillitis; cerebro/headache; rheumatism
Nutritional		**Physiological**	
Poor diet; lack of vitamins	Anemia; anger	High blood pressure	Headache; nerves
Skipping meals; irregular eating habits	Unspecified illness state; cerebro/headache		
Eating too much food or spoiled food that attaches itself to the stomach	Diarrhea; parasites empacho (bolus attached to the stomach)		

Table 5.1   cont'd.

Exogenous		Endogenous	
Cause	Illness	Cause	Illness
NATURAL CAUSES			
Eating wrong foods; e.g., <u>nopal</u> squash, peanuts; or eating at improper times; e.g. melon in the morning	Vaginal fluids; <u>empacho</u>		
SUPERNATURAL CAUSES			
<u>Aire</u>	Intestinal problems; dysentery, vomiting; diarrhea; pains in arms and feet; crooked mouth; paralysis of mouth; body paralysis		
Witchcraft	Illness unsuccessfully treated by physician		
Food given to a person to eat	Madness (<u>loco</u>)		

*<u>Cintura</u> refers to pain in the waist as well as lower back. Women frequently associate the pain in the waist with pain in the ovaries. This illness may be related to gynecological problems, including a type of pelvic congestion syndrome, which includes symptoms of abdominal and lower back pain.

6. PATIENTS AND THEIR PATTERNS OF RESORT

In Chapter 4, we saw the various therapeutic options available to the people of the region. Now our focus turns to the patients who patronize Spiritualist temples and physicians. Initially, I implicitly assumed that all temple patients follow a similar pattern of resort, and that all individuals from the region's lower socioeconomic sectors practice dual use. Accordingly, I postulated that Spiritualist healing was universally accepted within the peasant and wage-laboring sectors of the region, but that patients would present different symptoms to Spiritualist healers and to medical practitioners.

These assumptions were not fully borne out by my research findings, in fact, three separate categories of patients seek temple treatment with each presenting a different typology of symptoms and practicing a different pattern of therapeutic resort. Moreover, not all persons from the peasant and wage-laboring sector seek Spiritualist ministrations and there seem to be several unexpected behavioral and demographic dissimilarities between the temples' and physicians' patients.

In this chapter, then, I compare temple and physician patients[1] along sociological, demographic, and health-related dimensions that illuminate the similarities and dissimilarities between patients resorting to disparate therapeutic regimes. This comparison sheds light on the variety of contemporary treatment-seeking strategies encountered in an ostensibly homogeneous segment of a complex society. This is significant because it illuminates intracultural diversity. Too often, generalizations are made suggesting that responses to health-care choices are uniform within a given socioeconomic or cultural group.

57

TEMPLE PATIENTS

Turning our attention first to temple patients only, 58 percent of the temple clientele are adult females, 27 percent are children, and 15 percent are adult males.

Among these there are three categories of persons who resort to temple health care which I have designated as regulars, first-comers, and habitual temple users.

Regulars

Regulars are persons who have adopted Spiritualism as their religion and who participate frequently in temple rituals. Regulars include temple functionaries, curers, and persons who regularly attend Spiritualist irradiations. Unlike members of the other two groups, regulars usually consult temple curers first in all cases of illness. Hence, when an illness befalls a regular's household, the ill individual immediately seeks treatment at the temple. However, if a cure is not effected within a brief span of time, then the patient resorts to medical services. In fact, the temple curer may even suggest to the patient that he or she consult a physician. To cite but one example, albeit an uncommon one, Lupe, whom we have encountered earlier and will meet again later, gave birth to an extremely sickly child and brought the infant at one week of age to the temple for treatment. The baby was treated by several curers, including Lupe's own spirit protector. After about two weeks, when the baby was not responding to the various treatments administered in the temple, Lupe took it to the Children's Hospital in Mexico City where it died soon thereafter.

It may also happen that after a temple regular has seen a physician, he or she might return to the temple to confirm the physician's diagnosis. The diagnosis is confirmed or disputed depending upon the particular healer and his or her stance toward the medical profession. This point will be explored in Chapter 7.

Mexican physicians frequently complain that patients come to them as a last resort and fail to receive adequate medical care because of the folk practitioners whom patients prefer to consult first. Physicians claim that by the time a patient arrives in their office, his or her dysfunction is too far advanced for them to resolve it successfully. To the extent that this argument is valid at all, it only applies to regulars; and even among regulars, Lupe is unusual in that she put off taking the infant to the hospital for a long time. More commonly, regulars resort to medical treatment if after a week or so of temple therapy, the patient's condition has not improved. As we will see in Chapter 8, in the majority of cases the regulars' first contact with the temple occurs during an illness episode. Events follow a similar pattern for most : the individual is unsuccessfully treated by one or more physicians and even specialists, and he or she comes to the temple as a measure of last resort having been told about the temple's existence by a friend, relative, or neighbor.

First-comers

This brings us to the second category of temple users, the first-comers. Ironically, physicians and Spiritualist healers similarly complain that patients come to them as a last resort, when the illness is too advanced for either of them to effect a cure. The findings, however, support the healers assertion, but not the physicians'. As a general rule, first-comers include individuals who failed to respond to medical treatment and who as a final recourse sought an alternative mode of health care. Sometimes, these persons have been advised by a physician that their sole hope of a cure is a surgical procedure, which many patients fear. By their reasoning regarding the etiology of their illness, first-comers create an interesting symbiosis between medical practitioners and Spiritualist healers. As was noted in Chapter 5, in most cases, when an individual fails to be cured biomedically, the individual concludes that the illness was caused by witchcraft. We have seen that this type of reasoning creates a curious paradox, because Spiritualists repudiate the reality of witchcraft. Although we can assume that first-comers who never return to the temple remain convinced that their illness resulted from witchcraft, both regulars and habitual temple users tend to relinquish their beliefs in the malevolent powers of relatives, friends, and neighbors.

Successfully treated first-comers, then, become either regulars or habitual temple users, the last category for discussion.

Habitual Temple Users

Habitual Temple Users comprise the majority of temple patients. This category refers to persons who, having been successfully cured once by Spiritualist healers, return again on other occasions, though they are not themselves Spiritualists.

Of 1212 patients for whom I wrote prescriptions, only 135 or approximately 11 percent were regulars; the remaining 89 percent varied between first-comers and habitual users. Of those interviewed at the temple , excluding the regulars, 26.4 percent were first-comers; the remaining 73.6 percent were habitual temple users. Among the habitual temple users, 27.1 percent had been seeking treatment there intermittently for 1 year or less, 25.5 percent for 1-7 years, and 21 percent for 8-20 years. It must be emphasized that the term "habitual temple users" used in order to differentiate this group from the regulars and the first-comers, does not imply that this group resorts to temple treatment indiscriminately.

The pattern of resort of habitual temple users follows cultural notions bearing on the gravity or the non-gravity of a set of symptoms. Grave illness refers to life-threatening afflictions, illness episodes requiring confinement to bed, and sundry conditions involving fever. While fever alone, in the absence of additional symptoms, is not regarded as grave, fever is assessed as a grave symptom if associated with diarrhea, vomiting, or pain in other parts of the body. Significantly, absence of pain militates against the recognition of the seriousness of a given condition. For example, enteropathogens which, as we have seen, are endemic to the area but which frequently are asymptomatic, especially when not accompanied by fever, are not regarded as serious illness. In fact, individuals may often fail to mention to a physician or a Spiritualist curer that they have noted parasites such as worms in their own or their children's excrement, unless they have been suffering pain.

Twenty-eight habitual temple users of those interviewed indicated precisely what their households did during a given illness episode and the reason for the action. Their responses are shown in Table 6.1. Table 6.1 shows the type of illnesses regarded by the respondents as grave and non-grave and the type of treatment sought for each condition. The complementary pattern of resort by habitual temple users as shown in Table 6.1 exhibits great regularity and predictability. Interestingly, these findings coincide with those by Young (1978a, 1978b), who, using a decision model, also demonstrates that the complementary use of biomedical and nonbiomedical health-care services is predicated on similar distinctions of gravity/ nongravity. Habitual temple users' dual-resort pattern is evident from their responses pertaining to treatment-seeking behavior during a prior illness episode. Of our sample, 39.7 percent sought treatment from physicians during their last illness; 26.5 percent sought treatment at the temple, and the remaining 33.8 percent sought no treatment at all, with a few individuals attending a government health center.

In sum, the findings on habitual temple users suggest that patients seek out temple curers not only out of commitment to cultural illness (Schwartz 1973) and not only during cultural illness episodes such as *susto,* and *empacho* (Rubel 1960); but also, because of traditional definitions of grave/nongrave illness--which definitions, of course, are not necessarily congruent with medical evaluations, as, for example, in the case of parasitosis.

COMPLAINTS OF TEMPLE PATIENTS

The types of complaints brought to the temple by all three categories of patients are shown in Table 6.2, which is based on my observations during my apprenticeship at the temple.

Cleansings which will be described and analyzed more fully later, refers to an important symbolic aspect of Spiritualist treatment. The importance of temple patients' desire for cleansing as disclosed in

Table 6.2, provides an empirical basis for my later discussion on patients symbolic requisites for recovery.

The gastrointestinal dysfunctions reported in Table 6.2 include a wide array of illnesses frequently reported in terms of feeling bloated or of suffering abdominal distension or flatus. The musculoskeletal disorders are not clearly defined: patients report overall body aches, numbness (which most often is attributed to aire) in the upper or lower limbs or both, aches in lower extremities, or a general feeling of physical malaise. Significantly, the vagueness of musculoskeletal complaints presented at the temple contrast with the more specific symptoms reported to a physician at his office displayed later in Table 6.4. Skin eruptions and blemishes are more frequently presented at the temple than at the physician's office, as will be seen in our comparison of the two sets of data.

Surprisingly, a relatively small percentage of temple patients comes to seek advice for personal problems, as is evident from this set of data. In fact, many of those seeking counsel are regulars who tend to become dependent upon guidance from spirit mediums. Patients' dependence upon healers is explored in Chapters 9 and 10.

The small percentage of verbalized personal problems presented at the temple suggests that temple patients in the rural region seek an alternative healing mode not simply to deal with psychological distresses--as, for example, is the case with the Spiritualists in Wales (Skultans 1974) and Spiritists in urban centers (Harwood 1977a, 1977b)--but also to resolve physical complaints. Most probably, however, many of these complaints are somatizations of dysphoric affect or other psychological distress. Somatization is a common psychosocial adaptation in nonindustrialized societies where mental illness is not admitted (Eisenberg 1977) and where psychological problems are not viewed as medical ones (Kleinman 1980). Somatization is also common in cultures like that of Mexico, where, as we have seen, psychological states are given physiological expression.

Many disorders attributed to anger--*muina* and *coraje* or *bilis*--are directly associated with interpersonal strife, especially between men and women. In fact, the majority of problems presented to Spiritualist healers concern conflicts between men and women.

Types of personal difficulties presented to temple healers are set forth in Table 6.3.

The high frequency of conflicts between men and women re-quires some comments. Such hostilities often have economic underpinnings. Economic deficits directly affect the women, who usually are left with the responsibility to manage household funds. Additionally, heavy drinking is prevalent among men. This, too, takes its toll on the women, despite the fact that Table 6.3 discloses a small percentage of alcohol-related problems (heavy alcohol consumption is not always viewed as a problem).   Male-female tensions may also be related to changing family structure, a point made in Chapter 3. With a shift from extended to nuclear family arrangements, latent strife between spouses comes to the fore in the absence of authoritative persons in the household who mitigate interpersonal dissension.

Beside tensions between men and women, Table 6.3 reveals temple patients' other existential concerns, including monetary disputes among family members and women competing for the same man.   Other areas causing deep distress include, of course, loss of mother or of a child, abandonment by mate, as well as a felt loss of luck. Currently, children's performance at school is a concern, too, because, as we have seen, parents exert great efforts to maintain their children in school.

COMPLAINTS OF PHYSICIAN'S PATIENTS

Not all who live in the region seek treatment at Spiritualist temples, however. In fact, individuals from a control group of ostensibly healthy persons (N - 372) allegedly never sought temple tratment. Similarly, 89.9 percent of patients seeking treatment at a doctor's office claimed that they had always sought treatment from physicians. The remaining 10 percent included those who had never previously sought treatment outside the home and those who had gone to a temple for a cleansing. In sum, these data, as well as those obtained from the control group, suggest that the region encompasses individuals with distinctly different health-care preferences. This finding is very significant, because it reveals behavioral heterogeneity rather than homogeneity. I shall return to this issue in Chapter 9.

The data displayed in Table 6.4 are important for at least two reasons.   First,   they   disclose   discrepancies   between   patients' assessment of their conditions and the physician's diagnosis; second, when the data in Tables 6.2 and 6.4 are compared, they disclose similarities and dissimilarities between the two groups of resort.

A comparison between columns 1 and 2 in Table 6.4 reveals that the diagnosis of patients conditions provided to me by the physician reflect, but fail to correspond to patients self perceived symptoms, for which they had sought treatment. It can be seen that the physician   diagnosed   a   higher   incidence   of   gastrointestinal malfunctions   than   the   patients   and   identified   urinary-tract impairments of which patients were not cognizant. These findings are not surprising; they simply support the well-established fact that the biomedical and lay models of illness fail to correspond (Freidson 1970; Mechanic 1968) unless patients share similar social and educational backgrounds with physicians. In our region, of course, the subject population and the physicians originate from distinct social strata.

Different uses are made of medical and Spiritualist healers, as is made clear by a comparison between Tables 6.2 and 6.4. For example, we see immediately that as expected, doctors' patients fail to seek cleansings or solutions to personal problems. Life's problems are not categorized as medical concerns to be solved by physicians. Gastrointestinal disorders are frequent complaints presented in both establishments. But obstetrics-related cases are rarely brought before temple healers, whereas almost one-quarter of the physicians' practice is devoted to obstetric cases.

Accident-related injuries are rarely introduced at the temple. Impairments associated with bleeding and noxious pain are regarded as sufficiently grave to require immediate medical attention. In fact, I never witnessed a patient brought to the temple bleeding or wounded, and needing treatment.

Respiratory malfunctions associated with chest pains, coughs, and grippes are frequently reported in the region (see Appendix D), and these are reflected in Tables 6.2 and 6.4.

As mentioned previously, complaints of surface skin eruptions are more frequently presented to temple healers than to physicians, with physician patients attending to these by self-treatment. This simply supports another finding, that in cases of nongrave conditions habitual temple users seek temple treatment, whereas the physician's patients resort to various self-treatments.

To summarize the comparison made thus far, we note that conditions for which patients seek treatment from physicians involve insults to the organism associated with acute rather than chronic pain. Pursuing this line of thought further, I postulated that from a biomedical perspective, conditions treated by the physician were more life-threatening and more disabling than those presented at the temple. The latter assumption is attested to by several findings. First, while 79.9 percent of the doctor group indicated that they "couldn't do anything" when they had fallen ill during their last illness episode, only 42.6 percent of the temple group gave this response. Inasmuch as the subjects under discussion comprise an ethnically homogeneous group, it is unlikely that they respond differentially to illness episodes, in contrast to the case in Chiapas (Fabrega 1977), where different ethnic groups exhibit distinct patterns of disability. Second, the research tends to support the hypothesis that illnesses presented at the temple are types of impairments that linger on for relatively long periods of time, conditions which some have associated with neurotic behavior in general (Dohrenwend and Dohrenwend 1965) and others specifically with dysphoria (Blumer et al 1980; Sternbach 1974). This hypothesis is also supported by the Cornell Medical Index Health Questionnaire (CMI) mean scores for the two groups, as displayed in Table 6.5.

Although there are no statistically significant differences between the two groups' total scores, women in the temple group render significantly higher scores (.001) by the t test, than women in the doctor group on the emotional-disturbance section of the questionnaire. There is no statistically significant difference between the males in the two groups. Total scores, however, mask subtle differences between the two subject groups.

Perusal of responses on the separate subsections of the questionnaire permits closer scrutiny of the variations between the two groups' scores. These results come into view in Figures 6.1 and 6.2. Figure 6.1 discloses that men from the temple group tend to experience higher scores on the following sections: musculoskeletal, nerves, fatigability, inadequacy, depression, sensitivity, anger, and tension. However, the differences between the two groups are not statistically significant.

Figure 6.2 brings into sharp relief the significant differences using the t test, between the women's responses on the emotional disturbance section of the questionnaire, with the temple women scoring significantly higher on anger (.001); on inadequacy, depression, sensitivity, and tension (.01); and on anxiety (.05). Figure 6.2 reveals also somewhat higher fatigability scores, analogous to those in Figure 6.1. As among the men, among women the mean fatigability score is not statistically significant between the two groups. The fact that they are higher is not surprising, however, because fatigability tends to be associated with emotional disturbance, especially depression.

In sum, both temple and doctor groups tend to experience similar physical symptoms as measured by the CMI, with women from the temple group experiencing more self-perceived emotional disorders than women from the doctor group.

Additionally, women in the temple group tend to score significantly higher (.01) by the t test on the emotional disturbance section than men in the temple group, but there is no similar significant difference between the men and women in the doctor group. One important reason for this difference is no doubt related to the fact that a common syndrome suffered by persons in the region is nerves, a condition regarded as untreatable by physicians. Thus, while only one patient in the doctor's office came to alleviate nerves, two percent of the temple patients indicated that they came to seek treatment for this condition.

Although nerves is not exclusively a women's illness, more women than men tend to report this disorder. There are several reasons for this. We have seen before that, as an illness state, the etiology of nerves is anger and tension which subjects attributed to dissension with their spouses and also to their day-to-day interactions with their children, especially when children fight among themselves or fail to obey their mother. These situations provoke angry responses in both sexes, but, as indicated in Chapter 3, Mexican culture provides men with coping strategies that allow them to dissipate emotional strains with their cohorts. Women lack culturally equivalent outlets for expressing anger.

The preceding discussion illuminates the differential CMI results disclosed by the investigation. First, the significant differences between the males and females within the temple group simply reflect the fact that although men in this group may tend to suffer from depressive disorders, they can also deal with other emotional states including anger and tension, because Mexican culture facilitates for men more than for women ways for dissipating, if not eliminating such types of emotional impairment. Second, it elucidates why there is no significant CMI score difference between the males and females of the doctor group inasmuch as the women who suffer from nerves would not resort to a physician's services.

PATIENTS' EXPECTATIONS

The diverse disorders presented at the two health-care establishments mirror habitual temple users' disparate therapeutic expectations. When Kleinman (1980:288) describes how Taiwanese patients distinguish between traditional and Western physicians, he could be describing the Mexican rural population. As among the Taiwanese, habitual temple users assert that the major difference between the two therapeutic modalities rests on time factor alone. That is, temple treatment is viewed as resulting in slower recovery than biomedical therapy.[2]

Patients' differential expectations of physicians and Spiritualist healers are reflected in my findings. Those treated by a doctor reported that they had recovered within 3.3 days after biomedical therapy, whereas those who received temple treatment reported that they had recovered within 9.6 days. But the discrepancy in recovery time need not perforce reflect the superiority of biomedicine but rather a difference between the syndromes suffered by patients who patronize the two health-care systems. I propose that the symptoms perceived by patients as sufficiently grave to require biomedical attention correspond to those most amenable to antibiotics and other pharmacological agents effecting a speedy recovery. This is in keeping with my hypothesis, suggested by the findings, that temple patients seek treatment for chronic dysfunctions and physicians' patients for self-limiting dysfunctions. I shall return to this proposition in Chapter 9.

As I pointed out earlier, patients shop around for cures by going from doctor to doctor and may consult as many as four or more physicians, if an illness is not alleviated quickly. Curiously, patients' incessant quest for a biomedical cure leads them to mistrust the medical profession. People find it puzzling that each doctor prescribes a different medicine for what they experience as the same symptoms. This, in fact, undermines the medical profession's credibility and is an important reason for patients' mistrust of doctors' precriptions, which are even considered harmful.

The two perceptions, taken together, that doctors' medicines are harmful, but that they furnish a speedy recovery, are disadvantageous to biomedical practitioners and advantageous to Spiritualist healers, for the following reason: on the one hand, by expecting a slower recovery after consulting Spiritualist healers, patients are inadvertently allowing time for the disease to take its course and for the body to heal itself. The natural history of a disease is now an established fact, as is the fact that patients may recuperate in time with or without ministrations (McDermott 1977; Thomas 1974). On the other hand, by expecting a quick recovery from biomedical treatment, the patient's impatience to recover compels a search for a cure from different doctors. By so doing, the patient is also likely to be administered a large array of drugs in quick succession and consequently exposed to an iatrogenic combinative effect above and beyond the usual side effects of any medication. Not surprisingly, patients frequently claim that medical prescriptions make them ill, in contrast to herbal medicines, which are less likely to be injurious to the organism.

BEHAVIORAL AND DEMOGRAPHIC PROFILES

As I pointed out at the beginning of this chapter, I assumed that the population resorting to Spiritualist temples and physicians was behaviorally and demographically homogeneous. As a result, I set out to test the following two hypotheses:

1. I advanced the null hypothesis respecting contrasts between the temple and doctor patients along standard socioeconomic dimensions, including occupation, land tenure, family structure, education, religious affiliation, migration; along demographic variables such as age and household composition; and along cultural variables pertaining to illness attribution.

2. I anticipated a demographic difference along sex lines. I hypothesized (a) that more women than men seek treatment from both the physician and Spiritualist healers because as has been well documented, women more than men tend to utilize health-care facilities of every type the world over (Fabrega et al. 1967; Hinkle et al. 1960; Lieban 1978; Matarazzo et al. 1961; Mechanic 1976; Nathanson 1979; Whitehurst and Jaco 1979); and (b) more women than men seek treatment at the Spirituralist temple, because more women tend to be attracted to dissident religious healing movements (Finkler 1981a; Lewis 1971); but (c) proportionately more men than women resort to the physicians' services because men tend to suffer from illnesses that usually call for medical attention, including serious disabilities and injuries (Hinkle et al. 1960; Mechanic 1976; Nathanson 1979).

The research findings substantiate the null hypothesis only partially; they substantiate the second hypothesis fully.

First, the temple and doctor groups share the same etiological beliefs, as well as similar occupations. They are equally distributed among peasants, daily wage laborers, housewives, and self-employed indivduals. Both groups include, equally, both landless households and households with small land parcels (1-3 hectares).

Second, the population of neither group is integrated into the nationally institutionalized industrial labor force. This assertion is based on the fact that 83.9 percent of the temple group and 93.5 percent of the doctor group lack access to the national health plans available to permanently employed workers, as was noted in Chapter 4. Of those lacking access to the national health plans, 6.2 percent of the temple group and 8.3 percent of the doctor group are self-employed and would normally not benefit from national health plans. With the exception of the self-employed in both groups, the subject populations are relatively marginal to the national industrial economy, using access to national health plans as an indicator.

Attention should also be called to the 16.1 percent of the temple clientele that does benefit from health plans and that therefore can be assumed to form part of the industrial sector. These persons are relatively better situated economically than peasants and daily wage laborers. This, of course, supports the long-term observation that the majority of Spiritualist temple patients in the region are usually indigent, but that Spiritualist healers also attract persons in more advantageous economic positions. Third, patients in the two groups originate from similar types of families, with equal percentages stemming from nuclear, extended, and female-headed households.

Finally, the two groups do not differ in age. Based upon the present sample, however, it must be noted that a larger proportion of infants and young children are brought to the temple than to the doctor. In fact, the proportion of infants and children seen by temple healers (28.6 percent) is almost twice that seen by doctors (13.8 percent). This can be explained in at least two ways: First, infants and young children are usually taken to physicians when they are suffering from high fevers accompanied by other symptoms such as diarrhea. Light fevers or simple diarrhea are usually treated at home, or by women who specialize exclusively in children's cultural illnesses. Whereas habitual temple users take children suffering from these illnesses either to one of these women or to the temple, the doctor group may have children's disorders treated by these women specialists. Second, young first-time mothers receive helpful instructions from the healers in traditional childrearing practices, including, for example, how to deal with crying infants. A healer tends to allay a mother's concern when a baby cries excessively, which in this region is considered a sure sign of illness. This aspect of the Spiritualist healers role is important in light of the fact, noted earlier, that a majority (57 percent) of the entire sample population resides in nuclear families, away from their mothers and mothers-in-law. My observations suggest that young mothers may expect reassurance from health practitioners when their infants are sick, an aspect of the doctor-patient relationship found lacking among physicians in the United States, for example (Korsch and Negrete 1972). Concomitantly, a young mother may unwittingly attribute an illness to an infant for secondary gain in order to attract attention from her husband, who may otherwise not be very attentive. Husbands become very attentive, however, when one of their offspring becomes even slightly indisposed.

The preceding discussion respecting the children's mother calls attention to yet another difference, albeit not statistically significant, between the two sample populations under consideration. While the majority in both groups had no schooling whatsoever, mothers who brought their children to the temple tended to have less formal education than mothers interviewed at the doctor's office. Nine percent of the mothers from the temple group, but 20 percent of the mothers from the doctor group, had one to three years of elementary schooling. Ten percent in both groups had four to six years of elementary education.

More importantly, however, years of schooling discriminates between the subject groups as a whole. On first glance, the first hypothesis is supported by the finding that the two groups do not differ in education. As is shown in Table 6.6 approximately an equal percentage of individuals in both groups had no elementary education. But a closer inspection of the results reveals that years of schooling distinguish the two groups at a statistically significant level, with a higher percentage of medical patients having been exposed to more years of schooling than temple patients. (Ninety percent of the population in both groups had no schooling above the elementary level.)

These findings suggest that length of exposure to elementary schooling influences not only CMI scores (See Appendix A) but also treatment-seeking disposition. It is assumed that length of exposure to the public school system leads to increased absorption of the biomedical disease model, as well as to the importance of inoculations and preventive health measures. Importantly, these findings are also supported by Lieban's (1976) data demonstrating the importance of education in determining preference among Filipinos for biomedicine.

Yet another interesting contrast appears between the two groups relevant to household decisions about treatment choices. In nuclear and extended-family households with male heads, there is a statistically significant difference between the two groups respecting who makes treatment choices. As is shown in Table 6.7 spouses decide jointly where to obtain treatment in the majority of households in both groups. But in the remaining households, treatment choices are made by each spouse independently. Herein rests an interesting difference between the two groups. In the doctor group, more men select the treatment modality, whereas in the temple group, more women make corresponding choices independently of their husbands; they may even conceal the fact, as is done in other societies, e.g. Taiwan (Kleinman 1980).

This leads to yet another salient observation respecting various ways in which choice of treatment is transmitted, a subject which has not received much attention in the literature. For example, among habitual temple users, when married women come to the temple with the permission of their husbands or sometimes even accompanied by them, the man's mother assuredly also had sought treatment there at one time or another, hence demonstrating to her children her approval of Spiritualist temples. Otherwise, my observations reveal that husbands usually forbid their wives to go to Spiritualist temples for treatment, on the same grounds as those advanced by physicians and clergy.

In keeping with the male orientation toward doctors, it is noteworthy that the two groups differ in household composition: the doctors' patients come from families where there are twice as many male adults (1.9) as there are in the families of the temple patients (0.9).

Twice as many unattached females seek treatment at the temple as at physicians offices. Although there are various reasons why unattached women may come to the temple (including those experiencing amenorrhea who may wish to find out whether they are pregnant), within the context of the present discussion it can be inferred that unattached women enjoy greater freedom of choice in managing illness than married ones.

On the whole, more women resort to temple treatment than men, as the second hypothesis predicts. This is attested to by the high ratio of women to men at the temple. In fact, only 15 percent of those observed in front of healers during my apprenticeship and 26.4 percent of those randomly interviewed were males, whereas the group interviewed at the doctor's office was comprised of 37.2 percent males. (The methodology of subject selection is discussed in Appendix A). The fact that both health-care establishments service more women than men is not surprising, as was indicated when my hypotheses were stated earlier in this chapter.

Various reasons have been advanced for difference in health-care utilization of men and women (Mechanic 1976). Three reasons for the variance bear directly on the present findings. First, men and women report different symptoms. For example, men tend to suffer from more accidents than women do (Nathanson 1979). In the region under study, job-related accidents are common occurrences. Accidents resulting from violence are usually, if not exclusively, confined to men (Finkler 1974). As we saw earlier, injuries resulting from accidents are universally relegated to the biomedical domain, by both habitual temple users and regulars. This fact comes into view in Table 6.4, where we see that 9 percent of the doctor's cases include accidents suffered by males.

Second, while men tend to report fewer symptoms than women, their impairments tend to be more disabling than women's (Hinkle et al. 1960; Nathanson 1979). These are the types of dysfunctions that are usually regarded as sufficiently grave to require medical attention by the subjects studied.

Third, as alluded to earlier, fewer males believe in Spiritualist treatment than females. A similar phenomenon has been noted in other cultures (Kleinman 1980). While it is puzzling on first sight, it is in keeping with the fact that women tend to suffer more than men from depressive disorders and pain-prone disorders (cf. Finkler, in press; Rosenfield 1980; Weissman and Klerman 1977) not readily amenable to biomedical treatments. It is thus not surprising that they tend to seek Spiritualist therapy after biomedical intervention has failed, and therefore also be more disposed to it than men.

Perhaps the most important behavioral contrast between the two groups relates to their differential stance with respect to the Catholic church. In fact, my findings suggest that the two groups are differentiated by their disparate relations to the Catholic church. Behavioral and cognitive differences between the two groups respecting Catholicism emerged during the course of the research when it became evident that both men and women who were opposed to Spiritualism were also practicing orthodox Catholics, closely affiliated ideologically with the church.

I must stress that while the overwhelming majority (90 percent of respondents in both groups) identify themselves as Catholics, 62.1 percent of the doctor group reported they attend church weekly, but only 27 percent of the temple group responded in this way. This is statistically significant at the .01 level when a Chi square test is done of the frequency of church attendance by treatment sought. These findings, as well as my observations, suggest that Catholic orthodoxy is a critical variable militating against persons seeking alternative therapies of the Spiritualist variety. This is not surprising in view of the point made earlier on the antagonism between Spiritualism and Catholic orthodoxy.

But, aside from Catholic orthodoxy, absence of an "illness network" leading to temple treatment will similarly militate against patients' resort to temple ministrations. Recommendations to a Spiritualist temple depends largely on the individual's illness network--people with whom the sick person interacts during a given illness episode. Within the context of this discussion, the illness network refers to persons successfully treated in a Spiritualist temple. Such individuals usually refer others to the temple.

While the referral network embraces neighbors, friends, relatives, or ritual relatives, referrals to Spiritualist temples are frequently made by chance encounters. For example, in one case, a women was traveling on a bus from her town to Juarez, twenty-two miles away, to see a physician. She had already been unsuccessfully treated by doctors closer to her village. She sat next to a women who engaged her in a conversation, during which her fellow passenger told her about the Spiritualist temple in Juarez. The women arrived in Juarez and went to see the physician, who was not available at that moment. She then decided to go to the temple about which she had just learned rather than to wait for the physician. Subsequently, the women was treated and healed in the temple. As a result she became a habitual temple user. Thus, individuals may fail to pursue treatment at a temple simply because they are not aware of its existence. This is important because illness networks, in effect, mediate access to Spiritualist treatment.

Differential illness networks relate to one other important finding of my research. The data disclose that respondents from the temple group came from households from which at least one household member had sought migrant-wage labor outside of his or her natal town or village. In fact, a Chi square test of the migration variable by treatment sought reveals a statistically significant difference between the two groups at the .001 level. Thus, 55.6 percent of households in the temple group were exposed to wage-labor migration, in contrast to 37.2 percent of the doctor group.

Rural-urban migration has been invoked to explain differential resort (e.g., Press 1978) because, it is argued, migrants in cities tend to become alienated and in need of the personalistic health-care delivery presumably provided by nonbiomedical practitioners. While psychotherapeutic interpretations of this type often predominate in elucidating patients' preferences for nonbiomedical healing specialists, my observations indicate that individuals exposed to wage-labor migration enjoy extensive personal networks which become activated during a prolonged illness episode. We may assume that wage-labor migrants come into contact with many more people then do those who rarely leave their natal homes. Persons who are spatially mobile are more likely to encounter individuals who will direct them to a Spiritualist temple, or who may have told them about it in the past, than are those who lack similar mobility (cf. Waxler 1976). In fact, among habitual temple users, 52.6 percent reported that they had learned about the temple from friends outside their immediate circle of relatives and neighbors.

In sum, the results from the quantitative analysis suggest that both religious ideology and illness networks are critical variables determining resort to medical practitioners in this region of Mexico. Years of schooling also plays a role in militating against resort to Spiritualist therapy. Tentatively, we can anticipate that individuals strongly committed to Catholic orthodoxy with some education and with limited illness networks are more likely to resort to biomedical practitioners than to Spiritualist healers, irrespective of their occupation or economic circumstances.

EXISTENTIAL CORRELATES OF THERAPEUTIC RESORT

Therapeutic preferences must also be explored from the perspective of the individual's life circumstances, which are best gleaned with observational materials and life histories. So viewed, we discern that those who resort to biomedicine exclusively-- including those from the control group and those who have not had previous experience with Spiritualism--have not experienced prolonged or recurring illness, the type that lingers on, e.g., perpetual parasitosis or chronic pain related to physical impairment or to depressive disorder (Sternbach 1974).

And the quantitative materials fail to illuminate the existential distress and human tragedies propelling patients to Spiritualist healers, the sort of experiential difficulties that generate the deep emotional upsets to which Mexicans tend to attribute illness, including anger and bereavement. Emotional vents of this kind can be associated with symptoms and syndromes that resist biomedical cure, conditions that require the symbolic reordering provided by Spiritualist healers. The symbolic significance of temple therapy comes into full view in Chapter 9.

The experiential predicaments to which I refer involve the individual in long-lasting interpersonal conflict or personal loss--of either a parent or an infant--is the kind of loss that, profoundly affects us all. Loss--due to natural causes, to violence, or to abandonment--or serious interpersonal conflict may be responsible for ongoing symptoms for which biomedicine simply lacks remedies.

Analysis of life histories from the control group discloses that the two groups differ in exposure to life traumas and illness experience. For example, with few exceptions temple patients--especially regulars--have suffered the death of a child, whereas only three out of nineteen controls have known a similar loss. Additionally, the control group's illness histories reveal few illnesses in their families, including cultural syndromes related to witchraft or *aire*. Compared to the control-group, patients have more frequently experienced depressive disorders and other dysfunctions not readily curable biomedically. In fact, perusal of life histories of individuals from the control group reveals that they tended to lead a more peaceful existence than habitual temple users and regulars prior to their participation in the temple, a life less punctuated by tumultuous interpersonal relationships. A case in point is Emiliano, a man who, prior to the onset of his illness, experienced loss and interpersonal conflicts, change of residence, and subjectively felt distress, and who subsequently succumbed to somatization of a reactive depression.

Emiliano A Case Vignette

Emiliano, who is 47 years old, originates from the very poorest sector of Mexican peasant society. He is married, with five living children. He resides in an inaccessible village; it and the nearby land that he tills are 30 miles from the temple.

Emilano was brought to the temple by his wife a year after the onset of his illness. Previously he had sought treatment with physicians and a *curandera*, but he continued to suffer from his impairments. His symptoms included insomnia, severe headaches, lack of appetite, pain in the entire body, and generalized numbness. He urinated often and suffered from pain in his kidneys and liver. He also developed a large ball-like lump behind the ear. Additionally, Emiliano reported that he dreamed many evil dreams, such as being beaten up by his brothers and neighbors. He wanted to kill himself but was stopped by the thought of leaving his children fatherless. He described himself as having been very nervous, easily frightened, quarrelsome, and rude. He used crude language and easily lost his temper, especially when he got drunk. He used to drink two to three liters of *pulque* (a local alcoholic beverage) and *cubas* (rum and coke). Life went badly for him. Two of his children had died and the other five suffered from many illnesses.

Emiliano, a docile man who impressed me as a bit dim-witted, was next to the youngest of eleven children. His mother had died upon delivery of her last child. His father remarried, but the stepmother treated her stepchildren abominably. He recalls how she used to strike them, how she let them run around dirty in unwashed clothes. At 15, Emiliano left his village and moved to an industrial town about twenty-five miles north of Mexico City, where he worked as a mason for thirty years until returning to his village two years ago. Three of his adult children continue to live there.

He bought some animals and two hectares of land in the village. He built a little house on land he inherited from his father. He inherited one hectare of *ejido* land from his mother. Soon after he returned to the village he fell ill. The onset of his illness corresponded to the time of a violent dispute with his neighbors and brothers over land boundaries. He attributes his illness to the jealousies of his brothers and neighbors. He knows they gossip about him and even accuse him of being a "witch".

The doctors who had treated him took blood tests, according to the results of which there was nothing wrong with him. After a year of unsuccessful treatment with various health practitioners he arrived in the Juarez temple. Initially he came irregularly. He did not believe he would be cured here, and his condition went unchanged. After six months of sporadic attendance, the temple head suggested that he remain in her house so that he could receive treatments regularly and also save himself the exorbitant travel expenses from his village to the temple.

Upon taking up residence in the temple head's house, he was also ordered to enter development. Emiliano described his trance experience poetically. Briefly translated, he indicated that he <u>felt</u> a beautiful light appearing before him and that it felt good. He thinks it was the light of God, which entered his body, gave it a spark, and removed his pain. Following each development session he felt happy, and he experienced the feeling of a "fresh breeze" passing through his body.

I shall return to Emiliano in Chapter 10, where I will also introduce several other individuals whose lives were punctuated by turbulent interpersonal relationships and who felt stress, fell ill, and became Spiritualist regulars.

Table 6.1   Pattern of Resort of Habitual Temple Users

Illness episodes reported as grave for which biomedical treatment was sought	Illness episodes reported as nongrave for which temple treatment was sought
Pain in kidneys	Worms in stool
Bronchitis	Pain in feet, arms, head, lungs
Gastritis, diarrhea with fever	Diarrhea
Catarrh, cough, grippe, infection	Susto
Injury	Senile father
Pain in kidneys, hemorrhage	General pain
Intestinal infection	Lack of appetite
Fever	Infant with diarrhea attributed to teething
Pain in kidneys, high blood pressure	Diarrhea (empacho)*
Pain in stomach, gastritis, infant with fever	Growth on foot; has not menstruated
Fever	Growth on foot
Fever	Epileptic attacks
Bronchitis	Baby dribbles from teething and frightened (espantado)
Bronchitis	Pain in stomach
Grippe, high fever	Diarrhea (empacho)*
Cough, hemorrhage	General body aches
	Susto
Pain in liver	Pimples on the body, pain in one foot

Illness episodes reported as grave for which biomedical treatment was sought	Illness episodes reported as nongrave for which temple treatment was sought
Pain in liver	Eyes tearing, diarrhea, cannot sleep
	Catarrh, pain in lungs
	Grippe
	A little diarrhea, spitting blood because of the cold, blood in urine but no pain
	Baby cries, doesn't sleep
Swollen hand	Grippe
Bronchitis	Evil eye
Vomiting with fever	Susto
Diarrhea, vomiting and fever	Diarrhea, no fever
Parasites and pain in kidney	Susto, nerves
	Sweat, pain in back
	Grippe, pain in stomach
Stuffed-up nose, plugged-up ears, pain in ear	Pain in feet
	Grippe
Angina[†] with fever, pain in stomach, pain in liver, wound	Angina[†] without fever, pain in throat, grippe, stomach ache, catarrh, aire

*Most always pertain to children's diarrhea (usually without fever).

[†]Usually refers to tonsils or generalized throat pain regarded as having been caused by inflamed tonsils.

Table 6.2   Complaints Cited by Temple Patients (N = 1093)

Complaint		Percent
"Cleansing"		17.5
Gastrointestinal distress		17.0
Musculoskeletal distress		15.0
Personal problem		10.2
Respiratory impairment (chest pain, cough)		5.6
Surface skin eruption		5.3
Miscellaneous:	e.g., gynecological problem; headache and pain in cerebro; susto; nerves; depression; frequent anger episodes; suspicion of witchcraft; concern about taking physician-prescribed medicine; seeking treatment on behalf of another person	29.4
		100.0

Table 6.3   Personal Problems Presented to Spiritualist Healers (N = 112)

Problems		Percent
Male-female related		31.0
Interpersonal dissension with other than spouse or boyfriend		16.0
Disobedience by children		16.0
Accidents and misfortunes		13.5
Work and economic problems		11.1
Children's school		6.1
Alcoholism		3.8
Miscellaneous:	e.g., where to deliver a baby – at home or clinic; university student cannot concentrate on studies; child prescribed glasses but mother doesn't want him to wear them	2.5
		100.0

Table 6.4 Patients' Complaints and Diagnoses of Complaints
Presented to a Physician

Complaint	Patient's Self-Diagnosis Percent N = 183*	Physician's Diagnosis Percent N = 156*
Gastrointestinal distress	25.7	38.0
Obstetric	20.2	22.8
Accident	8.2	8.9
Respiratory Distress	8.7	5.1
Urinary tract impairment		4.4
Miscellaneous: diabetes; grippe; liver disease; anemia; skin-related problem	18.6	
Miscellaneous: tonsillitis; glandular infection; abscess		20.8
Musculoskeletal: feet distress; arms or lower back pain	8.2	
Unspecified	10.4	
TOTAL	100.00	100.0

* N = 183 represents the number of complaints presented by 156
patients.

Table 6.5 CMI Score Results: Temple and Doctor Groups

	Temple (First Comers and Habitual Temple Users)		Doctor	
	Male (N = 92)	Female (N = 257)	Male (N = 58)	Female (N = 98)
Physical	37.9	42.9	40.3	44.1
Emotional	19.1	23.8 *	18.4	18.3
Total	57.0	66.7	58.7	62.4

* Significant at .001 level.

Table 6.6   Years of Schooling of Patients

Years of Schooling	Temple (N = 389) (Percent)	Doctor (N = 156) (Percent)
0	29.0	34.0
1-3	38.6	22.4
4-6	32.4	43.6
	100.0	100.0

NOTE: Chi square - Significant at .001 level.

Table 6.7   Treatment-Seeking Decisions in Male-Headed Households

Who Decides	Temple (N = 229) (Percent)	Doctor (N = 113) (Percent)
Joint	54.6	50.5
Male	22.7	33.6
Female	22.7	15.9
	100.0	100.0

NOTE: Chi square - Significant at .001 level.

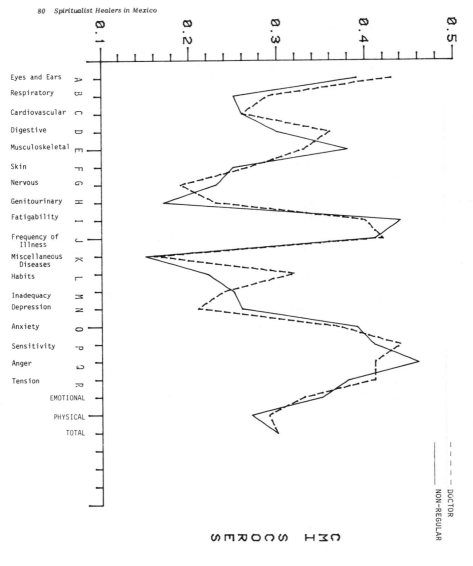

FIGURE 6.1   COMPARISON OF MALE PATIENT GROUPS

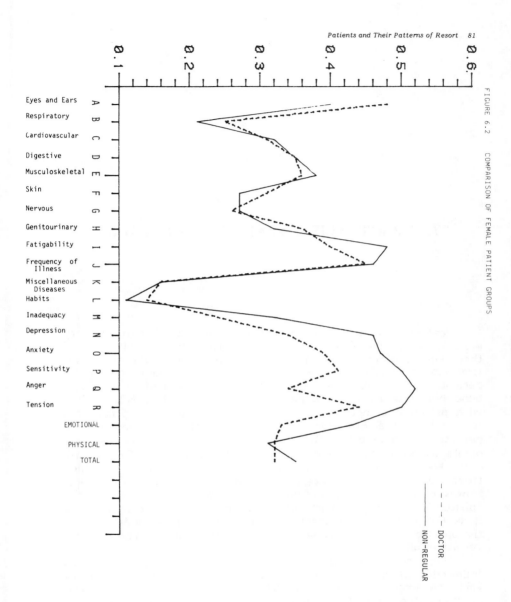

FIGURE 6.2   COMPARISON OF FEMALE PATIENT GROUPS

7. SPIRITUALIST HEALING TECHNIQUES

Healing techniques, the foundation of any health care delivery system, raise pivotal issues concerning the efficacy of a given therapeutic regime. Viewed from the individual patients perspective, first and foremost we must ask, what does a given regime do for the patient? What constituent elements of curing procedure are most beneficial to patients? How successful are the procedures in dealing with patients' complaints? To what degree do these procedures remove the causes of disease and to what extent do they constitute a palliative or a placebo? When approached from societal vantage points, as is done by some scholars (Fox 1974; Pellegrino 1979; Turner 1974; Wallace 1960), we must inquire as to the ways in which therapeutics affect and intertwine with other societal institutions. However, before we can deal with these questions within the Spiritualist context, we must examine their standard practices. Thus, it is the task of this chapter to identify Spiritualists' standard therapeutic techniques, as well as to call attention to some stylistic variations among healers

Every therapeutic system has a standard set of procedures followed in treating patients notwithstanding the wide range of variation among individual practitioners. In contemporary medical practice, for example, which is familiar to most patients of biomedicine, there are specific procedures a physician is expected to follow that normally include the taking of a patient's medical history, a physical examination, and laboratory tests. These are then followed by a diagnosis, a prescribed treatment, and, ideally, by follow-ups (Nobrega et al. 1977). Of course, individual practitioners vary in the degree to which they carry out these procedures as well as in the time they proportionately devote to each (Romm et al. 1976).

Similarly, Spiritualist healers follow standard treatment procedures. In fact, Spiritualist healers place great emphasis on treatment techniques by minimizing the importance of an individual healer's abilities. They usually stress that all healers are equally effective in treating patients, and by so doing they deemphasize the specific healer-patient relationship. This is an important point, to which I will return in Chapter 9.

Because different techniques are applied to nonregulars (first-comers and habitual temple users) and regulars, these two categories of patients must be discussed separately. I begin by focusing on the majority of temple patients, the nonregulars.

HEALING TECHNIQUES APPLIED TO NONREGULARS

Spirit protectors, through whom Spiritualist healers treat patients, and who are referred to as Brother or Sister So-and-So, manifest themselves on curing days after the healer has arrived in the temple, put on a white robe, approached the altar to listen to a brief prayer recited by the temple head, and entered the healing room. To summon the protector the healer sits down, closes her/his eyes, and mildly shakes the upper half of her/his body. The healer ceases to shake when the spirit protector temporarily settles in her/his body, identifies itself by name, and greets everyone present. Following this proceeding, which may take no more than a minute or two, the healer is prepared to receive patients.

Spiritualist healers usually treat patients in a room adjacent to the temple. On curing days the temple anteroom is transformed into a waiting room where long wooden benches are placed in separate sections for men and women with their children to sit separately, patiently waiting as long as two to four hours to be seen by a healer. Patients are often instructed to contemplate the altar and concentrate on it as they wait. According to some Spiritualists, the cure begins then, with the patient sitting silently in contemplation.

Seeing the large number of people that usually sit awaiting treatment is no doubt reinforcing to a new patient who may arrive with some grave doubts about the establishment because of the Spiritualists' reputation as witches.

Several curers sit side by side, each treating a different patient. The room is usually noisy, especially when one or more infants are being treated. In one of the temples, six curers usually work simultaneously: because of the large clientele there are two shifts, with each curer working, on the average, two hours a day. However, healers who have an especially large following may work unceasingly for as long as four to six hours a day. New patients are directed to the first available curer, and when they return for subsequent treatments they are directed to the curer who initially treated them. Thus, individual healers cultivate a clientele which they treat continually. Spiritualists believe that continuity of treatment with the same healer is essential to effect a cure. Patients may stop coming for treatment if their curer terminates his or her affiliation with the temple, as sometimes happens.

Curers are assisted by temple functionaries who are not in trance. It is the task of these functionaries to furnish the curers with special aromatic waters, which a few curers use for the purpose of cleansing the patient. The assistant also records on a piece of paper the medicines and treatments prescribed for the patient by the curer. A patient is expected to bring the prescription on return visits to the temple. Should a patient fail to bring the paper with the prescription, which frequently happens, the curer may angrily reprimand the patient or simply remind the person to bring the prescription next time. When the patient presents the prescription, the curer asks the assistant to read it out loud.

It can be supposed that by hearing the previous prescription the curer, who at all times sits with eyes closed during trance, is able to recognize the patient's previous condition, for which the prescription was given, and can thereby inquire of the patient about the symptoms he or she had previously reported. This is usually the main overt sign of recognition given the patient, except when curers reassure patients that the spirit world is with them and that the spirit world is omniscient, implying that the spirits are able to transcend the limits of time and space.

A personalistic relationship of the type described in the literature (e.g., Fabrega & Silver 1973; Metzger & Williams 1963), however, is not possible here for two reasons: First, curers in trance cannot admit to recognizing anyone, even including members of their own family, who are frequent patients; second, many patients come from numerous surrounding villages (in my sample forty separate villages are represented) other than the ones from which the curer originates. Thus he or she is not likely to have met patients prior to the treatment encounter or to interact with them after the treatment episode.

Subsequent components of the healer's strategy are singularly impersonal and also brief. In the temple where I worked, each curer sees an average of seventeen patients during the two hours he or she spends in the curing room. Thus, each healer spends, on the average, 7.1 minutes with one patient. The actual time spent with each patient varies, depending upon individual healers and the treatment given. Special types of treatments may take as long as three quarters of an hour. However, during the course of the day a healer typically devotes between 4.7 and 17.5 minutes to a patient. (Interestingly, the time a Spiritualist healer spends with a patient does not differ much in length from that of one local doctor, who indicated that he spends from fifteen to twenty minutes with a patient.) In fact, if a curer takes longer than the average number of minutes with a patient at a time when a room full of people is still awaiting treatment, the head of the temple, who oversees the curing sessions, approaches the curer and firmly tells the spirit protector to hurry up and not take up so much time with one patient. Alternatively, the head of the temple may reprimand the patient when the person is heard repeating again and again his or her complaint. The temple head urges the patient to get to the point quickly because there are still many people waiting.

While it is customary for patients in this region to seek health care accompanied by another adult or a child, patient-healer interaction is dyadic, in contrast to the situation in some cultural settings (Kleinman 1980), where related persons are involved in the therapeutic encounter. As a matter of fact, Spiritualist healer-patient interchanges closely mimic the medical model as described by Kleinman (1980) and Szasz and Hollender (1956). Following Szasz and Hollender's well-known four models of patient-doctor interactions, guidance and cooperation is the most common. According to this paradigm, the doctor-patient encounter sets the doctor up as ominiscient and the patient as the recipient of the doctor's superior knowledge. The superordinate-subordinate relationship requires the patient to follow the physician's orders without any attempt by the patient to have any control of the situation. Analogously, Spiritualist patients are expected to carry out the healer's instructions precisely and to the letter. In fact, when patients fail to do so, they are vigorously reprimanded by the spirit medium.

But whereas the Spiritualist healer and the physician both manage the therapeutic encounter authoritatively, Spiritualist healer-patient interaction departs from the medical model in at least two important ways. First, physicians, unlike Spiritualists, place no responsibility on their patients for their cure. On the other hand, Spiritualist patients are expected to have faith in the healer. Patients are incessantly reminded that in order to be cured they must have faith in the spirit world. If at some moment during the healer-patient encounter, the healer detects a lack of faith in the patient's voice or in his or her comments, the patient is immediately castigated by the spirit medium. Second, although both physicians and healers are regarded as all-powerful, physicians' patients do not regard the medical practitioner as capable of transcending spatial and temporal boundaries nor are clairvoyant powers attributed to physicians. Consequently physicians are not expected to know a patient's complaints without the patient's having stated them. In contrast, Spiritualist healers are attributed with supernatural and clairvoyant powers, with healers reinforcing the image by frequently reminding patients of their omniscience and omnipotence.

Importantly, patients' acceptance of healers' transcendent powers precludes the necessity for them to recite their problems, as it is assumed, that the spirit already knows them. Kleinman (1980) observed the same phenomenon among sacred healers in Taiwan. According to him patients are deprived of an opportunity to unburden themselves of their woes and thereby they are denied an important ingredient of the healing process intrinsic to some psychotherapeutic techniques. Based upon my observations, however, patients with problems of living and psychological problems demonstrated a sense of relief when the healer anticipated their predicaments and they were not required to say anything. The healer made them feel that their problems were being discerned by the spirit.

Paradoxically, in this type of exchange, or lack of it, the patient is afforded an opportunity to experience a passive form of catharsis, a feeling of a sense of release and relief without having said or done anything. As I observed nonlinguistic cues such as head shakes denoting agreement, or relaxation of facial muscles, patients conveyed a sense of comfort in this sort of "catharsis" based on passivity. The fact that patients are relieved from saying anything and yet made to feel that they have said it all is consonant with a common cultural pattern of social interaction in the rural region. Mexican rural populations and especially rural women are frequently reticent about personal problems (see Paz 1961 on this subject), especially those relating to male-female relations or those threatening loss of face. By not eliciting a narrative of the patient's anguish from the patient, the healer facilitates a customary response pattern.

Patients' confidence in their healers supernatural powers forms an important component of Spiritualist healing techniques in yet another way. Healers not infrequently inform patients that, unbeknownst to the patients, they are being treated spiritually away from the temple. To the degree that patients accept this as fact, it serves as a powerful placebo, a subject I will turn to in Chapter 9.

PHASES OF INTERACTION

Healer-patient interaction can be divided into four major phases. The first phase begins when the patient is directed to the healer by a temple functionary overseeing patients in the waiting room. Upon approaching the curer, a patient is required to recite a salutation that initiates a customary response from the spirit protector. New patients, ignorant of the salutation, are instructed by the assistant to utter the set phrase. Once the salutation is given, the curer moves his hands up and down the patient's body and recites a blessing. This phase of the treatment episode is referred to by Spiritualists as *desalojo* ("dislodgment") whereas patients refer to it as a *limpia* ("cleansing"). Some curers may even spend as much as half of the interaction time with the patient in administering a cleansing. Additionaly, most curers move their hands up and down the patient's body, lightly massaging the person throughout various phases of the treatment episode. Hence, curer-patient interaction is singularly tactile. Since curers have their eyes closed while they are in trance, patient-healer interaction lacks the eye contact sometimes deemed important in the healing process.

My observations suggest that the constant massaging of the patient has a tranquilizing effect on both adults and children. I will discuss the symbolic meaning of cleansing and dislodgments later; at this juncture it is important to emphasize that this aspect of the treatment, performed only at the temple, is regarded by patients as a major beneficial component of Spiritualist therapeutics. Also, to anticipate a point I will note later, tactile interaction is believed to be curative, and, of course, an important ingredient in less conventional psychotherapeutic techniques that emphasize touching and massaging (Krippner 1978; Krieger et al. n.d.).

The second phase of the treatment episode consists of the curer's inquiry about the purpose of the visit. The patient states the reason and usually describes his or her symptoms. Frequently the curer explores the symptoms by touching the affected part of the body. Some curers may anticipate the patient's symptoms when the latter nonverbally indicates the part of the body affected by pain. During the symptom-exploration phase of the patient-healer interaction, a curer may suddenly faint away and begin speaking seeming nonsense. Careful attention to the words spoken reveals that curers maintain a standard repertoire of set sentences that are uttered during a fainting incident, declarations such as, "What am I doing here?" or, "Take me away from this sacred place." These enunciations suggest that a foreign intruder has removed the curer's spirit protector and taken over the curer's body. The fainting episode is usually sustained from two to five minutes, at which time, attendants hurry over to the curer to recite a special prayer in response to which the curer's spirit protector returns and identifies himself by stating, "Here I am, back again in the service of humanity." Interestingly, few, if any, first-comers--but many habitual temple users--comprehend the significance of this brief ritual drama, which is only practiced by some curers. To Spiritualists, the event denotes that the illness possessing the patient has been literally transferred to the healer and manifested in an alien spirit who briefly possessed the curer's body.

Most patients, unless socialized into the Spiritualist culture, fail to understand the act of instant transference of an illness from patient to healer. Frequently, patients view this as strange behavior and stand watching the event with baffled expressions on their faces. Nevertheless, patients seem to accept the goings-on as part of the regular course of the curing procedure. This is an important instance supporting my view that healers and patients need not similarly comprehend the therapeutic intervention in order for the patient to seek the treatment encounter.

The third phase of the treatment episode follows. Once the patient's symptoms have been ascertained, the healer authoritatively prescribes a series of remedies. Prescriptions normally include massages, baths, teas, and--depending on the curer--pharmacological remedies. As I observed before, some healers include antibiotics in their pharmacopoeia in addition to herbal medicines; the spirits antecedents determine what is appropriate.

Of the 152 plants prescribed by healers (see Appendices B and C), the most common were rue (*Ruda*; Ruta chalepensis), rosemary (*Romero*; Rosmarinus officinalis), balm (*Toronjil*; Agastache Mexicana), camomile (*Manzanilla*; Matricaria chamomilla L.), basil (*Albacar*; Ocimum basilicum L.), and *Inojo* (unidentified botanically). These are usually utilized for teas and baths. Of the 221 varieties of pharmaceuticals, 26.5 percent included some type of laxative, the most common of which was Phillips Milk of Magnesia; 15.5 percent included lotions for massages; 6.1 percent, a variety of body-invigorating tonics, and 4.3 percent, appetite-stimulating vitamin tonics. The remaining 46.7 percent included a variety of medicines such as antihistamines, antibiotics, mild tranquilizers, and antidiarrheals such as enterovioform. Each curer had a favorite antidiarrheal medicine. Only two prescribed enterovioform, which is for sale in pharmacies in Mexico but has been banned in the United States because of its potentially adverse side effects. Purgatives are often prescribed to patients on their first visit to the temple. In cases of intestinal disorders, curers also recommend a food regime requiring the patient to eliminate from the diet such foods as pork and spices; men are prohibited from drinking alcoholic beverages.

Healers frequently deny a patient's sick role. For example, when patients report symptoms of depression or *susto*, the curer prescribes special teas and frequently also lets the patient know that there is nothing wrong with him or her. In the words of one favorite curer, "Go out and smell the flowers, and you will feel better."

Furthermore, curers are usually dogmatic with patients and will not permit any kind of challenge. For example, when a curer prescribes various ministrations, a patient may interject that he or she was previously prescribed a given medicine and that it failed to produce a beneficial effect. Most curers ignore the patient's assertions and insist that the patient "do as I say."

During the final phase of the healer-patient interaction, the healer recapitulates the prescription and instructions given the patient. This is followed by a blessing with the healer's hands over the patient's body. The patient is expected to give thanks to the curer, to which the curer responds with a standard phrase terminating the treatment. On leaving the temple, patients leave a voluntary contribution, which may range from as little as one peso to as much as ten pesos, or what usually equals to less than a dollar.

It is noteworthy that patients usually do not question the reasons for their affliction, nor do Spiritualist healers explain the etiology of the illness in the usual course of an interaction. Diagnoses are infrequently given. In fact, out of 353 patients, 215 (61 percent) were not given any indication as to what was the matter with them. In short, the interaction revolves around a patient's statement of symptoms and the healer's statement of remedies. There is little demonstration of compassion or support for the sick person other than inherent in providing a prescription for the symptoms and in assuring the patient that the spirit world is watching over him or her.

Having described the standard healer-patient interactional pattern, I hasten to note that each healer exhibits stylistic variations within the standard therapeutic format. Among healers cross-culturally, as among physicians, there exists a wide range of idiosyncratic healing repertoires within standard procedures. This point requires emphasis because discussions of healing techniques frequently ignore these important variations. Examples abound. Some healers demonstrate verbally and nonverbally greater comprehension of patients' problems than others and exude more personal warmth in their tone of voice. Some are brusque and angrily scold patients, while others speak in a soothing and reassuring manner. As a general rule the more experienced healers tend to spend the least time with a patient. For instance, the head of the temple devotes less than two minutes to a patient, whereas a new and inexperienced curer may attend a patient for as long as twenty to thirty minutes.

Healers differ in the type and number of queries they pose to patients, as will be seen shortly. Some question a patient exhaustively and even ask for the patient's name, natal town, number of times the patient had previously sought temple treatment, and other biographical data.

Others make few inquiries and even fail to ask the patient's name. In fact, I observed consultations in which the patient never uttered a word during the entire healing episode. In such instances patients come just to seek a cleansing or a "passive catharsis" for situational difficulties.

Various healers employ different healing props. Most use aromatic waters--concocted of ammonia, eau de cologne, and rubbing alcohol--for massages and cleansings, but others use no paraphernalia, not even the special branches that patients, especially newcomers, normally expect Spiritualist healers to use during cleansings.

Interestingly, some healers often resort to the "instant transference technique" of fainting away during consultations, whereas others use this procedure only occasionally; and still others, never. The differential use of this treatment technique is puzzling; as a general rule, however, it is used most by less experienced curers, suggesting that the fainting away provides more of a catharsis for the healer than for the patient. In fact, in Chapter 9 we shall see how, in the words of Spiritualists, "By healing others one also heals oneself," with this procedure being one facet of the therapy.

Significantly, the methods of performing a cleansing may vary as well. For instance, some healers use a "spitting" technique, noisily moving their lips up and down the patient's body, demonstratively and symbolically ridding the patient of undesirable substances occupying his body. More commonly, healers use their hands or branches to gently beat the patient. Those who use branches instruct their patients to bring such accoutrements, and sometimes patients bring branches and flowers for this purpose of their own volition. On the whole, flowers are an important ingredient in Spiritualist rituals, as we have seen previously, and they may be prescribed for cleansing the home. Some healers instruct patients to cleanse their homes with red flowers, said to possess the power to remove evil, or to display white flowers, said to protect from evil.

Some may hold the patient's head in their hands and rotate it on its neck, and others may occasionally lift the patient at the waist and instruct him or her to kick forward one leg at a time.

Some healers provide meticulous instructions for every prescribed procedure by specifying precisely when and how a ritual must be done at home, or the exact dosage of each ingredient in a prescribed tea, bath, or liquid for a massage. Others just order the patient to cleanse the home, or enumerate the ingredients for the prescription without indicating dosage, as will become apparent from the patient-healer encounter vignettes presented later in this chapter.

Significantly, healers also vary in the ways in which they deal with existential problems. To illustrate, one healer avoided dealing with any personal problems presented to her by a patient. She ignored any reference to a patient's mention of difficulties at home with a husband, or children, or family. When a patient asked, "What shall I do?" or stated "I feel desperate," this healer responded by prescribing what I would call "busy work." She instructed the patient to carry out a set of elaborate procedures away from the temple; this involved searching for special flowers in the fields, placing them in specific spots in the house, and cleansing the home with them. There was also an endless litany of tasks that had to be carried out in a precise manner. Keeping the patient occupied with complex sets of tasks may divert his thoughts from his problems or may afford him the feeling of doing something to alleviate them, a feeling which iteself becomes curative (cf. Thomas 1974).

Others deal with personal problems pragmatically. For instance, a woman living with a man in a common-law arrangement was advised to get married, not on moral grounds as is preached by priests in church on Sunday, but for legal reasons: It is "your and your children's best protection against abandonment." When a patient came to report that someone had stolen her money, the spirit medium responded with, "You will not get it back"; when a woman reported that her unemployed husband was beating her, the advice was, "Go to the local judge."

Most healers react similarly when women patients report tensions with their husbands. The healers usually blame the woman and instruct her to acquiesce in her spouse's wishes. These responses reflect a basic tenet of Spiritualist teachings, that a woman must please her mate. When a woman complained to a healer of her husband's infidelity, the advice was to ignore it, to greet him with flowers when he came home, love him, and avoid quarrels: if the wife is agreeable, the husband will stop being unfaithful.

The healer's advice to women reflects a broader emphasis on submission, obedience, and acceptance of the status quo. These teachings are important from the perspective of Spiritualism as a socioreligious movement in Mexico, and they will be discussed in Chapter 10. To cite but one instance, a man reported to a healer that he was not paid for overtime work. The healer advised him not to attempt to claim the extra pay: "God will repay you--don't protest to the boss."

Several spirit mediums inquire whether the patient has previously seen a doctor and what the diagnosis and prescription have been. Some encourage the patient to continue with the physician's prescribed treatment; others insist that the patient cease following the doctor's regime. By and large both healers and patients claim that it is harmful to take a physician's and temple prescriptions concurrently. Interestingly, the most favored curers are not necessarily those who devote the longest time to the patient, nor those who prescribe patent medicines. The curers preferred most are those who are "most spiritual," meaning, as it happens, curers who concentrate on cleansing and massaging the patient.

Patients are assigned to specific healers upon request; most patients tend to remain with the healer designated them on their first temple visit. This is important because, although one idiosyncratic healing style may be more attractive to a patient than another, it is a specific technique such as cleansing that brings patients to Spiritualist temples. It is Spiritualist therapeutic procedures rather than individual treatment styles that are valued. I will return to this point in Chapter 9.

The following vignettes of verbal interchanges between patients and healers were randomly selected--from the 1212 observations that I made during my apprenticeship at the temple in my role of assistant to the healers--to illustrate some of the points made pertaining to patient-healer interactions: i.e., the brevity of the exchanges, the relatively limited nature of problem exploration, the healers' failure to provide patients with a diagnosis, and their differential stance compared with the medical profession (for example, compare the healer "B" on p. 92-93 with (the healer "L" on p. 96-97). Of course, the vignettes cannot convey the ongoing tactile communication between healer and patient, the vocal intonations suggesting compassion or anger, or the use of a phrase that is uttered in the form of both a declaration and an interrogation. For instance, a healer may address a patient with the sentence "You are feeling better!(?)" which implies both a command and an attempt at fact finding.

Also, it is necessary to visualize the patient and healer both standing facing each other, with the healer gently massaging the patient's body, or the patient standing and the healer sitting and holding the patient's hands during part of the interaction.

Because all healers follow the same initial and final procedure, these standard exchanges are not presented here. A standard exchange must begin with the patient stating "In the name of God, all powerful, I salute you brother (or sister depending on the sex of the spirit protector). To which the healer replies "And I answer you. Speak to me." This is followed by a blessing as described earlier. The encounter ends with the healer reminding the patient to attend irradiations and the patient saying "Thank you brother for your charity to which the healer responds with "Don't thank me, thank my father" referring to God the father). In several of the following cases, patients murmured something to the healer that was inaudible to me and probably also to the healer; otherwise, the dialogues that follow are verbatim exchanges in translation.

HEALER: P

The patient is a young woman who came with branches and requested a massage and cleansing.

HEALER: You brought branches for the massage?
PATIENT: Yes.

The healer divided the branches into separate bunches, and as she was doing so she spoke to the patient.

HEALER: It's not the person whom you see in front of you who is preparing the branches, it is a sacred spirit. How do you feel?
PATIENT: The nausea has not gone away, *this patient had seen the healer a month earlier,* but the pain in my head is gone.
HEALER: Does your stomach hurt?
PATIENT: No.

PRESCRIPTION: Juice from three lemons to be taken on three mornings.

HEALER: B

In this temple, B is the only male healer. In other temples there is a higher ratio of male to female healers. The patient is a middle-aged woman.

PATIENT: My head hurts.
HEALER: Does anything else hurt you?
PATIENT: No, only my head and eyes.
HEALER: How long has it been hurting you?
PATIENT: Fifteen days. I went to the doctor who told me my headaches come from high blood pressure.
HEALER: Can you breathe? Does your heart hurt?
PATIENT: Only my head. The doctor gave me pills and injections, but I am still in pain.
HEALER: Do you have pain in your chest?
PATIENT: Yes.
HEALER: Do you feel heat in your stomach?
PATIENT: Yes; after the doctor gave me the medicine the pain went away, but it returned.
HEALER: With the medicine you felt worse?
PATIENT: Yes, I was afraid.
HEALER: It wasn't the medicine that harmed you. Doctors know much. They are men of science, but they make mistakes. You need Spiritualist healing. When you wake up your stomach is upset; it stirs; do you feel weak?
PATIENT: Yes, my joints hurt.
HEALER: How long have you felt this way?
PATIENT: Two months, but I didn't think about it before.
HEALER: Is this the first time you are here?
PATIENT: Yes.
HEALER: Who told you to come?
PATIENT: Someone recommended it.
HEALER: What you need is Spiritual healing; to listen to the Word which is charity *this refers to irradiations and God's word, which is regarded as charity, or "bread".*

PRESCRIPTION: *Three packets of sal de uvas (a laxative) in half a glass of water--recite the prayer.*

TEA: *Flower of (Sp.) azares (Citrus)*
    (Sp.) flor de tilia (Taonabo sp. or
       Ternstroemia
       pringlei)
    (Sp.) flor de junco (Aporocactus
       flagelliformis)
    (Sp.) flor de magnolia (Magnolia grandiflora)
    To be taken seven mornings.

MASSAGE: *With red flowers and alcohol.*

HEALER: T

The patient is an old man.

HEALER: What did you bring *referring to branches for cleansing?*
PATIENT: *Arbol de pirul (Schinus molle L.).*
HEALER: *angrily:* I told you *(Sp.) romero* <u>Rosmarinus</u> <u>officinalis</u>
and red flowers. I never told you to bring this. *She takes the
branches and gives the patient a cleansing anyway.* How are you
doing? You don't have the same inflammation?
PATIENT: No, not any more.
HEALER: Go on taking what I gave you. *The patient was
previously prescribed a laxative.* Where are you from?
PATIENT: *Names a relatively remote town.*
HEALER: Come on Sunday for an irradiation.

HEALER: X

The patient is a baby carried by his mother.

HEALER: What have you done? *This healer frequently opens the
exchange with these words, which mean "What is wrong with you?"
Some patients do not comprehend the meaning of this expression.*
MOTHER: I gave the child tea and his kidneys are now well.
HEALER: You see how, when you do it with love, God is the doctor
of all doctors. Prepare yourself. Give Him thanks.
MOTHER: The child has surface eruptions in the thigh area and I
couldn't find *(Sp.) yerba mora (Solanum nigrum L.), previously
prescribed by the healer.*
HEALER: Look for it.
MOTHER: He doesn't want to eat, and he cries.
HEALER: What has the doctor told you?
MOTHER: He didn't.
HEALER: You can feed him purees. How old is he?
MOTHER: One year old.
HEALER: You can give him papaya, oranges, gelatin, milk, mint
tea, all kinds of fruits; noodles, avoid giving him greasy foods and
beef. Give him only chicken.

PRESCRIPTION: 3 drops of Tri-Vi-Sol.

HEALER: K

*K is the head of the temple. The patient is a middle-aged man
from a distant village.*

PATIENT: I have pain in my stomach.

HEALER: How long have you had this pain?
PATIENT: A year.
HEALER: Did you go to the doctor?
PATIENT: Yes, but I stopped going.
HEALER: Did they do an analysis?
PATIENT: Yes, it was nothing. I wasn't vomiting.
HEALER: Nor do you have ulcers?
PATIENT: No; it only hurts in the morning.
HEALER: You are not hungry during those hours?
PATIENT: No.

The healer again examines the stomach with her hands and gives an especially vigorous cleansing in the stomach area.

HEALER: It's an infection of the prostate; you have an upset stomach. I will give you a cleansing.

PRESCRIPTION:	*1 bottle of Sal Hepatica in tepid water--to be taken in the afternoon.*
	In the morning, take a glass of orange juice.
	1 ampule of penicillin of 500--mg;
	2 cm in the morning;
	2 cm on Friday; and
	1 cm on Sunday. Return on Tuesday.
TEA:	*Root of (Sp.) malva (Malva parviflora)*
	Root of (Sp.) verbena (Verbena carolina L.)
	Root of (Sp.) yerba del negro (Sphaeralcea angustifolia)

HEALER: A

This is one of two healers whose tone of voice is reassuring and compassionate. The patient is a middle-aged man with crusts and lesions on his skin. He is accompanied by his mother.

HEALER: Since when have you been feeling like this? *Some healers open the first phase of the interaction with this statement, immediately suggesting to the patient that the healer already knows the patient's ailment.*
PATIENT: Since Friday. *The patient's mother had brought branches for a cleansing, and in the course of carrying out the procedure the healer fainted away. When her spirit protector returned, the healer revived.*
HEALER: Move your head well. You have not done anything?
PATIENT: Nothing.
HEALER: You eat well?

PATIENT: Yes. I have a question. A flower pot fell on my head
from nowhere.

MOTHER: He does not want to come on Sundays to the rituals. He
only drinks.

PATIENT: I didn't drink on Friday.

HEALER: I don't say you shouldn't drink at all. Don't be afraid.
Come at ten in the morning on Friday and Sunday. Bring flowers.
You lack vitamins. I know everything. Walk on your way smiling.

PRESCRIPTION:

TEA:	*(Sp.) ruda (Ruta chalepensis L.)*
	(Sp.) romero (Rosmarinus officinalis L.)
	2 drops of ether
BATH:	*Take a bath in the morning and at noon in liquid made from:*
	7 branches of (Sp.) romero (Rosmarinus officinalis L.)
	7 branches (Sp.) ortiga (Urtica dioica)
	7 branches (Sp.) ruda (Ruta chalepensis L.)
	7 branches (Sp.) arbol de pirul (Schinus molle L.)
	1 cup ammonia
MASSAGE:	*With a liquid made of aromatic waters and rubbing alcohol (consisting of agua safalica, agua sedativa, and espiritus de untar).*

*This is a very common prescription when the diagnosis is susto.
In this instance it is a likely reason for the patient's seeking
treatment, inasmuch as the patient reported that an unexpected event
had occurred: a flower pot fell on his head. But in this case, as in
many others, the healer does not state the diagnosis.*

HEALER: X

*The patient is an 18-year old boy, coming for the first time, who
has been brought by a temple regular.*

HEALER: What have you done?

PATIENT: I broke my foot on my job. I had an operation, but my
foot is still sore around the ankle. *He displayed his foot to the
healer. The healer called for a chair, and the patient sat down and
put his foot on her lap. She moved her hand around the affected area,
which had been bandaged with gauze. She gave him a spiritual
injection, mimicking the motions of a physician.*

HEALER: Don't cover this part. Uncover it so that air and humidity can penetrate. Only, when you go somewhere where there is dust, cover it up.

PRESCRIPTION:　　*Wash the wound. Prepare the liquid by boiling:*
3 leaves of (Sp.) aranto (unidentified botanically)
1 piece of (Sp.) flor de arnica (Mentzelia conzattlii; Zexmenia pringlei)
3 drops of salt in 7 drops of vinegar
9 drops of clarisol
Dry the wound and apply sulfatiasol (antiseptic).

TEA:　　*Look for:*
(Sp.) yerba marota (family Convolvulaceae)
1 piece of (Sp.) sangre de drago (Jatropha dioica L.)
(Sp.) flor de noche buena (unidentified botanically)

HEALER: A

The patient is a nursing infant carried by his mother.

HEALER: What's wrong?
MOTHER: Diarrhea and vomit.
HEALER: What made him sick?
There is no response from the mother.
HEALER: What made him sick?
MOTHER: I gave him beans.
HEALER: Don't give him beans. How many times does he make?
MOTHER: Twice.
HEALER: You got angry and then you nursed him. How many times has the baby vomited?
MOTHER: Twice.
HEALER: *Angrily:* Why did you get angry if you are nursing a baby? *The healer prescribed for the baby biotalidina (an anti-diarrheal pill) if the diarrhea should continue. If it didn't, the pill was not to be given. Additionally, she prescribed tea for the mother.*

PRESCRIPTION:

TEA (For the Mother):
to be taken three times a day for 7 days:
1 liter of water

pinch of *(Sp.) boldo (Peumus boldus)*
(Sp.) cuasia (Quassia amara L. or
  Picrasma excelsa)
(Sp.) aranto leaves (unidentified
  botanically)
3 pieces of artichoke
(Sp.) contra yerba (unidentified
  botanically)
(Sp.) inojo (unidentified botanically)
3 leaves of (Sp.) manrrubio
  (Marrubium vulgare L.)
(Sp.) anis de estrella (Star anise)
  Illicium verum or Illicium
  anisatum
(Sp.) canela
  Cinnamomum zeylanicum
  anis de magnesia anisada (a purgative)

TEA *(For the Baby):*   *(Sp.) inojo (unidentified botanically)*
3 flowers of (Sp.) bugambilia
  (Bougaembillia spectabili)
(Sp.) oregano chico (unidentified botanically)
(Sp.) yerbabuena (Mentha spicata)

HEALER: B

The patient is an old man who has come with branches for a cleansing.

HEALER: Is this the first time you are here?
PATIENT: No.
HEALER: Where do you come from?
PATIENT: *Names the town.* Last time I saw Sister So-and-So.
HEALER: Then go to her. *This type of dismissal is unusual.*

HEALER: Z

The patient is a baby, carried by her young mother.

MOTHER: Baby's stomach hurts.
HEALER: What are you giving it?
MOTHER: Rice.
HEALER: No, rice is too heavy for the child. Does she have diarrhea?

MOTHER: A little.
HEALER: Do you have a purgative?
MOTHER: No.

HEALER: Give her a purgative to clean what she has inside. How old is the child?

MOTHER: Eight months old.

HEALER: Give her milk with cornmeal. Stop giving her rice. She is too small. Do you breastfeed her?

MOTHER: Yes, but I don't have enough milk.

PRESCRIPTION:	Kitchen oil
TEA:	*oregano chico (unidentified botanically)*
	1 leaf of (Sp.) guayaba (<u>Psidium guajava</u>)
	(Sp.) flor de 7 colores (<u>Lantana camara L.</u>)
	3 flowers of (Sp.) plumbago (<u>Plumbago</u> [<u>capensis</u>]- <u>auriculata</u>)
	(Sp.) anis de estrella (<u>Illicium anisatum</u> or <u>Illicium verum</u>)
	Sulfadiasina (antibiotic)
	Enterovioform (anti-diarrheal)

HEALER: A

The patient, who is discussed more fully in Chapter 9, is a very wealthy professional man in his early 50's, who subsequently became a Spiritualist adherent but not a functionary. On this occasion he was introduced by the head of the temple to the healer, who was informed by the head, "He is Brother So-and-So's patient, but the medium is not here today." After giving the patient an especially vigorous cleansing, the healer asked the patient his name.

HEALER: What did Brother So-and-So prescribe?

PATIENT: Medicine, massages, and baths, and pill six-sixty-six; Reumofan [medication for rheumatism] for eight days.

HEALER: Have you finished it?

PATIENT: No.

HEALER: Stop taking the prescription for three days and then take it for three more days.

PATIENT: Brother So-and-So told me not to bathe for eight days, until today.

HEALER: Continue taking what Brother So-and-So told you. Did Brother So-and-So prescribe tea?

PATIENT: Yes.

HEALER: What?

PATIENT: Albacar (<u>Ocimum basilicum</u>).

HEALER: Take the tea with (Sp.) azares (<u>Citrus</u>) and (Sp.) inojo (unidentified botanically). Bring flowers for a dislodgement. How do you feel?

PATIENT: Bit better. When should I come again?

HEALER: Friday. You feel very tired and you feel your feet swollen.

PATIENT: Yes.

HEALER: Everything disturbs you, bothers you, and you are sad. You have no more illusions.

PATIENT: Yes.

HEALER: Come Friday for three disiodgments and you will be well. Don't be afraid. Carry a red flower with you in your pocket. This will protect you. Nothing will happen. Don't be afraid. The Spiritual world is with you. Do you agree?

PATIENT: Yes.

HEALER: Y

The patient is a little girl with her mother.

MOTHER: The child has a cough.

HEALER: How long has she had this cough?

MOTHER: A week.

HEALER: What have you given her?

MOTHER: A cough syrup, which didn't do any good.

PRESCRIPTION: *Cough syrup to be made from:*
(Sp.) arbol de pirul (Schinus molle
   L.)
3 cloves of garlic
1 spoon of honey
Lemon juice

HEALER: A

The patient is a 13-year old boy with his mother.

BOY: My stomach hurts.

HEALER: Does he have worms?

MOTHER: Yes.

HEALER: How many have you removed, and what kind of medicine have you given him?

MOTHER: It's been a very long time since I brought him here.

PRESCRIPTION:

TEA: *Tonic 3 times a day:*
Water from (Sp.) hipazote
(Chenopodium) and mint

This was one of the rare cases where the patient,-- i.e., the mother--was not satisfied with the interaction, and she sat down again to wait to be attended by another healer.

HEALER: W

The patient is a young woman.

HEALER: Is this your first time here?
PATIENT: Yes.
HEALER: Where are you from?
PATIENT: From here *referring to Juarez.* I have pain, mainly in the morning.
The healer attempted to localize the area with her hand around the pubic region.
HEALER: Inflammation is very strong in the stomach. Come back in eight days and bring your prescription with you.

MASSAGE:	*Creams described as made of lettuce, apples, oranges, and (Sp.) Belladona.*
TEA:	*1 liter of water*
	4 roots of (Sp.) malva (<u>Malva parviflora</u>)
	4 roots of (Sp.) endivia (<u>Sonchus deraceu L.</u>)

The temple head suspected, as I did, that this healer did not work <u>limpio</u>, meaning that she was not in a real trance. One reason for the temple head's suspicion was that the healer frequently prescribed 4 instead of 3 to a dosage. The number 4 does not form part of Spiritualist symbolism.

HEALER: Y

The patient is a teenage girl, accompanied by her mother.

MOTHER: She broke out in welts and her feet hurt *pointing to the gastrocnemius.* She has had this problem for a long time. She broke out in welts yesterday.
HEALER: What did you eat?
PATIENT: Eggs and a syrup somebody gave me. I think the welts resulted from my eating the eggs together with the syrup.
MOTHER: She had been to see a doctor to treat the leg problem. He diagnosed it as anemia; another doctor diagnosed the condition as worms; and a third, that she had sick veins.

HEALER: You have rheumatism.

The mother, addressing me, said that her family had spent a lot of money on doctors and that they were recommended to a Spiritualist temple.

MOTHER: I don't know.

PRESCRIPTION: *To take at night:*
                       Small bottle of Phillips Milk of
                          Magnesia

MESSAGE: *With 1/2 liter of rubbing alcohol*
                       8 pills (Sp.) alcanfor (Eucalyptus
                          globosus Labill.)
                       (Sp.) ruda (Ruta chalepensis L.)

                       Neovina cream

                       1 bottle of Mefezolidina
                       (antirheumatism muscle relaxer):
                       3 a day before meals

                       Three days later, massage with
                       alcohol--90 proof--and 20 heads
                       of garlic. Take 20 drops of
                       alcohol.

HEALER: Y

The patient is a young woman of about 25 from Juarez, coming to the temple for the first time. She has been brought by a cousin without her husband's permission.

PATIENT: I have pain in the chest and lungs, and I feel nausea.

HEALER: The nausea is from exhaustion.
PATIENT: I also have my period only one day.
HEALER: How many children do you have?
PATIENT: One.
HEALER: Wait another few days. You may be pregnant.
PATIENT: I want to scream and cry. My husband took me to a doctor, but I have not been improving. I feel terrible and I cannot sleep.
HEALER: Come for a cleansing. Come on a Sunday to hear God's words.
PATIENT: My husband does not understand about coming to the temple. The situation is very delicate: My husband is very Catholic.

HEALER: Continue the treatment the doctor gave you. Take the pills the doctor gave you.

PRESCRIPTION:

TEA:	*(Sp.) arbol de pirul (<u>Schinus molle L.</u>)* *(Sp.) ambar (<u>Scabiosa atropurpurea L.</u>)* *Almonds* *(Sp.) romero (<u>Rosmarinus officinalis L.</u>)* *Ether pills*
	Drink the tea three days.
MASSAGE:	*For the <u>cerebro</u>, the massage lotion is to be prepared from three separate lotions.*

I followed up on this patient informally at various times during my field stay, and she reported that her condition had improved.

HEALER: X

The patient is a 3-year-old boy with his mother.

MOTHER: I have been giving him a vitamin tonic. I couldn't give him the other medicine, a palmitate. I couldn't find it. I bought a substitute. The child's welts disappeared because I gave him the Phillips Milk of Magnesia that was previously prescribed by Brother So-and-So.

HEALER: Continue giving him his baths and the milk of magnesia every third day, and give him a massage after the bath.

MOTHER: He would not drink the tea because he doesn't like the other pill. How many cleansings does he still need to have?

HEALER: Seven.

HEALER: X

The patient is a young woman, who came with branches. She had requested this particular healer.

HEALER: Where are you from?

PATIENT: From afar. *Judging by the patient's dress, she had probably come from a village located twenty-five to thirty miles away. She had been directed to the healer by the head of the temple, who said that the patient had been hit and that as a result she gets* attacks. *As the healer was giving the patient a vigorous cleansing, the healer fainted, while the patient stood by, watching, with a puzzled expression on her face. Then, after a minute, the spirit protector returned and continued the vigorous massaging by picking the patient up by the waist from behind. She instructed the patient to kick her legs in a can-can style three times and to breathe deeply.*

HEALER: How do you feel?
PATIENT: Very good.
HEALER: What are you taking?
PATIENT: Vitamined milk, but no teas.
HEALER: Bring a branch for a cleansing on Tuesday.

PRESCRIPTION: *7 branches of (Sp.) romero (Rosmarinus*
                 officinalis L.)
              7 red flowers
              7 (Sp.) jarilla (Dodonaea)

TEA: *1 bottle of port*
              (Sp.) anis del chiquito (Pimpinella anisum)
              (Sp.) flor de azares (Citrus)
              (Sp.) flor de tilia (Ternstroemia pringlei)
              (Sp.) flor de manita (unidentified botanically)
              7 leaves of (Sp.) naranjo (Citrus)
              Drink 1 cup three times a day.

HEALER: Z

The patient, an adolescent boy who came with his mother, said nothing.

MOTHER: He has had bad luck. He was just released from prison. He was in a car accident and he smashed somebody's car; he had bad luck.

HEALER: His *cerebro* is unbalanced. There is no submission and obedience in young people; they are only interested in material things. That's why they become unbalanced--mad.

PRESCRIPTION:

TEA: *(Sp.) flor de azares (Citrus)*
              (Sp.) huizaches (Acacia shaffneri)
              (Sp.) flor de manita (unidentified
                 botanically
              (Sp.) jarilla (Dodonaea)
              1 bottle of vitamin tonic

MASSAGE: *He must do it exactly at noon, made of:*
              1 cup mescal

White wine
(Sp.) ruda (Ruta chalepensis L.)

The healer also instructed the mother to put a cross of rosemary in the house.

HEALER: X

The patient is a woman in her 40s. With her she brought her little boy, who, according to the mother, had been successfully treated at the temple for welts.

HEALER: How are you?
PATIENT: My throat is better. My gall bladder and kidneys are also better.
HEALER: Do you urinate a lot? The more you drink, the more you will urinate.
PATIENT: I couldn't find the plant named "To." (unidentified botanically)
HEALER: It is also known by another name *gives her the name.*
PATIENT: I still feel I have worms in my head, and when I am nervous I feel faint.
HEALER: Listen to the voice of God; move your head.
PATIENT: No, it no longer hurts.

NO PRESCRIPTION.

HEALER: W

The patient is a big, fat, middle-aged woman.

HEALER: First time?
PATIENT: Yes. It's been one year since I had my period, since my baby was born. Before I had the baby I was very sick. I was operated on, and then I got pregnant.
HEALER: Did you breastfeed the baby?
PATIENT: No, I didn't have enough milk.
HEALER: *As she moves her hand over the patient's stomach:* Are you pregnant?
PATIENT: No, I am fat; that's the way I am after I have relations with my husband. I sometimes bleed.
HEALER: He is not delicate with you. A woman is very delicate. Have you seen a doctor?
PATIENT: No, I took nothing because I am afraid. I have a headache.
HEALER: Do you have symptoms of pregnancy like vomiting, nausea in the morning?

PATIENT: No.
HEALER: *after giving her the prescription:* This will certainly induce your period. Once you get your period, stop taking the tea. Drink it daily until the next time; and bring lotion.

PRESCRIPTION:	*A very hot bath every morning.*

TEA:	*1 avocado pit*
	1 handful of (Sp.) santa maria (Chrysanthemum parthenium)
	1 handful of (Sp.) arbol macho (same as arbol de pirul Schinus molle L.)
	1 bar of chocolate
	1 handful (Sp.) hipazote (Chenopodium)
	1 handful (Sp.) romero (Rosmarinus officinalis L.)
	unrefined sugar

BATH:	*(Sp.) arbol macho (same as arbol de pirul Schinus molle L.) Four baths every third day.*

HEALER: L

The patient, a young man, came with branches. The healer fainted as she gave the patient a vigorous cleansing. After the healer's spirit returned, she requested a chair for the patient and asked him to sit down. She washed his face with the water that was prepared in the temple.

HEALER: How do you feel?
PATIENT: Better, but my head feels heavy.
HEALER: Come back Tuesday at noon.
PATIENT: My skin feels burned. *His face was inflamed.*
HEALER: That is because you are bashful.
PATIENT: I also cannot see in one eye.
HEALER: Wash it with black tea that you buy in the pharmacy.

PRESCRIPTION:

BATH:	*(Sp.) toronjil (Agastache mexicana)*
	(Sp.) albacar (Ocimum basilicum)
	(Sp.) ruda (Ruta chalepensis L.)
	Rubbing alcohol
	Massage face with three types of vegetable creams referred to as made of oranges, lettuce, and apples.

> *Wash eye with black tea in 1/2 liter of*
> *water before going to bed.*
>
> *Buy 1 10-ml. vial of Neurovion (a*
> *tranquilizer based on vitamins); 2m.*
> *every third day.*

TEA: *(Sp.) flor de tilia (Taonabo sp. or*
                        Ternstroemia pringlei)
                     Flowers of (Sp.) azares (Citrus)
                     (Sp.) toronjil (Agastache mexicana)
                     For your nerves.

HEALER: I give simple remedies. You don't need to spend a lot of money, and don't take the doctor's medicine; suspend it. If they told you you are not going to get well, don't listen; you will get well with faith. Don't take the doctor's medicine; it makes you ill.

HEALER: X

The patient is a woman.

HEALER: Move your head. Breathe three times. How do you feel?

PATIENT: Good.
HEALER: What have you done?
PATIENT: Nothing.
HEALER: *moving her hand around the patient's abdomen:*   This part of the stomach hurts.
PATIENT: No.
HEALER: *placing her hand on another area:* Here.
PATIENT: A little.
HEALER: You are not taking anything for nerves?
PATIENT: Yes.
HEALER: What are you taking?
PATIENT: A tranquilizer.
HEALER: When you feel like this, you cannot sleep. You feel alone. Your stomach feels empty. *This is not a uncommon phrase spoken to patients.*

PATIENT: Where are you from?
HEALER: I work here, but I am from--*a nearby town.* Come Sunday. This will be a medicine for the spirit, to tranquilize you, so you feel God is with you. Say invocation.

PRESCRIPTION:

TEA: *(Sp.) azares (Citrus)*

> (Sp.) *flor de manita (unidentified*
>   *botanically)*
> (Sp.) *flor de tilia (Taonabo sp. or*
>   *Ternstroemia pringlei)*
> *1/2 glass three times a day*
>
> *Passiflorine (a tranquilizer)*
> *1 tablespoon with 1/2 glass of tea*
>
> *Massage cerebro with lotion de caballoro*
> *and lemon juice.*

HEALING TECHNIQUES APPLIED TO REGULARS

Regulars come to the temple frequently to assist the healers, to seek treatment or advice. They usually come to consult with healers about every problem outside their day-to-day experience. Spiritualist treatment of regulars differs in several significant respects, three of which merit consideration: patient-healer interaction; "development"; and becoming a curer. The full importance of these treatment techniques is discussed in Chapter 9; here the modalities are briefly described.

PATIENT-HEALER INTERACTION

Compared with the interaction between healers and nonregulars, the interaction between healers and regulars is qualitatively more personalistic and sometimes even emotionally intense. The interaction tends to last, on the average, twenty-three minutes, during which time the regular presents his or her symptoms and any current problems of living, while the healer constantly reminds the patient that the spirit world is protecting the patient. Regulars, unlike other patients, sometimes report to healers their dreams, suggesting that they tend to be more atuned to inner psychic states. Most important, the patient receives lengthy cleansings, with the curer unceasingly massaging the patient's body. In fact, regulars tend to come to the temple frequently, if for no other reason than to receive a cleansing. I can add that once I was incorporated into the temple structure as a regular, I was incessantly being urged to have a cleansing on the grounds that "It restores one. It makes one strong." This is especially important because during these interactions the regular also becomes socialized into Spiritualism with Spiritualist symbolism being continuously reinforced and internalized by the patient.

"Development"

Whereas patient-healer interaction is an important component of a regular's therapy, "development" is equally so, because trancing, intrinsic to "development," is instrumental in altering psychophysiological states, as recent findings suggest (Benson et al. 1976; Gellhorn & Kiely 1972; Lex 1976). I shall explore this point in Chapter 9.

An individual remains in development as little as three months or as long as eight years or until his spirit protector identifies himself by announcing his name during a development session for all to hear and for the temple head to record. Once the spirit protector announces his or her name, the individual is ready to become a curer.

Significantly, regulars frequently attribute their improvement or recovery to development sessions. When questioned how they feel following a trance experience, regulars uniformly respond "invigorated," "accelerated," "happy." During prolonged trancing episodes, they experience an absence of hunger pains and other physiological needs. Paradoxically, in almost all cases, regulars report initial reluctance to enter development because, as they say, they fear "losing oneself." In fact, in some instances, the fear of development may provoke the emergence of new symptoms in the patient, as we see later.

Becoming A Curer

When a patient becomes a curer, not only does he engage in trancing, but concurrently the patient's sick role is converted into a health-providing one. The role reversal transforms a depressed individual into a valued knowledgeable person capable of alleviating the afflictions of others.

By way of illustrating the interaction between regulars and healers, I present four interactional vignettes. While in two of the cases the interaction was very brief contextually they differ from healers' interactions with nonregulars in that they are also more didactic in character and usually lengthy. The cases are followed by a presentation of the case history of Chucha. Her experience is particularly illuminating of the treatment of regulars, although her case is not typical because, unlike most regulars, she arrived at the temple traumatized by two brain operations. Her case is also an excellent example of the way in which the healing of regulars is a gradual negotiation rather than a drastic one-time miracle cure and also contrasts with the speedy treatment process of nonregulars.

HEALER: A[1]

The patient is a 19-year old man, the son of a devoted temple goer. He frequently comes just for a cleansing.

HEALER: How do you feel?

PATIENT: Murmured something inaudible to me and I suspect also to the healer.

HEALER: You have a beautiful gift. You have an open mind. It is time for you to enter development. You know a spirit brings you here.

HEALER: L

The patient is a male. He said nothing and seemed to have come only for a cleansing.

HEALER: Let him not be an egotist, a hypocrite, and have two faces; let him be full of understanding and honesty. If you want to call God, call yourself; if you want to love God; love yourself; if you want to be good, know yourself. Have you understood? Look at yourself and this way you will be a real Spiritualist.

HEALER: J

The patient is another curer.

PATIENT: I feel very bad.

HEALER: Did you have a laxative?

PATIENT: No.

HEALER: With grippe there is a lot of filth and dirt in the body. You need a laxative--not a delicate one. Take Sal Hepatica. You have to think and struggle; struggle that you don't catch an illness and that it becomes chronic. You, as a functionary, your protector is your husband. You have to help him. He cannot exist or speak without the body.

HEALER: X

The patient is the brother of a core temple member.

HEALER: Have you brought the branches? What have you done?

PATIENT: I injured my knee; I fell two months ago. My knee hurts. It has no force. A friend told me to put vinegar and Yodex--that it would do me well.

HEALER: *examining the knee with her hands:* You have liquid in the space *she was pressing her hands against the patella.* You thought it was an external injury but it was internal. *She symbolically sucked the water out by putting her lips close to the knee.* Did you hear how this part thundered? *She requested oil, which she applied* to the knee cap. *She instructed him to bend his foot, to bend down and squat.*

PATIENT: Now I can move my foot.

HEALER: I removed the liquid but you will get more water. You will note it is hot.

PATIENT: Yes, very true. Can I do heavy work?

HEALER: To let it deflate, don't do anything today. Tomorrow, massage it first with vinegar. Apply a new bandage. It's a wound.

PATIENT: Won't it harm me to do heavy work?

HEALER: No--a little rest--and a little exercise, but slowly.

PRESCRIPTION: *Boil vinegar*

TEA: *3 teaspoons of salt*
a little (Sp.) cancerina (Asclepias sp.)
(Sp.) flor de arnica (Mentzelia conzattii;
*   Zexmenia pringlei)*
Three spoons of vinegar for nine days on
an empty stomach with the tea.
Thirteen tablespoons Reumofan
(rheumatism remedy) once a day.

The preceding case vignettes suggest a qualitative difference between the way in which regulars and nonregulars are dealt with. They also provide us with a glimpse of regulars' and nonregulars' differential resort to temple healers. Unlike nonregulars, who come to treat specific symptoms, regulars come regardless of any symptomatic experience. They maintain an ongoing relationship with the temple, which (as is discussed in Chapter 9) forms part of their treatment.

Regulars' ongoing relationship with the temple can be gleaned from Chucha's case, which follows. I present her case at this juncture to illustrate in greater depth some of the healing techniques to which regulars are exposed. Chucha's case also illuminates several points made previously, as well as some that will be made later. For instance, by examining the vignette, we see how Spiritualists recruit patients, how they alter a patient's etiological beliefs, and also how they create internal conflicts for the patient hitherto not experienced by the patient.

Chucha

I followed Chucha's case intensively for thirteen months and intermittently thereafter for ten more. During my association with her at the temple and at her home, I watched the woman become transformed from a listless, depressed individual to a smiling, relatively energetic one even though she continued to report sundry physical disorders in various parts of her body. Yet, despite the alleged symptoms, Chucha frequently acknowledged that, in contrast to her situation prior to temple treatment, Chucha was satisfied with her day-to-day existence as never before. *This contrast was also apparent to even a casual observer.*

I must emphasize that the limited knowledge of Chucha's medical history prior to her contact with the temple adds some mystery to her case. Nevertheless, the case provides a compelling example of the changes experienced by patients in response to temple therapy. A one-year chronological description of Chucha's progress is significant because it stresses the importance of long-term observations of treatment procedures and outcomes. Had Chucha been observed only briefly, it could easily have been concluded that either she had been completely unaffected by Spiritualist treatment or she had been in fact cured, depending on the point in time at which the observations were being made.

Chucha, a heavyset 41-year-old woman, had been married sixteen years, without children. She had acquired a third-grade education. She arrived at the temple in 1976, after two brain operations had been performed in a large, well-known Mexico City hospital. When we first met, Chucha had been treated at the temple for nine months. My initial impression of Chucha, with her expressionless distant gaze and grimace, was that she was suffering from depression. Her bearing suggested that every utterance and every motion was an effort for her. At our first meeting, Chucha described her symptoms as headaches and pain in the *cerebro*, with occasional chest pains; she had no wish to live, and emphasized that she frequently thought of dying.

By way of a brief biographical sketch, Chucha originated from the very poorest segment of Mexican society. At age 12 she left her natal town and went to live with an aunt in Mexico City a hundred miles away. Her sister and mother soon followed, to escape, like Chucha, from the father who used to beat them, particularly after drinking bouts.

In Mexico City, Chucha worked at odd jobs until she was 17, at which time she found a permanent job in a downtown restaurant. She worked there for eighteen years, until her first major illness. She was soon promoted to chief cook, but the responsibility weighed heavily on her. She met her husband when she was 17, she became engaged to him at 22, and they were married when she was 25. Her husband, who worked as a messenger boy in a government office in Mexico City, is an extemely amiable and good-humored man. He dotes on his wife. Some observers even commented on his open display of devotion to Chucha because such overt expression of affection is unusual for men from his social milieu. Ever since Chucha was recruited into temple participation, he has accompanied her, and he was even mobilized to take an active part in temple rituals, which resulted in financial sacrifice to their household.

When Chucha was 35 she fell ill. She lost her balance and zig-zagged while walking, she experienced nausea, and she felt, in her words, as if "I had water on my brain." Three physicians diagnosed her condition as a subdural hematoma on the brain and, in consultation, all but one recommended brain surgery. One of the doctors was not convinced that there was anything wrong with her, but, according to Chucha, his opinion was ignored. Two operations were performed within a span of eight days. On every occasion, Chucha points to the two incisions in the parietal region of her skull. She claims that six separate incisions were made and that, each time, the doctors found no evidence of any disease. She frequently recalls the excruciating pain of the operations. Her unceasing references to her physical scars below the hairline suggest that profound psychological scarring resulted from these operations as well.

Following Chucha's release from the hospital she was told to return for periodic checkups, but she never did because she was terrified of the doctors. At present, she reproaches her husband for having given permission for the operations.

After Chucha's operations, her condition deteriorated. She continued to experience the same symptoms, nausea and dizziness, but additionally she also suffered from severe headaches. She sought treatment from various types of practitioners. Finally, one medical doctor advised her and her husband that there was nothing more to be done for her condition and that their best option was to move to a small town where she would be more tranquil and where the air was better. Consequently, she and her husband left their jobs in Mexico City and came to live in Chucha's natal town, where they, along with Chucha's parents and sister, currently reside.

Upon her return, Chucha continued to seek treatment from several types of nonbiomedical practitioners, including a Spiritist curer who absconded with a large sum of their money. Chucha then encountered a woman who told her about the Spiritualist temple, which was situated twenty-five miles from where they lived and at which the curers did not charge any money. Chucha hesitated to go because, as a devout Catholic, she had heard that Spiritualist curers were witches (*brujas*). As a last resort she decided to go to the temple after she had obtained permission from the priest. Initially she was disturbed by the neighbors' gossip about her affiliation with witches, but as her condition improved she ceased taking any notice of the criticism. In fact, both she and her husband frequently remarked that had they discovered the temple therapy sooner they would have saved themselves great suffering and heavy financial debts.

Shortly after Chucha began treatment at the temple, the healer who attended her ordered her to enter development. During one healing session the healer informed her that she must prepare herself for becoming a healer, because by healing others she herself would recover. Subsequently, God announced publicly during a Sunday irradiation that Chucha would become not only a curer but a leader of others, that she and her husband would found a new temple in their town, where there was none. But Chucha was afraid of the overwhelming responsibility of becoming a temple leader (Finkler 1981a).

A synopsis of my observations of Chucha reveals the tenuous nature of Spiritualist curing. During my entire association with her, she participated in weekly development sessions and received treatments, including cleansings.

Between October and December 1977 Chucha was extremely depressed; she felt dizzy, weak, and sad. She failed to carry out her household chores, which her husband and mother took over. She reported that she felt well only after development. During this period Chucha's attribution for her illness changed. She declared that whereas previously she had imputed her illness to the showers she used to take at the restaurant after a day's work, she now knew that her illness was being caused by evil spirits possessing her body, that she was in fact being punished for having at one time designated Spiritualists as "witches." Concomitantly, Chucha also expressed her ambivalence about joining the temple. She stated that her doubts about Spiritualism were impeding her speedy recovery.

By the end of December, Chucha's spirit protector identified himself by announcing his name during development. The spirit protector publicly assured Chucha that he would take charge of her cure. Following this important event, Chucha declared she was no longer suffering from headaches, but she continued to suffer from heart palpitations. During this period the temple head pressed Chucha to begin work as a curer, now that she had her spirit protector. At first she resisted the temple head's urgings, again because she was afraid of the responsibility.

Spiritualist healers are gradually incorporated into their new roles as curers, however. Novices initially attend patients who come for cleansings, and only after about a month or two are patients with all types of ailments referred to them.

In February 1978, after considerable hesitation, Chucha finally assumed work as a healer. This was a watershed in her career as a patient. She began arriving unaccompanied to the temple. She reported that she was feeling extremely well. She smiled and appeared jubilant for the first time. A week later, however, she reported that she was again feeling weak. She attributed her weakness to an evil spirit who was transferred from a patient to her during a curing session. When she was treated by her healer she reported pain in her throat and in the distal end of her tongue. The healer diagnosed the condition as an infection and prescribed patent medicine in addition to the usual herbs, massages, and teas. (The curer recommended dramamine as a tranquilizer, and penicillin for her throat). Two days later Chucha indicated that the patent medicine prescribed by the healer failed to alleviate her symptoms because she was being punished by the spirits for noncompliance with the spirit world; she neglected to take the teas prescribed by the temple healer. By the end of the month she reported that she was again feeling well, and she ceased to think about dying.

In March and the first two weeks of April, Chucha reported that all her pains had disappeared; but she added that when she was absent from the temple her aches recurred. Yet an extraordinary change had come over her: she was visibly happy, and her cheerful mood was reflected in her bearing, her posture, and her facial expression, in spite of her alleged intermittent aches. On April 18, however, Chucha suffered a major crisis, which lasted for over a week and which confined her to bed. Her fears of death returned, along with her old symptoms. But because she was anxious not to disappoint her patients, she returned to work at the temple after a week.

In May, the temple head initiated twice-weekly consultations between the head's and Chucha's spirit protectors. Chucha's spirit protector confessed to her counterpart that Chucha was having doubts about Spiritualism and that she was not being sufficiently submissive to the world of the spirits. Chucha reiterated her conviction that her doubts about Spiritualism were impeding her recovery.

During June, Chucha felt well, looked and acted cheerful, and was even active in doing her household chores. She reported, however, a pain in her skull, which she attributed to bumping herself inadvertently in her skull sutures.

In July, she reported pain around the heart area again and claimed that her head ached, especially when she had to do her household chores; yet, to her own surprise, when she worked in the temple as a healer she never felt any pain despite the physical exertion, especially when she was cleansing patients.

Between August and October, Chucha avowed that she was feeling very well. In fact, her husband was incredulous about the positive changes he saw taking place in his wife. But she continued to report intermittent pain in her eyes, her head, her skull sutures, and her foot, as well as occasional dizziness, which was alleviated after she finished a day of curing at the temple.

Chucha's story suggests a case of somatization of depression, whereby patients express dysphoric affect with physical symptoms. It is quite likely that Chucha's physicians failed to diagnose her depressive disorder, a common occurrence that has been reported to befall others in similar situations elsewhere, (e.g., "Mr. Hung's case" (Kleinman 1980:155-157). Chucha's clinical manifestations failed to respond to the medical therapeutic regime employed by her physicians to treat her condition. I might note that despite my close and extensive contact with Chucha, I was not able to establish the precise events which had led up to the onset of her illness. It is my impression, however, that Chucha's depression may have been connected with some type of endocrine dysfunction. Her physical appearance and her report that when she was in her early twenties she had suddenly gained sixty pounds after a tonsillectomy suggest glandular impairment. Chucha's report does not, however, suggest that she had been treated for her condition other than by surgery. Additionally, Chucha's depression may also be related to her childless state, a particularly unfortunate existential predicament in Mexico, where children are extremely valued, where the role of the mother is venerated, and where childlessness in a woman is considered a great misfortune.

Temple therapy and participation is sustaining her without internal medication, other than herbal teas and occasional patent medicines, thus avoiding further iatrogenic harm as a consequence of misdiagnosed depression. Chucha's condition has become so manageable that her day-to-day existence has become satisfying.

Chucha is a good example of successful Spiritualist therapy. Her case also demonstrates a concatenation of techniques used to alter her perception of her illness, if not actually to cure it. I shall elaborate on this point in my analysis of the several therapeutic components comprising spiritualist healing in Chapter 9. Before I do so, it is necessary to elaborate on Spiritualist therapeutic outcomes.

8. Spiritualist Therapeutic Outcomes

In the last chapter we explored Spiritualist therapeutic procedures and the ways in which they are applied to patients and their complaints. Now we can address the pivotal questions: What are the outcomes of Spiritualist treatments? What kinds of symptoms do Spiritualist healers succeed in alleviating? At what kinds do they fail?

Little is known about the efficacy of nonbiomedical therapeutics in general and Spiritualist ministrations in particular. No doubt the main reasons for this lacuna are the formidable difficulties related to defining and assessing outcomes. As Kleinman (1980) emphatically observes, the foremost of these and the central problem in the cross-cultural study of healing is how to evaluate therapeutic efficacy. Definitions and methods of outcome assessment present obstacles not only to anthropologists studying healing cross-culturally but also to medical practitioners attempting to evaluate biomedicine and psychotherapy.[1]

From a biomedical perspective, therapeutic efficacy is defined as the capability of an agent, demonstrably and measurably, to alter the statistically predictable natural history of the disease (Pellegrino 1979: 256). According to Pellegrino, effective medical treatment eliminates the primary cause of the disease and therapy alters its natural course. As Pellegrino and others (e.g., Thomas 1974, 1977) maintain, the aim of scientific medicine is to remove totally the cause of the disease. The fact is, however, that at present, with the exception of antimicrobial agents (such as penicillin, streptomycin, and sulfonamides, antimalarial agents, and antiprotozoan agents, there are no therapeutic agents capable of removing the causes of most diseases. Digitalis glycosides in heart contractions, diuretics promoting sodium extraction in coronary failure, thyroid hormone replacement in hypothyroidism, insulin in diabetes, and vitamin B-12 in megaloblastic anemia--all fail to eliminate the cause of the disease and are capable only of altering their course (Pellegrino 1979). However, there remains a large array of impairments that lack a cure comparable to that for microbial disease, such as cardiovascular, kidney, and liver diseases, cancer, arthritis, chronic pain, and acute respiratory infections such as grippe (Thomas 1977).

If the underlying causes of these pathologies cannot be eliminated, how then can effective treatment be assessed? Any measure of medical treatment outcomes has its pitfalls, not the least of which are the obvious facts that diseases are self-limiting and that in some measure the body heals itself with or without ministration. For these and other technical reasons it is difficult to establish the efficacy of any type of therapy. In fact, researchers undertaking to establish therapeutic outcomes of biomedicine have been locked in a controversy as to what, if anything, ought to be measured. Some argue that inasmuch as it is impossible to define efficacy, owing to a host of intervening variables, medical interventions can only be assessed by examining whether standard therapeutic procedures have been followed (McAuliffe 1978, 1979; Starfield & Scheff 1972), such as the use of medical histories, physical examinations, laboratory tests, and other technical diagnostic procedures. Alternatively, others fail to find any relationship (Lindsay et al. 1976) or only a tenuous one (Nobrega et al. 1977) between performance of medical procedures and outcomes; still others have found that therapeutic outcomes are dependent on psychosocial variables unrelated to the care received by patients (Cay et al. 1975). Donabedian (1978) takes a pragmatic approach to the controversy between the two positions--measuring process or measuring outcome. He proposes that it is unnecessary to choose between the two; assessments need to be done of whatever is more easily measured.

McDermott (1977:1380) cogently argues that linkage between process and outcome can be established when evaluating public-health measures because "...what is being measured is the presence or absence of particular diseases in a designated group and not the performance of a function" (a similar argument is made by Rutstein et al. (1976). McDermott rightly observes, "Broadly speaking, those components of the physician's performance that permit process-outcome linkage are again the easy things. As a result, if we try to focus on outcome on an individual basis, we once more end up with detecting minimal performance, but nothing more" (ibid.). Reasoning along the same lines as Pellegrino (1979) and Thomas (1977), McDermott considers that in current practice all doctors, both good and bad, similarly monitor episodes of acute distress that are self-limiting. The crucial test of management of illness is how it deals with chronic diseases or with those for which radical cures are unavailable at present--in fact, the types of illnesses that, as we have seen, Spiritualist healers must confront.

McDermott cites several impediments to validating treatment and assessing outcomes of chronic disease; according to him:

> If periods of months or years customarily elapse between the start of the disease process and the "outcome" in terms of death or permanent disability, a range of outcomes is possible. The outer reaches of that range can be very different: for example, survivals of fifteen or twenty years for some people are to be contrasted with survivals of one or two years for others. Yet all have the same disease. To be sure, the disease manifestations form patterns that can be refined into subsets. With chronic disease, the question then arises whether and how many subsets are sufficiently different from each other to have different outcomes, and how many of them are sufficiently different to be diagnosed in the living patient (ibid.:152.)

Additionally, in patients with chronic diseases, intervening conditions such as hypertension or kidney dysfunction may also affect differential outcomes (McDermott 1977).

If the task is problematic for medical practitioners, it is formidable for the anthropological study of nonbiomedical therapeutic regimes in the field and for the assessment of outcomes using scientific standards of evidence that aim at evaluating changes in patients' conditions. In exploring Spiritualist therapeutic outcomes, therefore, I made no attempt to deal with treatment efficacy of underlying biological and biochemical malfunction or disease. These considerations lead us to focus on subjectively determined criteria which ultimately lead a patient to relinquish the sick role. Importantly, under laboratory conditions, verbal reports measuring subjectively evaluated pain yield significantly finer stimulus discrimination measures than specific physiological measures (Pomerleau & Brady 1979).

This brings us to another important question: What subjective criteria ought to be used in assessing efficacy? Some regard effective treatment intervention in relation to the degree to which it produces desired effects, that is to say, patient satisfaction as the final criterion (Foster & Anderson 1978). Somewhat analogously, A. Young (1977) regards therapeutic efficacy in terms of whether it (1) enables people to deal with a sickness event and (2) provides the event with meaning; whereas Fiske et al. (1970), in their discussion of ways to evaluate psychotherapeutic efficacy, advocate the determination whether a patient achieves remission of target symptoms. Still others suggest functional and behavioral indices (Kane et al. 1977; Mitchell 1978). These criteria require that the patient's final health

status be at least equal to the status before the illness, and measurement of patient's compliance and satisfaction (e.g., Kane et al.
1977). By this definition, the patient is brought back to a premorbid
state and is restored to behavioral functioning.

In view of all such considerations, my concern is only with illness,
impaired functioning as perceived by the patient within a cultural
context. My data are based on patient-perceived symptoms or target
complaints and patient-perceived treatment outcomes defined as
symptom removal and restoration to usual behavioral functioning. I
measured successful outcome and attribution for recovery by using
the Cornell Medical Index and patients' verbatim reports about the
beneficial effects of the treatment and the alleviation of the specific
symptoms for which they had sought treatment. I assessed treatment
outcomes in two ways during two separate follow-up visits to the
patient's home--after he/she had been interviewed, using the CMI and
a socioeconomic questionnaire, at the temple on the day of treatment
(see Appendix A). During the follow-up home visits I readministered
the CMI health questionnaire, interviewed the patient, and engaged
him/her in open-ended discussion. I queried patients whether they had
carried out the healer's prescribed treatment. I explored with them
in great detail to what they attributed their recovery when they
reported that their symptoms had been either eliminated or
attenuated. But even this approach has its limitations.

The assessment of outcomes of first-comers and habitual temple
users utilizing these criteria was straightforward and presented no
difficulties. Application of the same criteria to the regulars became
problematic, however. Paradoxically, regulars frequently tend to
sustain their self-perceived symptoms, as seen in Chucha's case, for
example; yet they avow and also demonstrate that they have been
restored to functioning and health. In addition, regulars, unlike
nonregulars, are not restored to a premorbid social state, but in fact
they assume new social roles--as healers and temple functionaries.
Thus Spiritualist therapy leads regulars to a subjective state of not
being sick by promoting their state of well-being and expressed
satisfaction, although it frequently fails to remove their subjectively
perceived clinical dysfunctions. These findings lead me to assert that
renewal of behavioral capacities and restoration of the patient's
subjectively perceived state of health--of well being--(cf. Benfari et
al. 1976; Fabrega 1977; Finkler 1981a; Jilek 1974; Susser 1974) can be
accomplished not necessarily by the total removal of symptoms, but
by restructuring the patient's perceptions of his of her dysfunction
and condition. This is an important point and I shall return to it in
Chapter 9, in my analysis of the ways in which Spiritualists resolve
illness.

Because regulars and nonregulars respond differently to temple
treatment, they must also be dealt with separately when examining

treatment outcomes. The discussion focuses first on the nonregulars and then on the regulars.

TREATMENT OUTCOMES OF NONREGULARS

Table 8.1 presents the results of 108 follow-ups on all habitual temple users and first-comers not including Spiritualist regulars. The four separate categories of outcomes displayed in Table 8.1 emerged after the transcripts of the follow-up interviews were analyzed. I have designated these categories as follows: failure, success, inconclusive, and other.

Failure

"Failure" refers to individuals who sought temple treatment and administered it, but who reported that they were not cured by it. In these instances, the patients continued to suffer from the symptoms for which they came to be treated at the temple.

In all but four cases patients reported that they had continued to feel sick on the first follow-up. Even the four patients who claimed initial improvement later reported on the second follow-up, that they had failed to recover. This suggests that failure of temple therapeutic intervention is recognized right away, or at least within a fortnight after treatment, and that Spiritualist healers' sacred aura alone fails to dispose patients positively toward therapy by sacred healers as is sometimes held (e.g., Kleinman & Sung 1979).

Of the thirty-eight failures shown in Table 8.1, thirteen involve individuals with abdominal and stomach disorders manifested in symptoms such as blood in stools and diarrhea. The remaining twenty-five cases comprise a variety of maladies including a medically diagnosed case of terminal cancer (this patient subsequently died), an ear dysfunction, kidney impairment, abscess on foot, senile deterioration, severe psychosis, and female infertility. Of these thirty-eight, twenty-three were habitual temple users who had been successfully treated on previous occasions, ten were first-comers, and five were first-comers who have been coming for treatment of the same symptoms for a while.

Success

"Success" refers to those patients who reported that they had followed the prescribed treatment and that at the time of the interview they had recovered from the symptoms for which they had come to be treated at the temple. In most cases, as can be seen in Table 8.2, patients were able to designate which aspect of the treatment was instrumental in effecting their recovery. The majority of complaints, as shown in Table 8.2, revolve around pain in the abdominal region, with several patients reporting generalized body aches. This group is composed of fourteen habitual users and fourteen first-comers. The latter include three who came various times for treatment of the same ailment.

Interestingly, my findings demonstrate that recovery attribution is not related to the degree of experience with temple treatments, as one might have expected. In fact, I anticipated that of the 108 follow-ups the habitual temple users were more likely to report successes than first-comers. This, however, seems not to be the case, as can be seen from the almost equal distribution between habitual temple users and first-comers.

Inconclusive

The term "inconclusive" identifies patients who stated that they had recovered, but who had also sought medical treatment for the symptoms reported at the temple. Thus, patients in this group were unable to indicate specifically the source of their cure. (In two instances, only one of several complaints was removed by temple treatment.) Of the twenty-one inconclusives, the majority suffered from some type of abdominal problem; two children suffered from fright; and one woman was afflicted by a partial facial paralysis. Thirteen of the twenty-one patients were habitual temple users and eight were first-comers, of whom three came several times for treatment for the same ailment.

Other

The group categorized "other" includes a potpourri of patients, most of whom had not administered the prescribed treatment at the time of the first follow-up visit; one of the individuals, as it turned out, came only to seek advice, and four persons described themselves as believers in Spiritualist doctrine even though they did not, like the regulars, participate in temple rituals. I have not included the latter four cases in the success group on the assumption that these individuals' reports may not accurately reflect their current condition. Nine cases include patients as to whom, for one reason or another, it was not possible to ascertain whether or not their condition had changed since the initial interview, despite their lower scores on the CMI questionnaires elicited during the follow-up interview.

Successful Outcomes

We will now consider the twenty-eight successfully treated cases at the temple identified in Table 8.1. Table 8.2 displays sex, age, and marital status of these patients; CMI scores elicited at the initial interview and first visit; patients' symptoms reported at the first interview at the temple; medical treatment sought; medical diagnosis supplied by the physician, if any; treatment outcome; and recovery attribution reported by the subjects.

Data in several of the columns in Table 8.2 require elucidation and comment. With respect to the distribution by sex, the sample of twenty-eight patients is represented by 50 percent adult females, 39 percent children, and 11 percent adult males. The fact that males are underrepresented in proportion to the percentage of male patients come to the temple is explained by the fact that many of the male patients earmarked for follow-up visits were not at home during the day.

Whereas males are underrepresented, children are over-represented in the sample in proportion to the percentage of children brought to the temple. The fact that almost 40 percent of those successfully treated were infants can be explained by at least three interrelated factors: (1) Spiritualist treatments such as teas, massages, baths and enemas are effective means of dealing with many of the mild disorders of childhood; (2) many mild disorders of childhood are self-limiting; and (3) mothers' concern and agitation were alleviated by a visit to the temple, and consequently their perception of their children's symptoms was altered.

Most symptoms indicated in column 5 of Table 8.2 are self-explanatory. Those that represent specific syndromes in the region were discussed in Chapter 5.

Turning now to columns 7 and 8, analysis of the CMI scores has yielded results that tend to support the data gathered by direct interviews and open-ended discussion during the follow-up visits. Significantly, as can be seen in these columns, when the CMI was administered the second time there was a drop in the "yes" responses. I will return to the changes in the CMI scores shortly, when the data in Table 8.3 are examined.

Columns 9, 10, 11, and 12 are self-explanatory and require no further comment. Attention is called to column 13. Attribution is reported verbatim (in translation) wherever patients were able to identify the aspect of temple treatment instrumental in eliminating their perceived symptoms. In some instances, however, patients simply cited all the various elements of the treatment. These responses are designated by the term "prescription." In a few instances, patients could not verbalize what precisely had effected their cure except to indicate that their condition was alleviated. These cases were marked by a question mark.

The CMI scores shown in columns 7 and 8 of Table 8.2 do not require special interpretation. As can be seen, they are relatively high; however, it must be recalled that our tentative baseline of 50--established by using CMI data from a control group--is also higher than the 30 items established on the basis of the American sample population (Brodman et al. 1952). (For a discussion of how the baseline was established, see Appendix A.)

When we examine the mean CMI scores shown in Table 8.3, "Successes" and "Failures", some differences emerge between the groups. First, the mean figures from the first CMI suggest that both the successes and the failures were experiencing self-perceived disorders at the time of the initial interview, with the two groups' scores both being above the 50-item baseline and with the failures experiencing more disorders. The difference between the two scores, however, is not statistically significant. On the other hand, when the CMI was administered the second time, the gap between the mean scores of the successes and failures widened. In fact, the difference between the two groups is significant at the .05 level, using the t test.

Second, the results from the second CMI indicate that while the failure group continued to have a mean score above the 50-item baseline, supporting patients' verbal reports that they continued to suffer from many of their reported symptoms, the success group fell below that baseline, suggesting a greater decrease in symptoms among the successes.

In sum, the results lead to the conclusion that indeed there are greater symptom alterations among those individuals who report that they were effectively treated for their symptoms at the temple, compared with those who report that they failed to benefit from the treatments.

By way of illustration of successfully treated patients from the nonregulars, three case vignettes follow. The three cases demonstrate the ways in which routine ameliorative efforts positively affect patients. Jose's case is of special interest because it demonstrates that not only do infants seem to respond to temple intervention for the reasons cited earlier, but children of Jose's age tend to respond to symbolic aspects of therapy.

CASES OF SUCCESSFUL TREATMENT

Esperanza, a married thirty-six year-old woman, with eight children, is the sister of a very dedicated temple functionary, whose wife and children are devotees as well. Esperanza, however, has had very little contact with the temple prior to her most recent illness, chiefly because of her husband's vehement opposition to Spiritualism.

I was able to follow her case closely from its inception through its successful outcome three months later. Esperanza fell ill three days before she delivered her eighth (unwanted) child. When I first met her, shortly after the onset of her affliction, she was carried to the temple in a chair, her face contorted with pain. She was paralyzed from the waist down and her legs were in a semi-curled-up position. She also suffered from pain in the *cerebro*. Later she reported that when she was brought to the clinic to deliver her baby she was in such agony that the attending physician informed her husband that either she or the baby would survive but not both. She succeeded in delivering a healthy baby but after the birth she remained in the hospital, where she was treated for eight days. During the hospital stay she was told that her illness stemmed from the pregnancy. She was prescribed pills and injections, and she was eventually sent home to her village despite the fact that her condition had not changed. She remained paralyzed.

After she was brought home she was taken to a doctor near her village. This doctor diagnosed the problem as rheumatism (in her words *"rhumatismo bilioso,"* which is a native category for an extreme case of rheumatism). The doctor's medication failed to have any effect on her physical condition. A third doctor was then called in; he unsuccessfully treated her for a kidney impairment. Finally, a fourth doctor was consulted, who recommended that she be taken to Mexico City, where there were better medical facilities than in the small towns in the region. Her husband suggested that Esperanza be moved to Pachuca, the state capital, instead of Mexico City, because it was closer to the village. At this point her brother intervened. He argued that she would be neglected in the hospital, and that it was uncertain whether she would be brought back alive. He argued that she would be best treated at the temple and he brought her to his home over her husband's protest. There she was cared for by her sister-in-law.

Esperanza's treatment at the temple was dramatic, with three to four curers simultaneously working on her to dislodge her illness by the use of several dislodgement techniques employed in specially severe cases and by massages. During several of these curing sessions, her husband consented to accompany her, and at such times he too was given a cleansing. He also stood by watching the procedure while she was being treated. As she very passively received her treatments, Esperanza was visibly baffled by the procedures. In fact, later she indicated that she did not understand what was being done to her.

Nevertheless, I observed that after the first two treatments she abandoned the chair in which she was being carried and began moving around on crutches. However, her facial expression still suggested that she was in great pain. Progressively, with each treatment at the temple, supplemented by massages she was given by her sister-in-law at home, Esperanza was manifestly improving. Upon my last visit to her home, three months after the onset of her illness, she was perfectly well, smiling, going about her chores, and she called my attention to the fact that she was now even breast feeding her newborn infant, who during her illness had been cared for by her mother. She attributed her successful cure to the cleansings and massages she was given by her sister-in-law at home. Subsequent to her full recovery, Esperanza stopped coming to the temple, according to her brother, because of her husband's renewed opposition to Spiritualist temples.

Esperanza's case represents an example of somatization of a psychological condition caused by an event culturally conceived to produce illness, and it closely parallels the classical conversion reaction syndrome described by Breuer and Freud (1966) and others

(Ziegler et al. 1960). The onset of her illness coincided with the death of a young relative who resided in her house and who was like a member of her family. The boy had gone on a drinking binge resulting in a fatal fall into an irrigation canal. Esperanza thought a great deal about this relative at the inception of her affliction and although she was unable to pinpoint the reason for her illness, she associated it with *aire* connected with the boy's death; however, it might have been associated also with a wish not to have the baby.

Esperanza's second CMI score shows a drop of 22 points. The change in responses is concentrated in the section bearing on psychological symptoms; with responses to the physiological symptoms remaining largely unchanged. She voluntarily attributed the change in her responses on the second CMI to her cure.

Irene

Irene, a 36-year-old woman, is happily married with two children; she is economically well situated. Irene developed severe pain in her right arm as well as pain in her back and her *cerebro,* immediately after she moved to a new home removed from the center of town, where she had lived previously. Irene was afflicted with sleeplessness and a number of unspecified fears. She was treated by numerous doctors, including an acupuncturist in Mexico City, and her condition was variously diagnosed as related to her lungs, her chest, and her coccyx. Finally, one physician declared that there was nothing wrong with her. Yet she continued to experience the symptoms. After three months of treatment-seeking activity, a friend recommended the temple. After two treatments consisting of cleansing and massages, her ailment completely disappeared and she regained her usual cheerful mood. After her recovery, she stopped going to the temple, but she referred several new patients to the healers.

Irene's case suggests a mild somatized syndrome coinciding with her move to a relatively luxurious new house, totally isolated from friends and family. Significantly, she recalled that her father, whom she had attended until his death, had suffered a similar pain in his right arm at his death fourteen years earlier. The case suggests a somatized depressive condition precipitated by the loss of a home in which Irene had been very happy. It seems safe to say that the loss of her old home became merged with the loss of her father, as evidenced by her symptoms, which reproduced those of her dead father. It is not uncommon for depressed individuals to reproduce complaints of deceased loved ones (Freedman & Kaplan 1972)

As in Esperanza's case, Irene's CMI scores dropped by 24 points. Irene, like Esperanza, attributed the drop to her recovery at the temple.

Jose

Jose, an 8-year-old boy, second of three children, was brought to the temple by his mother at the suggestion of his elementary-school teacher. The boy fell ill several months after his mother had recovered from an illness produced by a series of dreams in which her dead father spoke to her. Jose's mother recalled that when these dreams began, two years after her father's death, she was feeling drowsy and very tired; she was treated at a temple where she was given a cleansing, and her dreams and tiredness ceased.

When Jose fell ill, he told his mother that he dreamt he saw his grandfather standing outside the house and wanted the latter to take him to school. Jose woke up frightened; he cried, his teeth trembled, and he lost his appetite. His elementary-school teacher, who was also the temple head's daughter, noted that the child was very pale, distracted, and pensive. The teacher summoned the mother and called her attention to the boy's listless state. The teacher was especially concerned about Jose because he failed to participate in recreational activities. The teacher explored several possible reasons for Jose's condition, including tensions between the mother and father at home. The mother explained that although her husband was a truck driver and poor, they were happily married and never fought. But her father had lived with them, and after his death she and her sister, who was also her immediate neighbor, talked a great deal about their deceased father. The child had been very attached to the old man and had spent a lot of time with him. In fact, the mother recalled, Jose had been the first to notice that his grandfather was in a deep sleep and wouldn't give him his customary kiss.

After the interview with the teacher, Jose's mother took him to a doctor who diagnosed the syndrome as nerves and prescribed vitamins. The boy's condition failed to change, however, and the teacher recommended that he be taken to the temple. On his first three visits, Jose was treated by one of the healers, one whom I was assisting the day he was first brought. I recorded in my notes my astonishment at the boy's stoic acceptance of the vigorous cleansing he was being given with branches and flowers as he stood half naked, in total silence, in a cold room on a very cold November day.

On my first follow-up visit, Jose and his mother disclosed that he had recovered. He no longer saw his grandfather in his dreams, and he played normally again with other children. I asked the child what had made him well and what, if anything, he liked about the temple treatment. Unhesitatingly he responded that he liked the flowers on the altar and the cleansing with flowers. On the second follow-up visit the mother reported that the boy was in excellent health and that the teacher was also satisfied with his behavior.

Jose had suffered from a typical case of *susto*. No doubt he became frightened by his bad dreams; and he emulated his mother's condition as well as her cure. As in the two other cases, Jose's CMI score dropped by 13 points. Jose's recovery within weeks suggests that Spiritualist intervention meets a recovery requisite that medical practitioners fail to furnish. It is, of course, possible that inasmuch as his teacher recommended the therapy, it bore greater weight for Jose than a routine visit to the doctor would have..

These three cases illustrate how patients with mild clinical syndromes respond quickly to routine temple treatment. They contrast, however, with the patients who are recruited into the ranks of the regulars. Whereas first-comers and habitual temple users tend to react favorably to temple ministrations, including teas, massages, baths, and cleansings, regulars fail to respond to these types of short-term therapeutic interventions. In effect, regulars are persons who suffer from disorders that are not readily cured either biomedically or by ordinary Spiritualist therapy. The healing requisites for regulars include ordinary temple therapeutic techniques but also involve extensive and continuous interaction with healers during cleansings, as well as participation in temple rituals.

TREATMENT OUTCOMES OF REGULARS

Regulars, in contrast to nonregulars, are exposed to diverse temple therapeutic modalities, and the nature of their recovery differs as well, as the cases of Chucha and Emiliano have compellingly illustrated. In Chucha's case, the symptoms have not been eliminated, but the patient was nevertheless restored to functioning by temple treatment procedures. In such individuals, recovery is slow, which brings into focus the types of intractable syndromes not readily amenable to the intermittent therapeutic regimes furnished to first-comers and habitual temple users.

Those who are selected and choose to become regulars, unlike other patients, tend to require continuous ministrations within the therapeutic environment. In fact, the regulars' ongoing contact with the temple brings them into a dialectical relationship with the curers and with Spiritualism, culminating in the transformation of the patient into a regular. The transformation signifies a new role for the patient, that of health provider-healer or member of a health-care establishment. By emerging as regulars, patients are in effect ushered into a state of liminality: neither healthy nor ill, as Chucha's case illustrates.

The same variables displayed in Table 8.2 for first-comers and habituals are shown in Table 8.4 for regulars. With respect to distribution by sex, the sample of thirty-one regulars consists of almost 33 percent adult males and 67 percent adult females. In contrast, first-comers and habitual temple users are 15 percent adult males, 58 percent adult females, and 27 percent children, suggesting that the ratio of females to males among regulars is more than double that for the other groups of patients. Although 27 percent of all temple patients are children, children are never recruited in the category of regulars. Spiritualists believe that only persons above the age of 12 should enter development. Moving to column 5 of Table 8.4, it can be seen that there is a high frequency of behavioral disorders (e.g., "went crazy," "desire to run") and syndromes revolving around dizziness and breathlessness--in short, types of symptoms frequently associated with a pattern of generalized anxiety (Freedman & Kaplan 1972) and depression (Sternbach 1974).

Perusal of column 7 of Table 8.4 reveals that in six cases the medical diagnosis was accompanied by recommendations for surgery, resulting in the patient's search for an alternative type of treatment. Column 8 shows that patients' afflictions persisted for an extended period of time prior to their coming to the temple to seek treatment. This further suggests that we are dealing with individuals who are suffering from pain-prone disorders associated with depression (Blumer et al. 1980; Sternbach 1974). Column 9 will be elaborated on a little later. Column 10 emphasizes that, as was the case among habitual temple users and first-comers, symbolic manipulations by cleansing and massaging are the stated reasons for recovery.

Significantly, when we turn to column 11 of Table 8.4 it can be seen that, unlike the situation among first-comers and habitual temple users, routine techniques among regulars fail to alleviate the patients' self-perceived symptoms. We see that in a few cases recovery is attributed to temple participation. In all other instances, regulars insist that they have recovered, but, as is shown, many simultaneously report that they continue to experience various symptoms. This important point will be explored more fully later. At this juncture an analogy can be drawn to pharmacological treatments of pathological syndromes. The drugs tend to suppress or calm the symptoms without curing the disease (Blumer et al. 1980; Davis & Cole 1975; Hogarty & Goldberg 1973). To cite but two examples: Prince (Leighton et al. 1968) describes an instance of a patient whom he treated with chlorpromazine and night sedation. Prince reports that the patient's symptoms abated as long as the patient received the drugs but reappeared in more intense form when he discontinued the medication; and Blumer et al. (1980) report that antidepressant medication "had to be continued (or resumed) in order to maintain the improvement" (1980:17). Similarly, as long as regulars sustain their contact with the temple, they tend to ignore or minimize their illness, as is the case with those who attest to good health yet report various symptoms when probed, particularly when they absent themselves from the temple.

In keeping with this point, we turn to column 9 of Table 8.4 which shows the CMI scores of regulars. Perusal of CMI responses lends support to the proposition that temple participation, in conjunction with temple therapies, tends to attenuate subjectively perceived symptoms. This is demonstrated when mean CMI responses of regulars are compared with those of nonregulars and of the control group of ostensibly healthy individuals. The data in Table 8.5 support findings by others (Kalimo et al. 1970; Mechanic 1976) that CMI mean scores correlate positively with sex.

Particularly interesting within the context of the present discussion are the lower mean scores, statistically significant at the .001 level by the t test between male regulars and nonregulars and female regulars and nonregulars: regulars' mean CMI scores correspond closely to those of the control group. This suggests that regulars exhibit significantly fewer self-perceived symptoms than nonregulars who came to seek treatment. The CMI scores of regulars and controls indicate that there is little difference between regulars and a healthy population in Mexico, confirming the regulars' claims of recovery to a state of perceived health--provided, of course, that they continue to be subject to the temple's therapeutic regime.

A comparison of the adjusted CMI scores[2] for each subsection of the CMI male and female regulars and nonregulars and male and female regulars and controls in Figures 8.1 and 8.2, respectively, reflect the differences in "yes" responses between the two groups. Although these graphic representations disclose similar curves, the responses by the regulars fall below those of the first-comers and habitual temple users on every subsection of the CMI questionnaire. Responses of the regulars--both males and females--closely parallel those of the controls, except subsection G of Figure 8.1, the nervous system.

Attention is called also to Figures 8.3 and 8.4 which disclose CMI scores on each subsection for the regulars and the doctor group. These figures demonstrate that the male regulars exhibit <u>lower</u> scores than the males in the doctor group on all subsections and (statistically significant at the .05 level by the t test) on six of the physical subsections (respiratory, digestive, musculoskeletal, genitourinary, frequency of illness, and habits). Similarly, female regulars exhibit lower scores than females in the doctor group on all subsections--eyes and ears (.05), respiratory, skin, frequency of illness (.01). Table 8.6 compares mean CMI scores between regulars and individuals drawn from the other two groups who reported that they were orthodox Catholics and attended Catholic church on a weekly basis or more often. This comparison is made with the assumptions that Spiritualist temples as religious establishments are structurally congruent to the Catholic church and that participation in rituals of either institution is instrumental in mitigating illness to some extent. Consistent with the other findings, the mean CMI scores of the regulars, both males and females, are lower by more than 10 points than the professed Catholic group of nonregulars; they are even comparable to the control group. These data suggest that the Spiritualist therapy adds additional dimensions to the healing process not provided by faith and religiosity alone.

The preceding materials demonstrate that regulars differ from sick persons and that they succeed in regaining and maintaining an ongoing state of self-perceived health. The case histories that follow are additionally instructive in at least two important ways. First, they illuminate the nature of the healing process of regulars, which, as already noted, includes a process of negotiation between the patient and himself or herself and between the patient and the spirit world. Spiritualist treatment of regulars is a slow process, leading to assimilation of a new sustaining idealogy and reinforcement of a new set of symbols. Second, the cases illustrate the fact that although temple treatments remove stresses that might have contributed to the patient's illness, the same treatments also create new stresses hitherto not experienced by the individual. Chucha's case, presented in the last chapter, is especially illuminating in this regard.

In the same way as Chucha's recovery was slow and dependent on ongoing contact with the temple, Emiliano (whom we met in Chapter 6) began to show improvement after several months; at that time he was beginning to feel well most of the time, but chiefly when he stayed at the temple. He no longer frightened easily or lost his temper; he had stopped being cross and quarrelsome and had also stopped drinking regularly: He might take some *pulque* occasionally, but he no longer became intoxicated. He also regained his appetite. The lump behind his ear diminished in size and although still visible, became unobtrusive. Emiliano felt well when he was at the temple, but when he returned to the village his body began to ache again. Significantly, at the initial interview, Emiliano's CMI score was 103. Four months later, when the instrument was administered the second time as a follow-up, his physical responses had not changed; however, his score on the emotional section of the questionnaire decreased by 20 points. Emiliano attributed his recovery to the cleansing and to his temple participation.

It will be instructive to present here several cases of regulars' treatments to illustrate further their illness resolution.

Jaime

Jaime, a 29-year-old man, single, with a fifth-grade education, resides in a small, relatively inaccessible village thirty miles from the temple site. He lives with his father and 15-year-old niece. For much of his adult life, Jaime worked outside his village as a brick layer; he also did odd jobs. He is a shy man. His illness was triggered by a fall from his bicycle. On the day of the accident he had consumed a bit of *pulque*, but he was not drunk when he fell. He broke his clavicle, which was promptly reset by a bone-setter. But he also felt faint and tired, and his hands and feet were numb. He suffered great pain in the right side of his chest, and he couldn't breathe. He felt asphyxiated, and he believed he was dying. His mouth felt very dry, and he was constantly thirsty. He also could not work.

Jaime fell ill a year after the death of his mother and two months before his wedding date. He indicated that he no longer thinks much about his mother, but that when he does, tears come to his eyes. After her death, he assumed the responsibilities for the household because his father was an alcoholic and incapable of any activity. His fiancee left him when he fell ill, and shortly thereafter she married someone else.

Jaime sought treatment with several physicians and later with nonbiomedical practitioners. Physicians prescribed numerous injections and pills but his condition failed to improve. The physicians concluded that nothing was wrong with him. When medical treatments failed to effect a cure, Jaime sought treatment with several *curanderas* in the environs as well as in a distant town. The *curanderas* informed him that he was bewitched by his fiancee and that this was the cause of his illness. Jaime objected to this diagnosis because, according to him, the fiancee was a very nice person and not likely to perform witchcraft, nor did she have any reason to do so, since it was she who had left him and not vice versa. After treatment by successive *curanderas*, Jaime developed three additional symptoms: headaches, pain in the *cerebro*, and insomnia.

Jaime suffered one crisis during his association with the temple when, after several months of treatment, he was ordered by the healer to enter development. According to Jaime, because he was afraid of development, he suffered a recurrence of numbness in his arms, and he couldn't open his mouth. He stated that he suffered an attack of nerves. He reported his condition to the healer, who assured him that it would disappear as soon as he started development sessions. Jaime mustered his courage and entered develoment. The symptoms brought on by fear of development disappeared, just as the healer had predicted, and in fact Jaime felt even more tranquil than before. He resumed work but continued to reside in the village so that he could attend curing sessions and rituals.

Felicia

Like Chucha's, Felicia's participation in the temple created a special conflict for her when she became a regular. Felicia, 21 years old, is an attractive unmarried woman who originates from a family of nine children. She resides in a town about fifteen miles away from Juarez with her parents and siblings. Her father, a truck driver, treats her well but her mother used to beat her frequently. Felicia was introduced to the temple by a neighbor who is a healer there. At the time of her initial visit to the temple she was very thin,[3] and she was feeling depressed. She could not breathe. She was desirous of sleep, but she would wake up in the middle of the night. She experienced a choking feeling, heart palpitations, dizzy spells, blurred vision, stomach upsets, extreme menstrual pain, nausea, and a constant bitter taste in her mouth. She also had pain in the *cintura*.

She had first fallen ill when she was 14 years old; before that time she was healthy and fat. The onset of her illness coincided with the time when her older brother beat her up and pushed her through the door. This episode brought about Felicia's menarche and caused her to bleed unceasingly for three months. Subsequently, she was treated by physicians who attributed her condition to low blood pressure and an infected kidney, contrary to her belief that her brother had caused the illness. One physician prescribed five injections, after which her condition improved. Felicia was told to return for further treatment but because of the high cost of the biomedical treatment, she went to the temple instead.

The temple healer who treated her, her neighbor, ordered that she enter development immediately. The healer attributed her affliction to low blood pressure (when healers provide a diagnosis they often repeat a physician's diagnosis as presented by a patient), and also to nerves, anger, and dark spirits. Felicia was prescribed various teas and tonics specific for anger and seven massages. She was also told to bathe with red flowers. The healer declared that it was not Felicia but her spirit that was sad and that she must go out and amuse herself a lot.

After Felicia spent several months in development and assisting healers, her symptoms disappeared. She attributed her recovery to her membership in the temple. In fact, when I administered the CMI questionnaire to her, she spontaneously added to numerous questions the response, "Now I don't feel like this, but I used to before."

For instance, Felicia no longer felt the choking feeling and no longer suffered from upset stomach. The latter change she imputed to a purgative prescribed for her at the temple. In fact, she noted that previously she could not eat "because my stomach was dirty inside," but that she regained her appetite once her stomach had been cleaned out by the purgative. Her menstrual pains were gone, and she no longer got sick repeatedly, as formerly. She still felt lazy, but the melancholia was gone and she even enjoyed speaking and joking with people. She used to get very angry with people, but not any more, nor did she feel a desire to die. She knew now that her spirit protector, who had not as yet identified himself, was nevertheless protecting her from all ills.

Despite the fact that her somatic symptoms were gone, Felicia repeatedly expressed to me her conflict about coming to the temple. Her parents approved of her going there, since they had previously sought treatment at a Spiritualist temple, but her boyfriend was an orthodox Catholic, and he absolutely forbade her to attend any religious establishment other than a Catholic church. When she accompanies him to church, she didn't feel very comfortable, because she was always being stared at.

Felicia consulted the spirit mediums about the internal conflicts that resulted from her fiance's objection to her membership in the temple and participation in its procedures. She was in a quandary as to what to do, whether or not to tell the young man that she came regularly to the temple and even assisted the healers. She repeatedly reported her dilemma to the spirit medium, who advised her not to say anything. Although all of Felicia's symptons were in remission and she felt tranquil when she was at the temple, she worried a lot about her problem with her fiance. Felicia stopped coming to the temple just before her wedding.

Bernardo

Bernardo's case is intriguing because he is one of a few regulars who seemed to be suffering from a serious organic dysfunction; however, his daily functioning was being sustained by the temple's therapeutic regime.

Bernardo, married, with two children, is 37 years old, illiterate, and one of the poorest peasants among the regulars. He has been suffering from attacks since he was 18 months old, but according to his parents, the attacks increased in frequency after his fifteenth birthday. When afflicted by an attack, he fell on the floor in convulsions, his vision became opaque, and he lost consciousness. He would bite his tongue until it bled. He was overtaken by attacks at unpredictable times. Attacks were preceded by a pain in the *cerebro,* which was Bernardo's sole warning of their onset.

His father had told him that when he was four months old he had been operated on for a tumor behind the ear; otherwise, he was healthy all his life, except, of course, for the attacks. Physicians diagnosed his condition as a cardiovascular dysfunction and impairment of the *cerebro.* He was treated with numerous injections and pills but continued to experience the attacks. When he reached the age of 20, his father declared that he could no longer spend any money on him. He had done what he could. Three years before I began my apprenticeship at the temple, Bernardo's wife and mother-in-law persuaded him to go to the temple. His father, a practicing Catholic, was against it.

When he arrived at the temple, he was immediately entered into development and was prescribed seven cleansings. Bernardo has never missed a development session since his first day, and he declares happily that he has not had an attack in three years. On his way to the temple he feels his arms hurt and his feet ache, but after a development session all his aches are gone and he feels tired no longer. In his words, "I leave feeling perfectly well."

Unlike his wife, Bernardo had never left his village because he was afraid he would suffer an attack while away from home. He worked most of his life for his father and on his own plot, 40 by 20 meters. He was a mild drinker, drinking usually made him sick, but he still liked an occasional glass of *pulque.* Bernardo reported smilingly how well he felt, yet he also noted pain in his kidney, chest, and *cintura.* He attributed these symptoms to his hard work and poor diet, because he regularly lacked money for food for his family. To deal with these pains, he takes an herbal tea; but he has no money to purchase the other types of medicines prescribed to him by temple healers.

Bernardo laments that he sometimes forgets things momentarily. He was sent to elementary school, but, owing to his affliction, only learned to sign his name, although he could remember the words to pretty songs. Now he can no longer memorize anything, including the invocation that a temple member is expected to know by heart. He has tried and is learning it with great difficulty (in fact, I heard the temple head reprimand him on various occasions for his failure to learn the invocation). Bernardo eagerly expressed his appreciation to the temple for his improved condition, and he was very clearly satisfied with the ongoing treatment that has contained, if not cured, his attacks.

Pancho

Pancho, married, 51 years of age, is--unlike Bernardo and the majority of regulars--a very wealthy man, whose standard of living is comparable to that of a middle-class American. He has a well established reputation in the city where he lives, twenty-five miles from Juarez. He is a professional man and a politically powerful one, originating as he does from a powerful, if minor, political faction in his town.

Pancho has been suffering from his disorder for twelve years. His wife, who learned about the temple coincidentally, urged him to seek treatment there but he refused. After several months of prodding he finally suggested that she go and inquire about a treatment for him. She did so, but the healer advised that Pancho must come personally. Feeling desperate, he went. Standing before the healer, he reported his symptoms as unceasing head and eye pain, dizziness, nausea, vomiting, sparks flying before his eyes, pain in the chest, and most importantly, excruciating pain in the lumbar region and lower rib cage. Pancho could not lie down, he was even forced to sleep sitting up. Also, he could not stand any noise, and he felt depressed, which was readily visible in his facial expressions and body posture.

The onset of Pancho's illness coincided with the time he decided to leave a government job because he felt that he was being exploited. He opened his own office as a builder-contractor. He had been treated by physicians who prescribed a variety of pills and exercises to relieve the back pain, and he was told that he would have to follow this treatment his entire life. One physician prescribed a corset, but this remedy was extremely impractical for a man with his occupation. One physician advised lower-back surgery, and another declared that Pancho was suffering from a kidney dysfunction. He was also treated with special machines by his son's professor at the medical school attended by the son.

I recall when Pancho came to the temple for the first time. He was brought before the curer whom I was assisting that day. Accompanied by his wife, he was ushered in by the head of the temple. He looked bewildered as he stood before the healer, who attributed his condition to nerves--nerves which, according to the healer, had resulted from incessant work. In addition to exploring Pancho's symptoms, the healer followed a procedure I had not witnessed before: she requested a shawl, a *rebozo*, which she put around Pancho's waist and pulled with great force, first to one side and then to the other. She also prescribed teas and massages made of ingredients that neither Pancho nor his wife had ever heard of before. Pancho was instructed to return on the following curing day.

To his and his wife's amazement, the pain in Pancho's waist, lower ribs, and *cerebro* disappeared. His wife said "who could ever have imagined that an ordinary *rebozo* could cure him?" For awhile he returned regularly on the days he was ordered to, and he also attended irradiation sessions. I saw Pancho on various occasions, and his facial expression had visibly changed; he smiled frequently and his wife attested that he no longer complained about his health. The family attributed Pancho's cure to the medium's pull of his waist with the shawl and to the massages that his wife faithfully gave him at home.

To summarize what has been said thus far, the results suggest that Spiritualist success in treating first-comers and habitual temple users is limited. Table 8.2 and other interview data on nonregulars disclose that therapeutic benefits tend to encompass four types of disorders: (1) diarrheas, probably those of nonpathogenic origin; (2) simple gynecological disorders; (3) somatized syndromes; and (4) mild psychiatric disorders analogous in type to those reported by others (Garrison 1977; Kleinman & Sung 1979). It might be assumed that treatment of diarrheas with teas and enemas are to some degree effective remedies. Similarly, gynecological problems of a vaginal variety appear to respond to douches prescribed in the temple.

In the majority of cases, however, by the patients' own accounts, Spiritualists fail to heal. In fact, it has been argued that although functioning may be improved by traditional curing techniques, the patient's disease has not actually been dealt with (Kleinman & Sung 1979). If the CMI results have validity, they tend to support this argument, as is made evident by the several case vignettes, including those of Esperanza, Irene, and Jose, who showed little change in their responses on the physiological symptoms. This argument might even apply to the other cases of patients whose symptoms and recovery attributions are displayed in Tables 8.2 and 8.4, who claimed that they had benefited from Spiritualist therapies.

On the other hand, it is also likely that the same symptoms will recur, not only because the disease was not dealt with but because the living conditions will not have changed. The underlying factors instrumental in producing the disease expressed in physiological or somatized symptoms continue in effect, including the unceasing flow of untreated sewage waters in the irrigation canals and the unremitting presence of disease vectors in the open garbage pits. Concomitantly, and equally to the point, violent deaths due to alcoholism and violence will continue, given the extant socio-structural conditions, which fail to militate against violence. In these circumstances, when one episode of *aire* is cured, another one may not be far behind.

Another observation relevant to the case materials is that, in all cases, the second CMI scores show significant drops. The change in responses is concentrated in the section bearing on psychological symptoms, with responses to the physiological symptoms remaining largely unchanged. Esperanza, Felicia, and others voluntarily attributed the change in their responses on the second CMI to their cure. This, of course, suggests that although they continued to experience physiological symptoms, the somatized condition was eliminated along with the psychological symptoms. Additionally, careful scrutiny of regulars indicates that while Spiritualist therapeutic modalities may address the illness, they fail to eliminate it. This comes into view with Chucha's and Jaime's cases, as well as with the data displayed in column 11 of Table 8.4, which show that in 50 percent of the cases patients continue to report symptoms, despite their avowals that they are not "feeling sick."

Yet, whether patients are successfully treated or not, many return repeatedly to seek Spiritualist ministrations, This then inescapably leads us to inquire what attraction Spiritualist healing holds for patients; how Spiritualist healers effect positive outcomes; and what the reasons are for their failures. The last question is especially interesting, because it is usually not raised, and it therefore opens new avenues for inquiry into folk therapeutic regimes.

The materials presented in this chapter lead to important conclusions bearing on the significance of symbols for recovery (Levi-Strauss 1967). In Chapter 9 I propose that illness along with recovery must be dealt with not only by concrete manipulation of physiological symptoms but also must involve symbolic manipulation in order for a therapeutic regime to do its job. Relevant to this proposition is the finding bearing on patients' references to the beneficial effects of cleansing. Perusal of Table 8.2 column 13 reveals that fully one-third of the patients attributed their recovery directly to symbolic treatment and cleansing. Additionally, as is displayed in Table 6.2, 17.5 percent of patients whom I observed treated by curers during my apprenticeship explicitly mentioned "cleansing" as their reason for coming to the temple. Even those who failed to benefit from temple treatment, as well as those counted as "inconclusives," indicated that what they liked most about Spiritualist treatment was the cleansings, although not all individuals attributed therapeutic efficacy to them. I postulate that the symbolic significance of this phenomenon is widespread within and beyond the subject population.   When questioned, patients could not always verbalize what they were experiencing during or after a cleansing. According to many, and especially the regulars, cleansing "fortifies one," "makes one strong," "restores one."   As I mentioned earlier, when I was incorporated as a regular, I was continually being urged to have a cleansing.   Why is cleansing beneficial to the healing process within the Mexican context; and, in what ways do Spiritualist treatments aid the patient in restoring his or her behavioral capacities and in diminishing the feeling of "being sick"?   These questions are addressed in the next chapter.

Table 8.1 Outcomes of Treatment at Spiritualist Temples:
Follow-up Interviews

Outcome	Number of Cases	Percent
Failure	38	35.3
Success	28	25.9
Inconclusive	21	19.4
Other	21	19.4
TOTAL	108	100.0

8.2 Successfully Treated Cases

1 Sex	2 Age	3 Marital Status	4 Number of Children	5 Symptoms	6 Length of Illness	7 First CMI	8 Second CMI	9 Previous Treatment for Symptoms	10 Medical Diagnosis	11 Outcome First Follow-Up	12 Outcome Second Follow-Up	13 To What Aspect of Temple Treatment Patient Attributed Success
F	1 yr.			No appetite; fever; stomach-ache		12				All symptoms gone	All symptoms gone	Prescription *
F	48	M	(all married)	Stomach pains; no appetite; insomnia; anger	Weeks	19	7	Medical	Colitis; high blood pressure	Feels better	All symptoms gone	Prescription *
F	7			Stomach pains; hands and feet; headaches; sleepy and lazy	Weeks	8	5	Medical	Anginas	Symptoms gone	Symptoms gone but no appetite	Prescription *
M	1 yr.			No appetite; nausea		7	1			All symptoms gone	All symptoms gone	Teas
F[1]	36	M		Stomach pain; feet, hands numb (See text)		72	48			All symptoms gone		Cleansing
M[2]	8			Frightened in sleep; dead grandfather appears to him; teeth tremble; loss of appetite; cries at night (See text)		17	4	Medical	Nerves	Appetite regained; sleeps better	All symptoms gone	Cleansing

1	2	3	4	5	6	7	8	9	10	11	12	13
F	36	M	3	Right arm numb; pain in back and cerebro	3 mo.	30	26	Medical	Nerves; nothing wrong	Feels better; can sleep	All symptoms gone	Cleansing
F	18	Single		Stomach pain; cannot breathe; nausea; loss of weight; sleepy; angry	1 yr.	91	72			Feels better; symptoms less severe	All symptoms gone	?
M	32	M	5	Itching inside body; feeling lazy; sleepy; angry; stopped working	6 mo.	33	20			Working; sporadic itching	All symptoms gone	Purge
F	2			Wakes up and trembles and talks at night	Weeks	10	6	Medical		Nerves; all symptoms gone	All symptoms gone	Cleansing
F	72	M	4 (Adopted)	Pain from waist down; legs swollen; lungs hurt; restlessness; sleeplessness; headache; constipation; frequent urination	?	75	67	Medical		Sleeps better; frequent urination ceased; constipation gone		Massages and baths
F	38	M	8	Womb infection; throbbing in stomach; burning sensation in vagina	Weeks	88	62			Burning sensation diminished	All symptoms gone	Vaginal douche

1	2	3	4	5	6	7	8	9	10	11	12	13
F	21	M	4	General lethargy; underweight	1 yr.	83	72	Medical		General well-being; feels stronger		Cleansing
F	48	Separated	9	Severe pain in stomach; stomach distention; excretion of worms	Days	54	15			All symptoms gone		?
M	13			White spots on skin; itching	Days	7	5	Medical	Lack of vitamins	White spots; itching stopped	All symptoms gone	Massages and baths
F	2			Pimples inside mouth, lips, throat; fever	Days	19	11			All symptoms gone, but now pain in stomach		Prescription and bicarbonate of soda
F	42	Separated	4	Pain in chest, heart; nerves; ache in cerebro, waist; pain in feet; feels tired; no appetite	6 mo.	65	47	Medical	High blood pressure	Well; regained appetite	All symptoms gone	Cleansing
F	7 mo.			Pimples in throat; diarrhea; slight fever		17	8	Medical	?	Diarrhea gone; pimples persist	Pimples gone	Prescribed aspirin massages, purge (olive oil)
F	9			Pain in stomach; fever	3 wks.	16	9	Medical	Infection	All symptoms gone	All symptoms gone	Enema (made of sugar, milk, and eggs)

1	2	3	4	5	6	7	8	9	10	11	12	13
F	50	Separated	4	Pain in feet; stomach distended		45	30			Symptoms gone; feet hurt	Symptoms gone	Cleansing
F	28	Separated	1	Nerves; pain in stomach & distended; nightmare; insomnia, headaches		89	70	Medical	Stomach ulcer; underweight	Nightmare gone; insomnia gone	All symptoms gone, except headache	Teas; massages
F	8 mo.			Constipation	2 days	**	**			Normal stools	Normal stools	Prescription* and olive oil
F	21	M	1	Vaginal secretions	15 days	15	11			Secretion ceased	All symptoms gone	Vaginal douche (boiled Rosmarinus officinalis L. and Acalypha langiana)
F	11½ mo.			Diarrhea; vomit; no appetite		6	2			Symptoms gone	All symptoms gone	Prescription (Bi-carbonate of soda and an antibiotic (palmitato de cloromiceatin)
F	37	Widow	2	Pain in kidneys, and legs; nerves; choking feeling; headaches; nausea	Months	89	65	Medical	Underweight	All symptoms gone, except pain in kidney		Prescription *
M	45	M	5	Tired; no appetite; could not raise arm, fingers swell	Years	13	7	Medical		Better	All symptoms gone	Cleansing; baths; massages and suppository

143

1	2	3	4	5	6	7	8	9	10	11	12	13
F	3 mo.			Light cough; born with two teeth		26	18			Cough disappeared; assured teeth will fall out		Prescription *
F³	36	M	8	Paralysis from waist down (See text)	3 mo.	51	29	See text	See text	See text	See text	Cleansings, massages

F¹ (Name: Irene)

M² (Name: Jose)

F³ (Name: Esperanze)

* A standard range of teas, baths, and massages.

** Unavailable

Table 8.3   Comparison of CMI Mean Scores:[1] Patient-Perceived
            Successes and Failures

	First CMI	Second CMI[*]
Failure	72.9	54.0
Success	61.8	38.8

*Significant at the .05 level.

[1]See Appendix A for the ways in which the mean scores were computed

Table 8.4 Regulars Treated at Spiritualist Temple

1	2	3	4	5	6	7	8	9	10	11
Sex	Age	Marital Status	Number of Children	Symptoms at Initial Contact With Temple	Reason for Illness	Medical Diagnosis as Reported by Patient	Length of Illness Prior to First Temple Visit	CMI Score at Time of Interview	To What Aspect of Temple Treatment Patient Attributed Cure	Symptoms at Time of Interview
F[1]	41	M		Loss of balance; zig-zagged when she walked; felt as if she had water on the brain; headaches and pain in cerebro; thoughts of dying	See text	See text	3 years		Development	Feelings of sadness still persist; symptoms re-appear when away from temple
F	44	M	3	Nerves; thinks evil thoughts; people want to harm her; feels all alone; has many fears; feels despair	First child's illness and subsequent death		Since her marriage 19 years ago		Cleansing	Symptoms continue but attenuated
F	34	M	2	3rd pregnancy; first two pregnancies aborted; feared 3rd abortion	Too much physical activity	Ulcers (re-quired operation)		34	Head of temple successfully delivered both succeeding infants	Ulcers
F	59	M	2	Body and teeth shiver; mouth crooked; couldn't eat; nose hemor-rhaged; foot swelled	Went out at night to tend her animals		3 weeks	6	Participation in temple	Intermittent depression; sweating; has no symptoms
F	67	W	3	Bronchitis; abdominal pain		Bronchitis	4 years		Aguamiel (cactus juice), egg yolks, vinegar -- on empty stomach	None

146

1	2	3	4	5	6	7	8	9	10	11
F	39	Abandoned	3	Pain in cerebro and headaches	Child's illness		1 month	33	Temple participation	Cries a lot
F	37	M	7	Back pain (cintura); cerebro; loss of orientation, went crazy	Death of mother-in-law; patient couldn't cry		18 months	10	Cleansing & bath	None
F	25	M		Attacks (falling & losing self)	Visit to cemetery				Cleansing	None
F	29	M	3	Abdominal pain; couldn't do anything		Liver: operation recommended	Several yrs. (treated by doctor 7 months)	78	Invisible operation and three months in development	Abdominal pains; can do everything
F	52	M	4	Back pain (cintura); tumor on navel size of orange; chest pain; sweating	Hernia due to lifting heavy things	Cancer: operation required	Years	14	Baths; invisible operation; cleansing	All symptoms gone but heavy sweating
F	43	M	6	Lost all her senses; pain in thighs and hips; could not sit; could not walk; nerves	Death of an infant	Rheumatism		44	Cleansing; pills given by doctor	Back pain (cintura)
F	37	M	9	Nausea; no appetite; headache; couldn't sleep; body felt hollow	Illness followed pregnancy accompanied by susto (husband lost job)			85	Cleansing; massage; development	No specific symptoms
F	65	W	3	Pain in feet, arms, cerebro, lungs, eyes; feelings of asphyxiation; sick heart				75	Massages; teas	Pains when she works a lot (patient has a severe limp)

147

1	2	3	4	5	6	7	8	9	10	11
F	48	M	8	Feelings of fear; blurred vision; no energy (long history of illness related to liver)	Ate something that didn't agree with her; vomiting and diarrhea	Diseased liver	8 years or longer	44	Purgatives	General poor state of health related to liver problems
F[2]	21	Single		Low blood pressure; headaches; depression; loss of weight; nerves; trembling hands; nausea; feelings of breathlessness; death wishes	Brother hit her, which caused her premature menstruation resulting in her illness	Very low blood pressure; poor diet	7 years	21	Massage; teas	Still feels suffocated; distended; still sad but now she can talk to people; no longer wants to die
F	60	M	7	Headaches	Because she must fulfill God's work or she falls ill		3 months	77	Participation in temple	Continues to have headaches
F	48	M	4	Four premature spontaneous abortions	Witchcraft		Years	85	Cleansing; development (subsequent to temple participation gave birth to 4 healthy children	Gets angry; recently had gall bladder operation and gynecological surgery (uterus removed)

1	2	3	4	5	6	7	8	9	10	11
F	23	M	2	Stomach distention	Ovaries overworked from lifting heavy things	Appendicitis; operation recommended	3 years	56	Cleansing	Abdominal--food makes her sick; feet swell; swelling removed following treatment at temple. (At the time of interview, patient was pregnant, temple never prescribes anything to pregnant women except cleansing)
F	60	Single	4	Pain in liver; ulcer; couldn't eat; couldn't urinate; nausea and diarrhea		Gall bladder; operation recommended			Teas, purgatives	Symptoms recur when away from temple
F	31	M	4	Heart palpitations; trembling; desire to run into street; nervous breakdown; couldn't sleep; felt persecuted (children would get sick a lot)	susto	Intoxication of noxious carbon	months	84	Cleansing; teas	Suffers from nerves; (children no longer get sick)
M	47	M		Pain in body; in cerebro; kidneys; cannot sleep at night; gets angry	Dispute with neighbor over land	Nothing wrong with him	12 months	82	Cleansing	Body aches; pain in cerebro when away from temple
M[3]	37	M	2	Pain in head; feels dizzy; epileptic attacks		Epilepsy (See text)	Since 1½ year old infant	24	Cleansing; development	All symptoms gone

1	2	3	4	5	6	7	8	9	10	11
M	30	M	1	Sprain in arm and and rib fracture				13	Symptoms not alleviated in temple but by bonesetter	None
M	23	M	1	Feelings of asphyxiation; depressed; back pain (cintura)	Lifted heavy things		15 days	10	? (Is in development	None
M	22	Single		Open wound in ankle	Accident at work		Several months	15	Massages; bath	None
M	40	M	8	Incessant headaches	Nerves; exhaustion		Months	55		Continues to suffer headaches when he is at work teaching school
M	46	M	5	Trembling	Had to stop drinking because he was dying from overdrinking			19	Temple participation, prescription and treatment	Pain in legs
M[4]	29	Single		Faint; ideas of suicide; pain in arms, hands, and chest; feels tired; thirsty; afraid; feelings of asphyxiation	Fell off bicycle (See text)	Nothing wrong (See text)	1 year	47	Cleansing; teas	Most symptoms largely disappeared but still feels sad; symptoms reappear when away from temple
M	51	M	3	Back pain; could not sleep; pain in cerebro; always tired; could not abide any noise		slipped disc; rheumatism; kidneys; back operation recommended			Temple treatment; cleansing; massage; baths	All symptoms gone

1	2	3	4	5	6	7	8	9	10	11
M	56	M	14	Shivering; grippe; fever; headache; fainted		Typhoid	1 month	52		Feels perfectly well; occasional grippe
M	52	Single		Two months after appendix operation some symptoms returned; abdominal pain and vomiting; couldn't eat or drink			Months	21	Tea; cleansings	None

F[1] (Name: Chucha)

F[2] (Name: Felicia)

M[3] (Name: Bernardo)

M[4] (Name: Jaime)

151

NOTE: Mean CMI Score (Entire Sample) = 43.3

Mean CMI Score (Female) = 49.7

Mean CMI Score (Male) = 33.8

Table 8.5   Mean CMI Scores by Temple Use and Sex

	Regulars		Non-regulars		Controls	
	N	Mean	N	Mean	N	Mean
Males	15	43.4*	90	59.8*	36	39.2
Females	23	51.9*	255	71.4*	336	50.0

* Significant at .001 level

Table 8.6   Mean CMI Scores by Religion and Sex

	Regulars		Professed Catholics (Non-regulars)		(Controls)	
	N	Mean	N	Mean	N	Mean
Males	15	43.4	18	54.1	16	36.3
Females	22	51.9	79	68.2	151	50.0

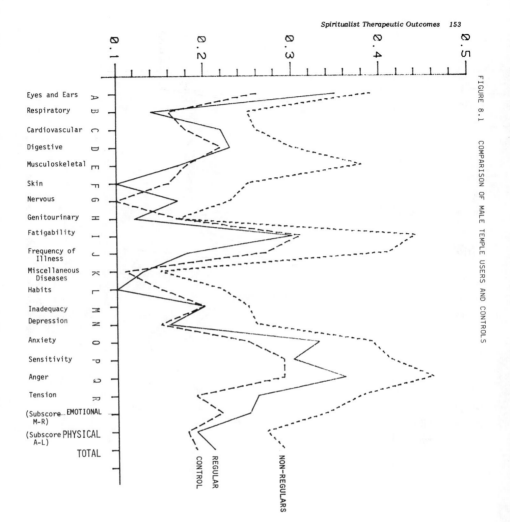

FIGURE 8.1   COMPARISON OF MALE TEMPLE USERS AND CONTROLS

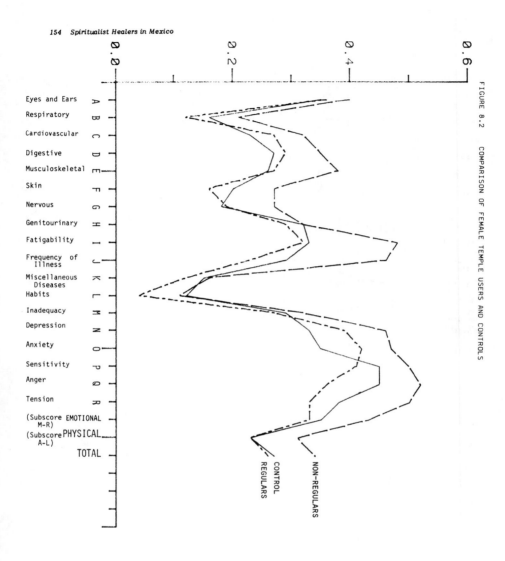

FIGURE 8.2 COMPARISON OF FEMALE TEMPLE USERS AND CONTROLS

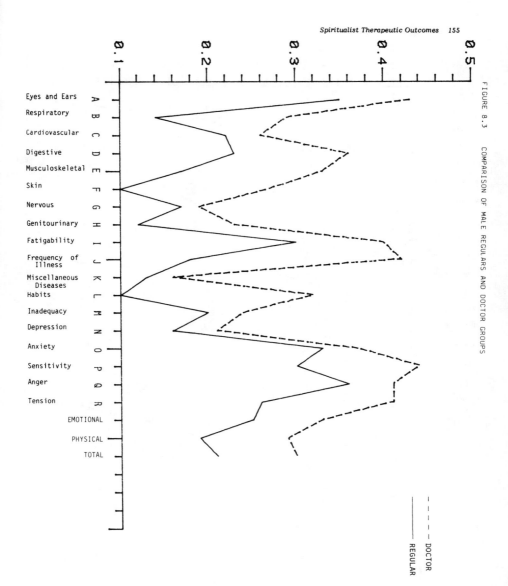

FIGURE 8.3 COMPARISON OF MALE REGULARS AND DOCTOR GROUPS

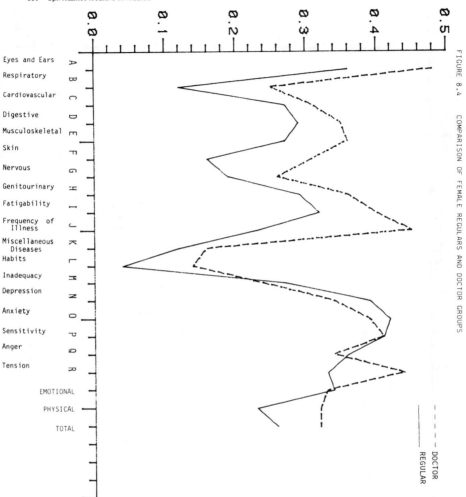

FIGURE 8.4   COMPARISON OF FEMALE REGULARS AND DOCTOR GROUPS

9. How Spiritualist Healers Heal

In this chapter we turn to the ways in which Spiritualist healers achieve therapeutic results. To scrutinize this problem is to illuminate how folk practitioners restore patients to health concomitantly, to embark on a first step in ferreting out the therapeutic elements of a nonbiomedical system within a specific sociocultural setting. Once the therapeutic benefits are assessed in many different cultural contexts, it will be possible to unveil the universal underpinnings of the health-restoring process. This avenue of inquiry is compelling from a theoretical and a clinical perspective because it enables medical practitioners to maximize health-care delivery to the advantage of both patient and healer. However, it is still open to question which aspects of a given therapeutic regime, separately or in unison, produce beneficial effect.

All therapeutic regimes are comprised of numerous intricately related elements in influencing therapeutic outcomes, including interactional and procedural components that possess symbolic significance. For heuristic purposes, I have divided the therapeutic encounter into three broad components: the doctor-patient relationship, techniques and procedures, and patient characteristics and syndromes. This categorization enables us to rank the different components in importance within the context of a specific therapeutic regime, and also to compare different regimes along these dimensions. My concern in this chapter is to rank these three components in Spiritualist healing and to compare them, briefly, with biomedicine. I will argue that patient syndromes and patient characteristics are the primary determinants of the efficacy of Spiritualist healing. Analysis of Spiritualism, however, leads me to conclude, as have others, that in healing systems associated with

157

religious ideologies, specific techniques and procedures tend to be dominant in the symbolic influence of outcomes; by contrast, in biomedicine the doctor-patient relationship assumes central symbolic importance in the healing process.

Before turning to the ways in which Spiritualist therapeutic regimes produce their effects, brief consideration needs to be given to the symbolic aspects of biomedical therapeutic procedures and the doctor-patient relationship.

BIOMEDICAL TECHNIQUES AND PROCEDURES

Clearly, every therapeutic modality can be identified by its standard procedures, but to what degree its customary techniques affect patients in a symbolic or real way is not fully understood. In fact, scholars in various disciplines have addressed this issue (Engel 1977; Glick 1967; D. Kennedy 1973; McAuliffe 1978; McDermott 1977; Pellegrino 1979; Romm et al. 1976; and others). McDermott's discussion (1977:136) is especially illuminating in this regard. He has identified two major components of clinical practice that he calls "technological" and "samaritan." In his words:

> Everything the physician does is some combination of technology and what we might call "samaritanism". Technology includes all those products of medical science that are useful in preventing or altering disease in a specific fashion. "Samaritanism" is the collection of acts that provide reassurance, or at least support, to someone troubled by disease or illness. These two functions--the technological and the samaritan--are separable in theory but not in practice.

Alteration and cure are limited to a number of diseases. Pellegrinos' observations cited in the last chapter must be recalled in this regard. He indicates a selected number of pharmaceutical agents capable of fully eradicating diseases of known etiology or diverting their inexorable course (Pellegrino 1979; Rosenberg 1979; Thomas 1977). There remain, however, a residual category of incurable dysfunctions ". . . effective means have not been found for coping with the stubborn complex of chronic and social illnesses that now predominate in economically advanced countries" (White 1973:3), and a large array of diseases for which current therapeutic measures have not been validated, including coronary heart disease, rheumatoid arthritis and cancer (Kleinman 1974; McDermott 1977; Pellegrino 1979; Rosenberg 1979; Thomas 1977). According to McDermott, "Roughly three-quarters of the nonsurgical physician's care today (both general and specialist) is not curative but supportive" (p. 141). The latter refers to prolonging of a patient's condition before he succumbs to it, or, in Pellegrino's words, cases in which drastic treatments prolong life without curing "the illness" (1979:262). McDermott, however, provides the following qualification (1977:141):

> To say that the principal contribution is "supportive" is not to say that it is unimportant, nor that it does not require mastery of the technology. On the contrary, the pattern of disease that has been shaped by our economy and our public health measures has created a situation in which supportive therapy that is largely, though not exclusively, technological becomes the physician's major function. In other words, the physician is left to alleviate these impairments with pharmaceutical palliatives, technological manipulation, and samaritanism.

In retrospect, fifty years ago or less most medical practice was a form of samaritanism. Treatments were developed in ignorance of the etiology of the natural course of the disease (Frank n.d.; McDermott 1977; Pellegrino 1979; Thomas 1974), in much the same ways as they are contemporarily for the diseases just cited. In fact, in McDermott's words, "At any one time, therefore, the body of knowledge that forms the practice, especially the therapeutic practice, of medicine is a curious mixture of a highly effective technology interspersed with islands of dogma, empiricism, conventional wisdom, and, at times, superstition" (1977:143).

In the final analysis, besides some types of surgical and a handful of pharmacological agents that effectively deal with disease, much of medical practice constitutes diagnostic procedures, some of which are not even calculated to affect outcomes (McDermott 1977). In large measure, then, the modern physician's function is chiefly diagnostic, and he relies on complex technology and laboratory measures (Engel 1977; Mechanic 1968) essentially comprising symbolic rather than real intervention. In fact, more and more scholars have come to recognize that much of biomedical practice constitues symbolic healing (Comaroff 1978; Jospe 1978; Kleinman 1980; Moerman 1979; A. Young 1976). Comaroff rightly observes, "In fact, such phenomena as the perpetuation of relatively ineffective therapeutic techniques, the ever-present optimistic bias of medical belief and the widespread use of placebos all point to the need to examine the ontological role of rituals in Western medical contexts" (p. 250).

Craine (1975) has attempted to describe the symbolic ambiance of the modern health-care delivery establishment and to demonstrate "that medical personnel are functionaries in a very significant symbolic system--for the patient, themselves, and ultimately, society" (p. 497).

I will make no attempt here to describe biomedical procedures that serve as healing symbols except to note that patients are confronted by such symbols in the guise of complex and imposing machinery from the moment they enter a contemporary medical establishment. The technological accoutrements encountered in modern health-care delivery facilities constitute an awesome array of healing symbols, especially for persons reared in industrial societies where all aspects of life are governed by technology and are technologically managed by institutional arrangements which flow from the technology (cf. Berger et al. 1974; Cohen 1968). Additionally, in Pellegrino's words, "The chemical agent becomes the symbol of the doctor's concern and power, and without it the transaction is considered ineffective" (1979:261). Hence, the proverbial placebo pill. In fact, it is claimed that the doctor-patient relationship itself is crucial in biomedical and psychotherapeutic practice.[1]

THE DOCTOR-PATIENT RELATIONSHIP

Some scholars maintain that the doctor-patient relationship per se is essential in the healing process (Anderson & Helm 1979; Fabrega & Silver 1973; Gill 1976; Haynes 1976; Pratt 1976) and in promoting successful treatment outcomes (Anderson & Helm 1979; Gill 1976; Pratt 1976). Pellegrino makes the significant assertion, "Equally essential is avoidance of a theory of medicine which excludes those human needs not susceptible to technological solution, which require personal interactions, or a more general integration of psychological and physical measures in healing" (1979:263).

Scholars, however, disagree on which elements of the doctor-patient relationship aid in fostering positive outcomes. Some suggest that physicians with the most faith in the efficacy of their treatment achieve the best results (e.g. Benson & Epstein 1975). Others emphasize the importance of communication between doctor and patient, especially when the physician facilitates the patient's understanding of his impairment, of what must be done to effect recovery, and of the likely outcome of the therapy (Haynes 1976). Pursuant to these considerations, Inui et al. (1976) propose that by informing patients of their condition, physicians foster patients' compliance and cure, while others (e.g. Egbert et al. 1964) cite physicians' encouragement and instruction as all important.

Still others give primacy to an egalitarian relationship between patient and doctor (Anderson & Helm 1979; Pratt 1976), whereas some contend that a modern patient places his "confidence in the physician and his imputed status, and, indirectly, in that of science itself" (Rosenberg 1979:21). According to this view, the physician's authoritative stance vis-a-vis the patient enhances the patient's confidence in the physician and also thereby effects a cure (Parsons 1975; Siegler & Osmond 1974). In short, whatever the doctor does must be curative.

Focusing, for a moment, on psychotherapy, with which Spiritualist healing is sometimes likened, Werner (1980) and others contend that by adopting the role of powerful healer, psycho-therapists, like shaman, exude great authority and affect patients in a positive way (Hughes 1976; Lieban 1977). Others have argued that the doctor-patient relationship alone, to the exclusion of any specific therapeutic technique, is instrumental in producing favorable outcomes (Strupp 1980e). Again, within the psychoanalytic context, the question arises as to what aspects of the relationship are most influential in effecting positive results. Opinions vary.

Although some scholars have asserted that selected helping persons succeed equally in assisting patients with their problems (Bergin 1971; Glasser 1977; Luborsky 1975; Strupp 1980a, 1980b, 1980c, 1980d, 1980e), others have found that therapists resembling their clients in ethnicity, age, and social level attain more positive therapeutic results than when patient and doctor are not similarly matched (Smith & Glass 1977). In sum, various investigators assessing different schools of psychotherapeutics reach essentially a similar conclusion: that individual practitioners rather than specific methods of treatment determine therapeutic effectiveness (e.g., Bergin 1971; Frank 1974; Marshall 1980a, 1980b; Werner 1980).

Great emphasis has been laid upon this idea of patients' and healers' sharing a common set of understandings. "The sharing of a common belief system facilitates communication and rapport between patient and physician, which in turn enhances the patient's confidence in his doctor" (Obeyesekere 1977:178). (See also Fabrega & Manning 1979; Kleinman 1980; Mechanic 1968.)

But after all is said and done, whether we are looking at biomedicine or psychotherapeutics, Donabedian may be correct when he observes, "It must be recognized, however, that our knowledge of how the attributes of the patient-physician interaction relate to 'health' outcomes is very fragmentary indeed" (1972:116-17).

The Spiritualist materials are instructive in this regard. Analysis of them leads me to assert that healing associated with religious ideologies tends to depend more upon specific healing techniques and procedures for relieving illness and less on the healer-patient relationship (cf. Bahr et al. 1974). In fact, as we saw in Chapter 7, the healer-patient interaction is relatively impersonal, especially among nonregulars. Spiritualist healers are only minimally reassuring, nor do healers and patients share similar models of illness etiologies. We have seen that Spiritualist healers themselves deemphasize the curer's role by claiming that all healers are equally effective. More pointedly, the Spiritualist healer-patient relationship per se is secondary to Spiritualist techniques in effecting positive outcomes.

The doctor-patient relationship has been emphasized in biomedical practice in industrialized societies for two interrelated reasons. First, because where normally social relationships are atomized and strong social supports may be lacking, patients may look toward the physician for affective support. Or, as Ben-Sira (1976) asserts, because patients fail to understand a physician's strategies, they look to him for emotional encouragement. Second, and related to the first point, industrialized society gives primacy to individual, personal emotional concerns and to ego-centric interactions as is embodied in the doctor-patient relationship, and the doctor-patient encounter is expected to generate emotional tones. On the other hand, while we have seen that rural Mexicans frequently attribute illness to emotional distress, nonregular patients seek emotional supports during an illness episode from their families rather than from the physician or healer from whom emotional support is not usually expected. Patients are almost always accompanied to a therapeutic encounter by some othe person who assists them by their presence. For the regulars the temple is an analogue of the family and their emotional supports are attained through their participation in temple rituals and membership. I posit that the nonregular patient, and even the regular one, looks toward the Spiritualist healing techniques to alleviate illness, of which cleansings are a major component.

ANALYSES OF SPIRITUALIST HEALING TECHNIQUES

Viewed analytically, Spiritualist healers achieve beneficial effects by an amalgam of techniques, which require four separate modes of analysis. I hasten to stress, however, that to distinguish these modes does not suggest that they should be separated.

SOCIOLOGICAL ANALYSIS

Viewed sociologically, the act of cleansing a patient suggests a symbolic termination in public of the patient's sick role. The sociological theory of the sick role proposes that patients assume a sick role usually for secondary gain (Parsons and Fox 1952). While the pay-offs for assuming the sick role are not always discernible, eventually the role must be discontinued for daily life to continue. Sigerist (1977) astutely observes that illness "throws us off our accustomed track" (1977:389). The sick role must be abrogated for life not to be excessively thrown off its accustomed track. In effect, Spiritualist healers symbolically efface the sick role in a culturally meaningful way, thus enabling the person to proceed with day-to-day affairs without further disruption. With symbolic termination of the sick role, the patient is restored to a level of functioning, if only temporarily.

There is yet another social psychological dimension to Spiritualist therapeutics which may be instrumental in abrogating the patient's sick role. It has been observed that patient's somatic complaints and chronic illness are frequently reinforced by family and social networks as well as by biomedical practice. A family's sympathetic supports to the patient's complaints reinforces somatization as do physicians who treat physical complaints rather than the depressive disorders with which these complaints are often associated (Katon et al. 1982a, 1982b).

I have emphasized earlier that, contrary to the usual view of folk healers, Spiritualist healers frequently fail to support the patient's sick role and tend to minimize the patient's complaints. While within the popular doctor-patient relationship paradigm Spiritualist healing techniques of this type may be regarded as dysfunctional, from a social psychological perspective their behavior may have a positive effect. The fact that Spiritualist healers are often less than sympathetic to patient's complaints will tend not to reinforce the patient's illness behavior. This lack of reinforcement from a sacred practitioner may facilitate the symbolic meaning of cleansing further and lead the patient to put an end to the sick role, particularly among patient's who may be somatizing a depressive disorder, as we have seen in Chapter 6.

The preceding discussion is, however, more applicable to the first-comers and the habitual temple users. Looking at the regulars, the sick role is not actually terminated when the individual is brought back to his premorbid role; rather, the patient emerges in a new role as health provider, healer, or member of a health-care establishment who serves others as a temple functionary (cf. Bourguignon 1976; Crapanzano 1973; Harwood 1977a). By emerging as regulars, patients are in effect ushered into a state of liminality--of being neither healthy nor ill. The impact of the new role on the patient can be seen in numerous instances--for example, in the case of Chucha, who felt compelled to return to the temple to fulfill her obligations as a curer to her clientele despite her professed condition of great weakness. In conjunction with their new roles, such patients acquire a new set of relational networks, which lead to new friendships, new responsibilities, and new ritual kinship ties (*compadrazgo*), with these networks furnishing a new social matrix.

The social matrix of which regulars become part generates several types of changes simultaneously. We turn our attention therefore to the regulars who are affected by Spiritualist treatment techniques and procedures that operate on several physiological and several cognitive levels at the same time. To reiterate, the various components of Spiritualist therapy are closely intertwined, although I deal with them separately here for purposes of analysis.

PHYSIOLOGICAL ANALYSIS

The large pharmacopoeia utilized by Spiritualists (discussed in Chapter 7 and listed in Appendices B&C) requires investigation under controlled conditions of its physiological effectiveness. We may assume that some of these plants are pharmacologically active but probably incapable of eradicating the causes of the diseases for which they are prescribed.

The Role of Trancing

It is quite likely, however, that Spiritualists induce physiological changes by their reliance on trancing during their rituals. I have noted earlier that participants express feelings of contentment and elation after trancing, a phenomenon that has been observed cross-culturally (Lewis 1971). Based upon all that we know currently, altered states of consciousness have their physiological correlates (Zinberg 1977), and there has been a growing interest in the physiological effects of trance and meditation (Benson 1974; Benson et al. 1976; Gellhorn & Kiely 1972; Glueck & Stroebel 1978; Lex 1976, 1978; Maupin 1969; Prince 1968; Wallace 1972; R. Wallace & Benson 1970; Zales 1978). These studies indicate that the therapeutic value of trance and meditation is linked to their effects on the autonomic nervous system and EEG patterns (Benson et al. 1976; Gellhorn & Kiely 1972). Gellhorn and Kiely conclude that meditation may be effective in the treatment of psychosomatic tension states, anxiety, and phobic reactions, the types of psychiatric disorders encountered in temple regulars.

Altered states of consciousness achieved in various ways--including trancing (Ludwig 1968)--affect the trophotropic system, which acts reciprocally with the ergotropic system (Gellhorn 1967). The ergotropic system involves the sympathetic nervous system, and the trophotropic system encompasses the parasympathetic nervous system; the two together comprise the autonomic nervous system. Normally, the ergotropic system increases its activities when the organism is under stress by augmenting the sympathetic nervous system's actions, as expressed in accelerated pulse rate, increased respiratory activity, increased blood pressure, sweat secretion, and raised blood lactate, and concurrently in inhibited gastrointestinal and motor activity (Benson et al. 1976; Lex 1978; Pelletier 1979).

Alternatively, trancing stimulates the trophotropic system by increasing the parasympathetic nervous system's activities, resulting in reduced heart rate, lower blood pressure and respiratory rate, and increased gastrointestinal motor and secretory functions. Concomitantly, striated muscles become relaxed, decreasing blood lactate levels. Cortical excitation is diminished (Benson et al. 1976; Lex 1978), as reflected in changed EEG patterns from the normal state (Pelletier 1979). Much data has been brought to bear on the positive effects produced by increased trophotropic activity (e.g., Pelletier 1979) fostered by trance and meditation. Benson et al. observe that this type of relaxation is "of considerable therapeutic and perhaps preventive value to the many individuals faced with situations in which excessive sympathetic nervous system activity is present and undesirable" (1976:445). Moreover, not only is trophotropic activity pleasurable in its own right (Lex 1976) but it is also useful clinically in treating the psychosomatic tension states, anxiety, and phobic reactions (Gellhorn & Kiely 1972) resulting from meditators' decreased lactate levels (Pelletier 1979).

It must be pointed out, however, that although findings that suggest these physiological changes have received wide currency, they have not been accepted unanimously. Some have argued that the beneficial effects of meditation and trance result from accompanying changes in life-style rather than from monitoring neurophysiological patterns (Pelletier 1979). Pelletier enumerates such life-style changes as reduced alcohol usage, reduced cigarette smoking and coffee drinking, and changes in diet. Even if this argument has validity, in the case of Spiritualist healing it would apply to men but not to women: It is true that men who become regulars decrease their alcohol consumption, but women normally refrain from drinking alcoholic beverages and smoking under any circumstances. Food intake remains the same for both men and women. Their interactions change, however.

We may assume then, that the changes reported by regulars after healing and irradiation rituals are attributable in some measure to physiological modifications achieved by trancing.

The Therapeutic Touch

Yet another aspect of Spiritualist procedures may have its physiological correlates and merits brief attention. We have seen that tactile communication of the type that takes place between healer and patient during cleansing, for example, including constant massaging of the patient, allows for bodily relaxation (Krippner 1978), which also may be associated with autonomic nervous system function. Others have observed that massage is a satisfying aspect of nonmedical therapeutics (Gillin 1965), and, in fact, recently Krieger et al. reported, "Therapeutic touch has proved itself most useful as an adjunct to orthodox nursing practices..." (n.d.:3). Therapeutic touch as described by these authors involves a healer scanning the patient's body with the hands in much the same fashion as in the patient-healer interaction in the temple described earlier, especially when the healer is cleansing the patient. The therapeutic touch seems to relax the patient and to produce responses analogous to trancing. Finally, the therapeutic aspect of massaging may also be related to the fact that the skin itself plays a role in inhibitory and excitory interaction and in mitigating pain, since pain tends to have cutaneous origin (Melzack & Wall 1975). In fact, it has been found that direct stimulation of the skin by vibration is an effective method for decreasing pain (Melzack 1976), but temple therapeutic procedures tend to mitigate pain in yet other important ways, which must be viewed from a psychological perspective.

PSYCHOLOGICAL ANALYSIS

Temple therapeutics have a differential psychological effect on nonregulars and regulars. The nonparticipatory nature of nonregulars' contact with the temple limits any meaningful psychological influences on this group of patients, whereas the regulars are affected cognitively and affectively in several important ways.

Pain Perception

Participation in Spiritualist healing and ritual influences perception and response to pain. It is well established that illness and perception of pain--all-encompassing experiences that include sensory, physiological, and behavioral components (Pomerleau & Brady 1979)--are culturally determined (Fabrega 1970; Wolff & Langley 1975; Zborowski 1952, 1968; Zola 1966, 1973); however, members of a given culture respond differentially to it by exhibiting varying pain thresholds (Tursky & Sternbach 1975).

It is perhaps a truism that "...pain is a private datum--not directly measurable. Because different individuals have undergone unique past experiences and have been subject to varying social and cultural influences, it is to be expected that they perceive pain in different fashions" (Wolff et al. 1980:83-84). However, there are several varieties of pain, with the major distinctions made between acute and chronic pain.

Scientists speak of a three-tiered system of pain distinction: sensory discrimination, motivation and affect, and cognitive evaluation, the last encompassing cultural and environmental factors. On a sensory discrimination level, the pain response follows a noxious stimulus. The affective level, related to motivational aspects of behavior, is not always easy to connect with a triggering stimulus. The cognitive-evaluative level interacts with the other two levels (Wolff et al. 1980).

Acute pain is related to the sensory level of discrimination, whereas chronic pain results from cognitive regulation of pain-related responses (Wolff et al. 1980). Hence, acute pain that results from tissue damage by "noxious stimulation" and that fails to respond to treatment may lead to chronic pain (Wolff 1980). Acute pain is transient pain that suggests tissue damage but that diminishes in the course of the natural healing process, whereas chronic pain is persitent and fails to disappear as the healing process progresses (Zimmerman et al. 1980). Additionally, researchers have found that although anxiety increases and then decreases with noxious pain, chronic pain is marked by an ongoing anxiety state (Pomerleau & Brady 1979).

Especially interesting about chronic pain is the discrepancy between observed and measured pain stimuli and the frequently immeasurable quality of chronic pain (Pomerleau & Brady 1979:12).

For this reason, chronic pain which "persists constantly or intermittently for several months or more" (Sternbach 1974:3) and is benign rather than life threatening (ibid.) has also been associated with depressive disorders (Blumer et al. 1980; Pomerleau & Brady 1979; Sternbach 1974); in fact, it has been found that chronic pain diminishes or disappears with psychopharmacological treatment for depression (Blumer et al. 1980; Sternbach 1974).

Weisenberg (1977, 1980), reviewing numerous studies dealing with pain regulation, emphasizes that a major ingredient of coping with pain is the degree to which the individual perceives control over his/her pain sensations. A similar proposition has been advanced by others (Antonovsky 1980; Melzack & Campbell 1975). All these studies suggest that pain tolerance is increased when a patient feels that the pain will and can be controlled by someone, "whether the patient himself or a trusted other person, such as a competent physician or other health provider, to whom he has yielded his own power of control" (Weisenberg 1980:112).

Perusal of the data in Table 8.4, column 8, suggests that we are dealing with chronic pain patients (Blumer 1980) whose disorders are linked to emotional states. This, in fact, is also recognized by the healers, who regard regulars as suffering from afflictions of the "spirit." In light of these findings, it can be asserted that by submitting themselves to the control of the temple and to the control of the spirits, regulars tend to minimize their self-perceived symptoms. The significantly lower scores of the regulars on the CMI as compared with nonregulars--and comparable with the controls--lend support to this contention. Although regulars still complain of their symptoms, they tend to give their symptoms minimal importance and to associate their condition with a state of well-being. Hence, while symptoms continue, behavior is improved and somatization is decreased as part of this change.

Physiological Correlates of Pain Reduction

Psychologically mediated pain may have its physiological underpinnings as well. In recent years a body of biochemical data has emerged showing that physical stimulation, including acupuncture, can produce analgesia by stimulating the organism to manufacture endogenous opiates. "Stimulation of certain areas of the brain and of peripheral nerves can modulate pain, as can administration of certain drugs. The presence of endogenous opiate-like substances that have similar effects to morphine lends credence to this proposition" (Willis et al. 1980:261; cf. Snyder 1977a, 1977b). Some of these opiate substances (e.g., enkephalins) have a transient analgesic effect; others (e.g., endorphins) produce a much longer-lasting analgesia (Akil & Watson 1980). It is hypothesized by some (Akil & Watson 1980) that endogenous opiates may control pain in phases, with release occurring during (1) stimulation that produces intense pain (2) stress, or (3) manipulation that alleviates pain by activating certain brain regions (Zimmerman et al. 1980). It is quite possible that whereas on lower phylogenic levels a physiological stimulus triggers opiate production endogenously, on the human level not only physiological but symbolic stimulation can trigger such opiate production. This is particularly pertinent in light of the conclusion of Levine et al. (1978:656) "that the placebo effect is endorphin-mediated."

The Placebo Effect

It is worth pausing for a moment to examine the placebo effect within the context of the psychological as well as the cultural level of analysis, to which I shall turn shortly.

What anthropologists call "symbolic healing" medical and other researchers refer to as the "placebo effect." While the power of symbols in healing has been long recognized by anthropologists (e.g., Levi-Strauss 1967; cf. Moerman 1979), the ways in which symbolic healing becomes translated into physiological processes is only currently coming into light. In succinct terms, the placebo effect is any therapeutic intervention that alleviates patients' symptoms within a healing context without removing the cause of the dysfunction. This follows Brody'a (1977) somewhat lengthy definition, which proposes that the placebo effect occurs for a given condition when a person believes that he or she is in a healing context and is administered an intervention that either totally or partially changes the condition, with the change attributable to the symbolic import of the particular intervention and not to any known pharmacological or physiological property (Brody 1977; cf. Jones 1980).

There is a considerable body of literature on placebos and their effects (Benson & McCallie 1979; Benson & Epstein 1975; Hahn & Kleinman 1981; Mechanic 1972; Moerman 1979; Rhein 1980; A. Shpairo 1959, 1971). Briefly, the placebo effect is present in hope, transference, encouragement (Egbert et al. 1964), and in the doctor-patient relationship itself, as well as when a patient feels himself in control or has yielded mastery over his condition to someone he trusts (Beecher 1962; Brody 1977; Shapiro 1971).

Until recently, little was known about the ways in which placebos produce their results on a physiological level, although it has been well established that the placebo effect emerges under conditions of stress and anxiety (Rhein 1980; Casper & Philippus 1975; Mechanic 1972); and chronic pain (Pomerleau & Brady 1979), but that the placebo effect is not generated in psychotic patients (Casper & Philippus 1975; Shapiro 1978; Rhein 1980), including schizophrenics (Jospe 1978), or in the absence of stress and anxiety (Beecher 1962), as, for example, under experimentally contrived conditions (Mechanic 1972). In short, pain associated with high anxiety, such as chronic pain, is also responsive to the placebo effect (Beecher 1962; Rhein 1980).

Until recently, medical researchers usually dismissed the placebo effect as a nuisance impeding laboratory testing of "real" cures (Benson & Epstein 1974; Jospe 1978). Currently, however, the placebo phenomenon has stimulated interest in its own right (e.g., Brody 1977; Jospe 1978), possibly owing to recent discoveries of the endogenous opiates within the context of the placebo effect (Levine et al. 1978). For example, Levine et al. (1979) found that high doses of naloxone (an opiate antagonist) cancels the placebo response, suggesting to these investigators that "only in placebo responders are endorphins released and thus low-dose naloxone only produces analgesia in placebo responders" (p. 741).[2]

At this juncture, a relation between symbolic phenomena and their physiological correlates such as opiate manufacture remains conjectural. It leaves a myriad of unanswered questions, including the ways in which placebos achieve their effects, perhaps through involving many diverse organ systems. For example, according to Benson and Epstein (1975:1225), "placebos provide relief in cases of angina pectoris, rheumatoid and degenerative arthritis, pain, hayfever, headache, cough, peptic ulcers, and essential hypertension," and they also deal effectively with anxiety and depression (ibid.). But, as Levine et al. suggest, "...If the analgesic effect of placebos is based on the action of endorphins, future research can proceed with an analysis of variables affecting endorphin activity rather than simply recording behavioral manifestations of placebo effects" (1978:657), including the symbolic activation of endogenous opiates.

The exciting research on endogenous opiates may furnish a concrete basis to symbolic healing phenomena. Thus, coupled with the physiological effects of development,[3] Spiritualist therapeutic techniques could be operant on several physiological levels, including the neurological and biochemical. Admittedly, at this juncture the foregoing hypotheses rest more on conjecture than on solid scientific evidence.

Affective Correlates of Spiritualist Therapeutics

Turning to yet another facet of the psychological level of analysis, one that may also be indirectly related to achievement of a positive placebo effect provoked under conditions of anxiety, it is useful to recall the case of Jaime. Jaime's case clearly demonstrates that traditional curers in Mexico tend to instill or reinforce an ideology of witchcraft, with its accompanying anxieties, in contrast to the Spiritualists under study here, who deny the existence of witchcraft. As was discussed before, the Spiritualist denial of witchcraft abates suspicion of others and fosters a more favorable social environment in which the patient may function, thereby eliminating possible future illness episodes. Paradoxically, however, although regulars may relinquish their anxieties about witchcraft, they become subject to dysphoric affects generated by temple participation and Spiritualist ideology.

The fact that nonbiomedical therapeutics do not always reduce anxieties, but rather provoke them, is important and has also been noted by others (Obeyesekere 1977). While Spiritualist therapeutic procedures, including both the regulars' interactions with the healer and development sessions, tend to reduce anxieties, temple participation tends to bring out strong emotions of guilt and anxiety, especially when persons fail to meet their obligations to the temple or the spirits. Chucha's and Felicia's cases are illuminating in this regard, especially Chucha's ongoing feelings of guilt for not having been sufficiently obedient to the will of the spirits. All regulars reported feelings of distress when they failed to meet their obligations to the temple as defined by Spiritualist ideology or by the temple head.

Nonetheless, the dialectical relationship between regular and temple must be regarded as an important ingredient of Spiritualist therapy because it promotes the internalization of a new system of symbols. Berger and Luckmann's (1967:114) suggestion is worth noting:

> Under the pressure of this guilt, the individual will come to accept subjectively the conceptualization of his condition with which the therapeutic practitioners confront him; he develops "insight" and the diagnosis becomes subjectively real to him. Successful therapy establishes a symmetry between the conceptual machinery and its subjective appropriation in the individual's consciousness; it resocializes the deviant into the objective reality of the symbolic universe of the society. There is, of course, considerable subjective satisfaction in such a return to "normalcy."

We may thus conclude that while, on the one hand, temple participation and treatment tend to reduce anxieties, they tend, on the other, to precipitate new stresses, which become allayed with dependency upon the temple and its spirits.

CULTURAL ANALYSIS

Similarly, in analyzing Spiritualist therapeutics from a cultural perspective, it is noteworthy to keep in mind that the symbolic aspects of healing may have their physiological underpinnings as well, as we saw in the discussion of the placebo effect. Now let us consider the special importance of cleansing for all regulars and nonregulars from a cultural perspective. I postulate that cleansing nurtures symbolically a Mexican cultural imperative. The healer must provide proper symbols to effect therapy (Turner 1967). As Turner (1967, 1968) and others (e.g., Cassell 1976) have pointed out, symbols reach us at the deepest level, and "assuming reinforcement takes place at necessary intervals, the symbols increase their dimensional efficacy" (Chapple 1970:314).

The usual reference to cleansing in the literature is within the context of Mexican traditional healing practices (Ingham 1970; Madsen 1955), but its special significance was unexpected. It does, however, suggest the cognitive correlate of recovery and the interrelationship between illness, healing, and sociostructural phenomena. This connection between sickness and social structure has been recognized by many scholars (Adams & Rubel 1967; Currier 1966; Ingham 1970; Lieban 1973; Turner 1967, 1968).

In the Mexican context, cleansing may be considered a form of external purification, which, as noted earlier, is sometimes recognized as complementary to the use of purges as a form of internal cleansing. Purification, it is proposed by Douglas, restores order "on an inherently untidy experience" (1966:4). The cleansing act terminates the illness, the sick role, an untidy experience from the start. However, the order that needs to be restored may bear not only on a personal level of experience but also on the patient's social context. Here we see the interaction between the individual health experience and the social structure, because the order that must be restored relates both to the illness episode and to the prevailing sociostructural framework of the society of which the person is part. Although Nahuas and other Meso-American peoples practiced rites of purification prior to the Conquest (Diaz 1979; Orellana 1977), cleansing and purification may also respond to cultural imperatives rooted in Mexico's more recent history. We have seen in Chapter 3 that Mexican history is replete with upheavals from the time of the conquest until the present, because of the compelling changes that are currently taking place as a result of Mexico's economic and industrial growth.

Thus, the disorders an individual encounters in his or life--be they produced by the ecological and sociostructural matrix within which the individual exists, or on a personal level of experience, or both--are relieved by symbolic manipulation through purification by cleansing. Hence, the patient gains relief, if only temporarily, before another illness episode strikes.

Symbols, of course, are transmitted in various ways, such as during healing and religious rituals to which only regulars are continuously subject. Temple participation thus forms an intrinsic part of the treatment; it exposes participants incessantly to healing and religious rituals. The exposure facilitates incorporation of Spiritualist symbols that is also linked with cognitive reorganization of perception. By way of illustrating with one example the ways in which Spiritualist symbolism becomes transmitted during treatment, in Chucha's case the curer linked Chucha's heart-palpitations to crystalline drops falling into an empty glass, the drops symbolizing God's words transmitted during irradiations and Chucha representing the empty glass. Later, Chucha frequently referred to these metaphors.

More important, the regulars' state of liminality, cited earlier, exposes them to communitas, to social interaction based upon unstructured, informal camaraderie (Turner 1969), and "...it involves the whole man in his relation to other whole men" (ibid.:127). Poor social relations are replaced by new ones, and individuals may emerge "revitalized by their experience of communitas" (ibid.:129). Moreover, participation in communitas generates cognitive and affective reorganization by symbols and new ideologies (A. Wallace 1966). As noted in Chapter 2, Mexican Spiritualists emphasize that they are the "chosen people" and promote vehement nationalism. Their symbols aim at restoring a collective dignity and self-esteem to their adherents that has been lost historically.

Communitas also forces its participants to redirect their attentions from idiosyncratic emotional preoccupations to a higher supernatural symbolic order. By so doing, the participant's focus is turned away from preoccupation with self and toward external concerns. Significantly, regulars are incessantly reminded by the temple head and by healers to concentrate only on God and the spirit world during development and curing sessions. In fact, Petra, whom we shall meet later, frequently lamented that her personal concerns interfered with her power of concentration, and therefore she failed to improve like Chucha and other patients. Along with ceaseless reinforcement of Spiritualist symbols, these modalities furnish a cultural and sociopsychological substratum conducive to the *attenuation* of dysphoric affect, perceived pain, and the feeling of "being sick." This, of course, is an ongoing and sometimes even painful procedure rather than one that takes place in a few dramatic episodes as in other ethnographic instances (e.g., Gillin 1965; Metzger & Williams 1963).

Two important questions of theoretical importance require examination. First, do all individuals in the same sociocultural enclave seek similar symbolic reordering for every illness episode? And do all patients respond equally to symbols furnished by Spiritualist healers? That is, are the same healing symbols universally shared by Mexicans?

SYMBOLIC SHARING OF EXPERIENCE

In Chapter 6 we have seen that the groups designated as physicians' patients and controls eschew Spiritualist ministrations. Although they originate from the same socioeconomic and sociocultural segments of the population as do Spiritualists' patients, these groups tend to use biomedical treatment primarily. This fact implies that not all members forming part of the same sociocultural enclave are similarly impelled to seek symbolic resolution of their illness (cf. Fernandez 1965). In light of this evidence, we could conclude that not all Mexicans require symbolic mediation of illness. In a complex society such as Mexico, it is logical to assume that there is cognitive diversity (A. Wallace 1970) even within a social sector.

It could also be argued that the institutional church assists its followers--including the doctor and control groups--to symbolically restore order during illness crises, but that it fails to do so for the population that has become estranged from it, including the temple-patient group. In fact, as we saw earlier, differential commitment to the Catholic church coupled with an adequate illness network distinguish those who seek medical treatment from those who avail themselves of both medical and Spiritualist therapeutic modalities. However, as was emphasized in Chapter 6, this distinction is derived from evidence yielded by using quantitative data-collection techniques (Appendix A). When individual patients' (regulars') life histories are examined and compared with those from the control group, an existential dimension comes into view that is masked by data gathered with interview schedules and questionnaires. As I have previously noted, life histories of persons from the control group disclose that these individuals and their families have been confronted with relatively few traumatic episodes, such as the death of children, life-threatening disease, or even extreme alcoholism. Compared to those who became regulars--like Lupe, Emiliano, and the others we encountered earlier--members of the control group lived a less turbulent existence than did Spiritualist adherents prior to joining the temple, and, similarly; a less turbulent existence than persons who turn to Spiritualist ministrations only occasionally. In sum, those who seek biomedical health care exclusively have not previously experienced sufficiently disruptive afflictions to necessitate the symbolic manipulation that touches the person at the deepest level (Cassell 1976; Turner 1967).

Most likely, a cultural imperative--e.g., in the Mexcian case, the restoration of order through purification--is shared by a large proportion of members of the culture. Such imperatives, however, become activated and come to the fore in the patient when life's equilibrium is severely upset either by chronic illness or through life traumas. Symbolic sharing thus flows from common existential experiences and illness episodes when shared symbolic meanings are drawn upon from a pool of cultural symbols available to members of culture.

Those who resort to biomedicine exculsively may never have experienced prolonged or recurring illness, the type that lingers on and throws the sufferer off his routine course, whether perpetual parasitosis, chronic pain related to depressive disorder, or physical impairment. We may assume that even orthodox Catholics will resort to Spiritualist healers in the event that they are faced with serious existential problems. In sum, while cultural imperatives associated with health restoration need not be shared within a given cultural group, they <u>become</u> shared when a prolonged illness experience (to which all persons are potentially exposed) is brought on, whether by endogenous factors, exogenous ecological or socioeconomic factors, or a combination of both.

One more point is relevant to the present discussion. There is some suggestion in the literature that health restoration associated with the theme of purification is found in other cultures, as, for example, in Africa and among American Indians (Bahr 1974; Hudson 1975; Janzen 1978). It is even tempting to contemplate that the imposition of order is not only a cultural imperative found in a few cultures but a universal human imperative (Berger & Luckmann 1967; Leach 1976; A. Young 1977), perhaps even a "human 'cognitive imperative' defined as the innate human necessity to order sensory experience" (Lex 1978:294). These are empirical questions upon which we may speculate for the time being, but which may be answered in the future.

SYNDROMES UNRESPONSIVE TO SPIRITUALISM

Turning to the question whether all patients respond similarly to symbols supplied by Spiritualist healers, it is evident that Spiritualists do not treat everyone; further, not all temple patients' ailments are removed by temple ministrations. In fact, only a minority of first-comers and habitual temple users claim that their symptoms have been alleviated. This suggests that not all illness episodes are amenable to Spiritualist therapeutic intervention. Earlier, I noted that individuals with fewer self-perceived symptoms are more likely to obtain relief from Spitirualist treatment than persons with a greater number of expressed symptoms. We have seen also that persons such as Emiliano, Chucha, and others who are recruited to become regulars are individuals who require ongoing ministrations themselves, including temple participation, frequent exposure to cleansing, and ritual trancing and development.

But there are those with syndromes that fail <u>totally</u> to respond to temple therapies and the types of patients who fail to respond to the symbolic manipulations furnished by Spiritualist healers. My observations of those who were selected to become regulars but who failed to respond to various temple ministrations and failed to be incorporated into the temple community, support the proposition that although temple treatment techniques assist individuals with dysphoria, mild psychiatric syndromes, and mild ongoing complaints, they fail to assist individuals incapacitated by psychotic syndromes. A corollary to this assertion is that while symbolic manipulation by healers is crucial for perceived treatment efficacy, a patient's <u>capacity to respond</u> to these symbols is equally crucial. Thus, although Turner (1967) rightly suggests that the healer must provide the proper symbols in order to effect therapy, it must also be acknowledged that not all patients or their syndromes have equal capacities to react to a set of symbols.

Analogously, we have equated symbolic healing to placebos and we may assume that much in the same way as placebos have their limitations (Jospe 1978; Rhein 1980; A. Shapiro 1971), so does symbolic manipulation (McCreery 1979). A. Shapiro (1971) indicates that psychotic patients react negatively to the placebo effect, as they do to other types of nonpharmacological therapies (May 1976). Similarly, the data from the Spiritualist temple suggest that patients unresponsive to symbolic manipulation fail totally to respond to Spiritualist therapeutic intervention.

Interestingly, in two out of four cases I encountered in the temple, the temple head made strenuous efforts unsuccessfully to involve the patients in training and trancing, and the head of the temple facilitated special elaborate rituals of cleansing and purification in addition to the routine massages, teas, and baths. In one case, that of a 70-year old man suffering from senile deterioration, the patient was given seven special dislodgements and other therapy with no visible effect. Similarly, in the cases of Petra and Concha, temple therapeutics produced no effect on the latter and only minimal effect on the former.

Petra

Petra's case merits consideration because she represents the temple's limited success in dealing with borderline psychiatric dysfunctions. Petra is especially interesting in light of her repeatedly expressed frustration with her failure to get well; yet, in the final analysis, her syndrome has been unresponsive to temple ministration.

Petra, 44 years old, married with four children, always well dressed and coiffed, is situated better financially than the average temple patient. Her husband, a bus driver with relatively good wages up until recently, was unemployed during the period I knew Petra. The family owns a little candy store adjacent to their well-furnished house, which is located a stone's throw from the temple. Petra is the youngest of nine children--four brothers and five sisters--and was raised in a poor and very Catholic home. She went to church frequently and belonged to a young woman's church auxiliary. Petra dates the onset of her disorder to the time immediately after her marriage, when she was 25 years old. She recalls, "As soon as I got married, I became nervous." She also remembers, however, that even prior to her marriage, when she went to church she asked God why she saw evil things when she wanted very much to see beautiful things. The saints consoled her, but after she married, the bad spirit within her became more forceful and led her to do bad things. Her condition intensified when her first-born child fell ill, and it became critical upon the child's death at the age of 9. According to Petra, the child was born lacking oxygen. After he developed meningitis in the hospital, he became paralyzed in the *cerebro.* She took the child to many physicians as well as to a temple, and she attended him faithfully, but he never developed normally like other children.

Petra described her symptoms at the onset of the more severe phase of her illness, after her child's death, as follows: She walked aimlessly in the street; she suffered from undefined fears; she was afraid of everyone, especially anyone walking behind her, because she thought she would be harmed. When she went to the market, she felt terrible any time someone approached her. "I don't know what I had imagined when I went there, but I didn't want anyone to come near me." She asked herself why she was so terribly afraid, afraid of being grabbed and hurt.

To conceal the fact that she attended a Spiritualist temple, she avoided going to the one near her house. Initially she went to a Spiritualist healer in the state capital (about sixty miles away), where she had taken her sick child before his death. There she was told that she was possessed by a dark spirit and, to her surprise, that she had a gift: "Who would have imagined I had a gift," she said. However, she says that she really didn't believe any of this.

Eleven years ago she began attending the temple in Juarez, where her disorder was similarly attributed to the possession of her body by a dark spirit. She was entered into development but failed to participate in it with love, because she didn't feel any. Nevertheless, being in development made Petra less nervous. When her protector identified himself--as an Indian of unknown provenance--she ceased feeling persecuted and stopped thinking and seeing evil things. Yet there are times, she says, when she still fails to feel the way she ought to; in fact, she is not happy. She inquires of the curers what is wrong with her, and they tell her to recite the invocation; but when she tries to concentrate on the invocation other thoughts creep into her mind--"material" thoughts, as, for exmmple, what happened to her on the street or in her house. At such times she feels even more desperate and in more pain than normally.

At each of our various encounters, a recurrent theme of her narrative is that she would like someone to help her but knows no one. She is totally alone; she is surrounded by people who hate her; there is no one to inquire what is happening to her, why is she suffering; no one to give her advice, to assure her that nothing evil will happen. The development, dislodgement, and irradiation sessions do help her somewhat; she feels well for two days after dislodgement, then she is in pain again. She wishes to be like the other healers, who, unlike her, are all well; but she fails to recover, and the more she tries the more desperate she feels; she gets nervous and starts crying. Sometimes she thinks that she will remove herself from everything and stop going to the temple, but she continues to attend because she feels guilty when she fails to do so. She frequently accuses her husband and his relatives, who are also her neighbors, of hating her. But she adds that she cannot identify any specific harm they have done to her.

She has worked as a curer, but she feels that, unlike the others, she is not working "cleanly" (*limpio*); she is not really in trance with her spirit elevated to God--she knows that she is not in real trance because, when she treats patients, she can hear and see everything that takes place around her. Petra wishes to speak to the head of the temple about her problems, but the woman is always occupied, surrounded by people; and besides, she does not pay any attention to Petra; moreover; according to Petra, the temple head is also a "despot."[4]

I inquired whether Petra could speak to her husband. She said that he is unresponsive to her suffering; even he fails to notice or understand her. However, Petra hastened to add that he has never treated her badly by beating her. Granted, he is a womanizer, but he is a good provider, and has always given her money for the household's financial needs. Her husband, whom she characterizes as being very smart, is an atheist and is vehemently opposed to her attendance at the temple. In fact, until recently she used to go secretly to the temple, but since he has been unemployed and has remained at home he has learned about her attendance there. Petra adds in a matter-of-fact way that her husband believes that the temple head exploits everyone who works for her, but Petra discounts this allegation by concluding that her husband must be possessed by an evil spirit and therefore is not responsible for what he says.

Petra has never consulted a physician about her fears and emotional pain. She usually seeks medical treatment when she is physically sick. Significantly, Petra is one of the very few temple patients who has not somatized her condition. In fact, while she states that she rarely sustains any physical symptoms, concurrently she reports that she has parasites in her intestinal tract, that she suffers from frequent stomach upsets and headaches, that she sweats a lot, and that she wishes to sleep a lot. She attributes her failure to recover in the temple and to be like the other healers to the absence in her life of anyone with whom she could discuss her beliefs in Spiritualism.

Petra impressed me as intelligent, extremely articulate, and communicative. In some ways, such as her overall bearing and speech, she stands out from the others in her milieu. She could be regarded as a person who is alienated from her culture and responds to it atypically. Consider, for example, that Petra is the only patient I encountered with an acknowledged affective disorder who failed to somatize her condition. As one who feels completely alone, she is isolated from the culture in which she exists, and for this reason she also fails to respond to the cultural symbols furnished by the temple. This is a significant point, to which I will return later in this chapter.

Viewed from a psychoanlytic perspective, Petra may belong to a category of patients suffering from a borderline personality organization disorders,[5] which Kernberg defines as neither neurotic nor psychotic but as characterized by a "typical symptomatic constellation" (1975:5). Included among the symptoms attributed by Kernberg to borderlines and also exhibited by Petra are chronic and diffuse free-floating anxiety, multiple phobias related to social inhibitions, and paranoid trends, as well as obsessive-compulsive symptoms. According to Kernberg, the borderline's capacity to test reality is preserved, in contrast to patients with psychotic reactions. In reference to the obsessive-compulsive symptoms, Kernberg notes that there is "a quality of 'overvaluated' thoughts and actions although reality testing is maintained, and the patient wants to rid himself of his absurd thoughts or acts, he also tends to rationalize these acts" (p. 10).

Along similar lines, E. Shapiro (1978) describes borderline patients as having difficulties in interpersonal relationships, particularly in terms of their pervasive sense of aloneness and their tendency to see difficulties as emanating from outside themselves.

On the whole Petra's recurrent refrain of perceiving herself alone and her obsessive wishes to be like the other healers correspond to symptoms displayed by borderline patients. Her excessive accusations against affinal kinsmen and neighbors and her frequent fears of public places such as markets betray her paranoid tendencies and poor social relations.

Borderline patients like Petra demonstrate "good reality testing" (E. Shapiro 1978), and this is evidenced in Petra's assessment of her husband, the temple head, and even her neighbors, who she realizes, have not actually harmed her despite her evaluations that they hate her. However, as Shapiro points out, borderline patients "are likely to regress to transient psychotic states under stress..." (p. 1306). This is in line with my observations that Petra's obsessive symptoms constitute a defense against a repetition of the temporary psychotic episodes which, by her own account, she may have suffered when she lost her bearings and wandered through the streets. In fact, I anticipate that if Petra should suffer a tragedy similar in intensity to the tragedy of the loss of her child, or if she should suspend her contact with the temple, her impairment will impede her from successfully functioning in her day-to-day existence. For the time being, Petra's ongoing exposure to temple therapeutics tends to keep her afloat without medication by sustaining her in her day-to-day functioning. She attends to her daily chores and to her children. She also fulfills her obligations as a wife by meeting her husband's demands.

If we compare Petra's case with that of Chucha or one of the other patients presented earlier who had suffered mainly from dysphoria, we must conclude that whereas temple techniques have aided Chucha and the others to cope with their dysfunction, even to master it, in Petra's case they have failed to do so. The two women display an important phenomenological difference, both tend to function normally in their day-to-day tasks, but Chucha is content with her existence, because of her temple participation, whereas Petra continues to suffer intensely from her affliction.

Petra provides us with a good example of a patient whose syndrome is only minimally managed by temple therapeutics, whereas Concha, a 16-year-old girl described by her mother as "crazy," furnishes us an example of a patient whose syndrome stubbornly fails to respond to temple therapeutics.

Concha

Concha, with her manifest intellectual and affective deficits, was the only patient I ever witnessed standing before a healer openly smiling, her inappropriate affect being my first indication of the severity of her dysfunction. She had been brought to the temple by her mother after having been treated by various nonbiomedical practitioners, including a *curandero*. Concha's mother took her to a *curandero* for treatment because, according to her, Concha had been bewitched by her father's girlfriend, who had deliberately fed the girl food that had brought on her condition.

I never heard Concha speak, but her mother recounted Concha's symptoms. These included the fact that: (1) she smiled to herself; (2) she had to be addressed like a baby or she failed to comprehend what was said to her; (3) she rarely spoke; (4) she was always very angry and sometimes also violent; and (5) she picked her nose constantly and continuously looked at herself in the mirror. Concha insisted that she was very ugly, and she therefore hid so that no one could see her; she failed to fulfill any of the household obligations expected of a young woman her age.

Ironically, inasmuch as Concha failed to respond to Spiritualist therapy, her mother became absolutely convinced that the girl's perturbed state resulted from witchcraft. The mother, whose husband had abandoned her, eked out a very meager livelihood by selling tortillas, washing laundry, and other similar endeavors. She was at her wits' end as to what to do about Concha. At a cost of several thousand pesos, she took Concha to yet another curer, but this curer's ministrations precipitated in Concha one more violent episode. At my last meeting with the mother, the woman told me that she had exhausted all her economic resources and now despaired of seeking treatment for the girl. Concha's condition, however, continued to deteriorate, to the desperation of her mother.

To even a casual observer, Concha's generalized schizophrenia is readily apparent, and it can safely be asserted that temple therapeutic procedures have no effect on such patients, those with severe psychoses. This was as true for Concha as it was for the 70-year-old man.

Of the three components constituting a therapeutic encounter that were identified at the outset of this chapter, the patient and his/her syndrome together with the therapeutic techniques determine the outcome of Spiritualist therapy. In fact, Petra's and Concha's cases lead to the conclusion that the temple's failure to heal is as much the limitation of its therapeutic regime as it is associated with the patient and his or her failure to draw from the available pool of symbols furnished by traditional Mexican culture and which symbols have been extracted and highlighted by Spiritualist healing techniques. In the case of Petra, her sense of isolation has alienated her from her milieu and has impeded her from sharing in the symbolic meanings of her culture. Concha's cognitive and emotional deficits hinder her response to any common shared symbolic understandings that could potentially alleviate her symptoms. Significantly, Strupp (1980a, 1980b, 1980c, 1980d) argues along these same lines when he reports the successes and failures of psychotherapy, as do Luborsky et al. when they examine the predicability of outcomes of psychotherapy. They state "Patient characteristics made up the bulk of the basis for prediction; therapist and treatment characteristics seemed to add little" (1980:480).

SPIRITUALIST THERAPY COMPARED WITH PSYCHOTHERAPY

The preceding conclusion invites comparison of Spiritualist therapy with psychotherapy, to which other nonbiomedical therapeutic regimes including Spiritism have also been compared (Garrison 1977; Harwood 1977a, 1977b; Kiev 1973; Torrey 1972). For brief comparison I have selected two points: treatment outcomes and therapeutic strategies of the two modalities.

Despite the fact that psychotherapy and Spiritualism are based upon disparate assumptions respecting illness etiology, with the former founded on the premise that affliction is largely generated by unresolved endogenously produced psychic conflict and the latter on the premise that the afflicted is the victim of possession by evil spirits, the two modalities share similar results, as has been observed by others (Garrison 1977; Harwood 1977b).

The materials presented on the regulars suggest that therapeutic outcomes are similar to those of psychotherapy. This assertion derives from canvass of the literature on therapeutic outcomes of psychotherapy: by and large, the data are controversial and inconclusive with regard to psychotherapeutic efficacy. Truax and Mitchell's (1971) evaluation of psychotherapeutic outcomes points out that while some therapies produce positive client change, the majority either effect no change or lead to client deterioration (see also Frank 1974; Torrey 1972). Bergin (1971) is less definitive in his assessment of psychotherapy but nevertheless concludes that, on the average, psychotherapy has positive effects (see also Glasser 1977). Other recent studies, however, demonstrate that, at least with respect to neuroses and depression, any type of psychotherapy is better than none, but that in the case of depression specifically, psychotherapy in conjunction with psychopharmacological therapies attains the most positive results (Luborsky et al. 1975; May 1976; Weissman et al. 1979). In sum, we see that psychotherapy is effective in dealing with anxiety states, phobias, and reactive depression (Marshall 1980b; Weissman et al. 1979), but much less effective in dealing with psychotic episodes (Hogarty & Goldberg 1973; Siegler & Osmond 1974; May 1976; Marshall 1980b). Spiritualist therapy of regulars conforms to this pattern of effectiveness.

Notwithstanding their shared aims to enhance patients' coping abilities, however, the two modalities differ by their emphasis on disparate coping strategies. The disparate coping strategies reflect important differences between the two sociocultural systems in which the two therapeutic regimes are embedded.

While there are many schools of psychotherapy, generally speaking they share a similar aim: to foster behavioral independence and autonomy. In Kiev's words, "The notion of individual susceptibility or vulnerability to stress which is heightened by the individual's failure to act autonomously, independently assuming control over his own destiny is quite central to psychiatric theory" (1973:226). Central to psychotherapy is that to achieve autonomy is to achieve insight. "No doubt the most influential contemporary explanation for the value of psychotherapy in the Western world has to do with insight" (Prince 1973:309). "The final result of this insight is hoped to be the creation of a self-determining individual who can see people and relationships as they objectively are" (ibid.).

Ideally, then, in order to accomplish insight, the individual must understand himself (Freedman & Kaplan 1972). For example, psychoanalysis provides an explanation or rationalization for the patient to explain why he is the way he is and why he will improve in treatment (ibid.). Some kind of explanation for undergoing change seems necessary for all methods of psychotherapy. A cure is effected when the patient becomes self-sustaining, in control of existential dilemmas in much the same way as scientists assume control of nature (cf. Bloom 1963): scientists unravel the laws of nature; patients in psychotherapy unravel the laws that govern their own behavior.

Behavioral autonomy is, of course, the *sine qua non* of psychosocial adaptation to a modern industrial society based upon atomistic relationships (Cohen 1968). Mastery of oneself and all situations, attaining growth and development, and liberation as a person (Kiev 1973) through insight, are in fact highly desirable in an industrial society, where individuals are freed from many prescribed cultural rules, and where they must frequently learn to improvise a new set of rules by adapting behavioral responses to various new and often unanticipated situations. Achieving self-reliance, individual responsibility, and control of one's own actions allows social maneuverability and facilitates the development of new behavioral strategies appropriate to unexpected situations and changing conditions. In sum, psychotherapy seeks to prepare the individual for autonomous action adapted to a constant flow of changing situations inherent in indusltrial society (cf. Berger et al. 1974).

From the foregoing discussion, it can readily be seen that Spiritualists, in contrast, are not concerned with subconscious motivation, nor with patients attaining insight into the reasons for their behavior. Spiritualist ministrations address a Spiritualist-construed reality that regards the universe as populated by evil spirits inclined to possess a person's body and removable only by Spiritualist healers. Nor do Spiritualists aim at behavioral independence. Unlike patients in psychotherapy, who ideally must find their own *modus operandi* for dealing with all life's circumstances, Spiritualist patients are provided with rules and guidelines with which they are already familiar--for example, women are encouraged to submit to their mates' will.

When, however, these rules fail to solve a given dilemma, the Spiritualist patient returns to the spirit for advice. It is not surprising that every time a regular is confronted with a new situation he consults with the spirit, because regulars are taught specific behavioral codes rather than generalized behavioral strategies. As a result, dependency upon continuous contact with the temple and with its healers is built into Spiritualist therapeutics, as became apparent in our discussion of temple participation. Spiritualist therapy aims at fostering dependence which conforms to societal behavioral patterns. In nonindustrialized societies and industrially developing societies such as Mexico, the individual is socialized to be dependent within both domestic and societal settings. Reliance on the family unit even among nuclear families is encouraged, and independence is frequently regarded as recalcitrance. In sum, scientifically legitimized therapies aim at advancing psychic autonomy and behavioral independence, but Spiritualist therapy aims at fostering psychological and behavioral dependence in ways that conform to Mexican societal patterns.

Viewed historically from a societal perspective, individual Mexicans, especially the peasant and rural wage laborers, have always been dependent on persons structurally more powerful than themselves. Indeed they have been subjected to dependency promoted by a patron-client relationship (Finkler 1978, 1980a; Foster 1963; Wolf 1959). Temple therapy emphasizes this dependency, with the temple becoming structurally congruent to the family and the spirit protector becoming analogous to the patron. Thus, fostering reliance on the temple must be viewed as consonant with the Mexican social and cultural model of individual behavior, and not necessarily as a shortcoming, as such therapeutic effects are sometimes regarded (e.g., Leighton et al. 1968).

To sum up, I argue that Spiritualist healing techniques operate in tandem with patients' capacities to respond to them, to advance the healing process. Nonbiomedical therapeutic modalities aligned with religious ideology owe their attraction, then, to ritual techniques and procedures, and their success is attributable to the liturgical order that implements the healing symbols, contingent, of course, upon patients' receptivity to them.

Behavioral dependence on the temple has economic consequences, however, that reflect on individual economic mobility and bear on social change. I briefly address this issue in the next chapter by reviewing some points I touched on earlier.

10. THE SOCIAL CONSEQUENCES OF WELLNESS

In the previous chapter I focused on the ways in which Spiritualist treatment procedures affect individual actors. In the discussion that follows I explore the consequences of this treatment on society as a whole. Numerous anthropologists have probed into illness phenomena by scrutinizing societal structures (e.g., Fox 1974; Turner 1974): however, less has been said about what I term the social consequences of wellness. By this I mean the effects on the aggregate of the healing mode. What are the consequences of health restoration, using Spiritualist techniques and procedures on Mexican society at large? How do the regulars fit into Mexican society, and how do they differ from the rest of the populace, if at all?

The focus here is on the regulars: their cures, unlike those of first-comers and habitual temple users, entail role change. We have seen that successfully treated first-comers and habitual temple patients are restored to a premorbid state whereas the regulars' daily lives are transformed in the health restoration process. By and large, temple regulars form a community of individuals who have succeeded in changing the sick role into a publicly acknowledged health-providing one. The case of the temple regulars exemplifies an obvious and important contrast between nonbiomedical practitioners and medical practitioners the world over. Nonbiomedical practitioners are usually recruited into the healing role after an illness episode (Lewis 1971), whereas medical practitioners enter medicine only after having passed rigorous examinations attesting to their physical and psychological health.

Among scientifically sanctioned health practitioners, only psychoanalysts, as a rule, undergo treatment--i.e., psycho-analysis--themselves before they become therapists. By contrast, the self-perceived health state of Spiritualist healers is contingent upon their becoming healers and upon their continued participation in religious rituals. Most important is the fact that one aspect of the therapy requires patients to internalize beliefs in their own powers to summon and control spirits at will, powers, neither legitimized nor even recognized by the larger contemporary Mexican society.

Inasmuch as regulars acquire new roles and new capacities to influence supernatural powers, it is necessary to ask in what ways, if any, their transformation from afflicted to healer and functionary impacts on the larger society. This is especially significant inasmuch as we are dealing with thousands of people and not just a few individuals. Related to this question is also the issue concerning Spiritualists' emotional and psychological health. Spiritualists restore patients to health by imbuing them with beliefs that human beings can communicate with spirits; how do persons with such beliefs fit into Mexican society? To what degree do these people stand apart from other Mexicans of the same social strata? It is true that, although an ideology of the existence of spirits is not alien to Mexican traditional thinking (witness, for example, the belief in *aire*), Mexicans do not ordinarily believe, as Spiritualists do, that humans can communicate with these entities. In light of such apostasy it could be said that by joining the ranks of regulars, afflicted persons shed one illness only to acquire a new one, creating an aggregate of individuals who are emotionally and psychologically unstable.

Numerous scholars have addressed this dilemma (Fabrega & Silver 1973; Kleinman 1980; Lewis 1971) and some (Silverman 1967; A. Wallace 1966) have suggested that folk practitioners of this type suffer from emotional disturbance or even psychopathology. Like shamans, everywhere, Spiritualist healers proudly acknowledge that they became healers because of a bout with an afflicition which, as we have seen, is quite likely linked with a somatized condition associated with dysphoria or other emotional disorder. In light of this fact, Lewis (1971) rightly argues that by mastering his affliction and becoming a shaman, a nonbiomedical practitioner of this type is more rather than less than the other men in his society.

By and large, scholars fail to find psychopathology either among participants in religious groups in general or among nonbiomedical practitioners in particular (Fabrega 1974; Garrison 1977; Kleinman 1980; Ness 1980). Ness, for example, using the CMI, found that participants in religious groups tend to report fewer emotional disturbances than nonparticipants. Kleinman recounts that of twenty-five shamans he observed in Taiwan, "None exhibitied any evidence of significant psychopathology nor gave any history of major psychiatric problems. Most were rather remarkable individuals who possessed strong personalities and many adaptive coping skills" (1980:214).

My data, too, lead me to conclude that Spiritualist healers are psychologically as sound as ordinary rural Mexicans represented by a control group. In fact, as seen in Chapter 8, where the health profiles of regulars and controls were compared, the former tend to exhibit no more self-perceived physical and emotional symptoms than the latter. Indeed, to observe regulars' behavior is to observe women like Mariana, the head of one temple: energetic, intelligent, and self-sustaining (Finkler 1981b).

Directing a temple large or small requires enterprise and the ability to manipulate the social environment. Women who become temple heads, perhaps more than the rest, display exceptional abilities. Mariana is a case in point. In her middle fifties, literate, she was a renowned curer in the region before she established her temple. She is remarkably active and alert, as is reflected in her penetrating gaze. For persons like Mariana, if not for most of the congregants, becoming a temple head is also an avenue of economic mobility from extraordinary poverty to minimal material wealth and entry into a somewhat higher socioeconomic class. In fact, Mariana often reminisces about the economically harsh conditions of her childhood, looks proudly at her cinder-block house, adjacent to the temple, and concludes "Look how far I have gotten!" (ibid.).[1]

And whereas female regulars do not display any behavioral differences from nonregulars, male regulars differ from nonregulars in at least two ways that are not reflected on CMI scores. Male Spiritualists tend to abstain from alcohol use and are also less macho. Men who are recruited and who choose to become regulars usually have a history of alcoholism. In my sample, 33 percent of male regulars, or five of the fifteen men, were alcoholics at their initial contact with the temple. Women in the region may drink, but they do not usually become alcoholics. As has been noted, Spiritualists are not teetotalers, but the twenty-two injunctions includes a prohibition against drunkenness. In becoming a regular, a man relinquishes his drinking habits and thereby becomes unlike the majority of Mexican men, whose drinking patterns define them as men.

In fact, whereas Spiritualists emphasize traditional female behaviors, they attempt to remodel male conduct by deemphasizing masculine behavioral traits associated within the local culture with machismo. A macho male, it will be remembered drinks heavily, and has many women. Such men believe that they may beat their wives providing they support them financially. They take pride in not allowing themselves to be bossed around (*uno que no se deja mandar*). Normally, these men are not likely to be attracted to Spiritualists, as the religion requires them to be submissive and obedient to the spirit world and the temple head, but those who do become Spiritualists seem to relinquish their machismo. A case in point is Manuel, who at age 69 was reputed to be a grand macho. He occupied a secondary political role in the municipality, and he was a henchman of local political bosses. He was by his own admission a heavy drinker and a womanizer. He had left the region some years ago and had taken a government post in Mexico City, where he had also become relatively wealthy. When Manuel was 68, his wife of many years died, and he acknowledged that he had treated her badly. After her death he was left completely alone. Even his children abandoned him, and he developed a severe depressive disorder. He came from Mexico City to a temple for treatment. The healers and temple head insisted that in order for him to be rid of his unhappy state he must "rid himself of his machismo." Manuel's depression was eventually alleviated, but because he resided in Mexico City our intermittent contact left me only with the impression that he became less obdurate and less macho.

Perhaps paradoxically, whereas some men's dissipation and machismo bring them to the temple, others--like Luis whom we met in Chapter 2--are attracted to Spiritualism precisely because there they can avoid drinking and can sidestep the macho role for which not all men are suited. In fact, my observations of male adherents suggest that they tend to exhibit fewer macho traits. For example, unlike most rural Mexican men from the same social strata, male adherents interact with their wives in a relatively egalitiarian way, refer to them as "my companion" rather then the customary "my woman", and, untypically for the region, tend to spend their lesiure time with their families. This is important because as more and more people find themselves residing in nuclear rather than extended families because of circumstances resulting from industrialization (Cohen 1968; Goode 1963), concerted activities by the family unit through harmonious male-female interactions become highly adaptive. In addition, the change in drinking patterns imposed by Spiritualists provides an economic advantage to the household, and for the women there is the added benefit that they are subject to less or no physical abuse at the hands of a drunken spouse.

Decreased alcohol consumption among Spiritualists, along with boasts such as one hears from Mariana about her improved economic situation, would suggest that Spiritualists are relatively well situated economically. Let us then consider what kind of social and economic positions Spiritualists occupy in Mexican society. To address this issue I will first compare Spiritualists and nonadherents along standard socioeconomic variables and will then examine their relative social and economic positions.

COMPARISON OF REGULARS AND CONTROLS

Sociologically, our sample of regulars consists of 38 out of approximately 50 core participants and 372 respondents in the control group. I compared the two groups along standard socioeconomic and sociocultural dimensions including age, family structure (that is nuclear, male head, extended, female head or female head extended (i.e., grandmother type), education, household composition, occupation, relational networks, religious affiliation, type of land holding, marriage, number of children in school, migration pattern and length of absence from natal community.

The findings disclose that regulars and controls share more similarities than differences. The sociological variables indicate that regulars and controls differ in marital status (.01 by difference of proportions test), church attendance (.001) migration, type of land tenure,and relational networks (.05 by the Chi square test).

Comparatively more temple regulars, both male and female are unmarried than is true of the control group.

In addition, 60.5 percent of the regulars, as compared with 41.9 percent of the control group, report that at least one member of their household migrated in search of wage labor at some point. There are no statistically significant differences in occupation between the two groups, or in the size of their landholdings (a majority in both groups hold between one and two hectares of irrigated cropland); however, more regulars (26.3%) than controls (14.2%) identify themselves as peasants with the remaining responses dispersed among various occupational designations, including domestics, wage laborers, and self-employed.

An important, if subtle, difference between the two groups is the fact that fewer regulars hold *ejido* lands than do nonadherents. Thus, 42.1 percent of the regulars report that they hold no *ejidos* as compared with 22.8 percent of the control group. Since *ejido* lands legally belong to the state and are managed by the national political apparatus, thus exposing *ejido* holders to contact with the national bureaucracy, it has been argued the *ejido* tenure tends to integrate the peasantry politically and socially into the national structure (Finkler 1980b; Stavenhagen 1970; Wolf 1956). Persons with less access to *ejido* lands can be assumed to be more structurally marginal, as they enjoy fewer sociopolitical networks and less access to national institutions (Finkler 1980b). Although these findings do not warrant the conclusion that structural marginality alone is a sufficient precondition for becoming a regular, it can be argued that individuals with structurally marginal positions are more likely to be attracted to a marginal religious movement.

It is important, if not surprising, that the majority of Spiritualists (71.9%) report that they never attend church services, with the remainder attending only upon invitation to a special occasion such as a marriage or baptism, whereas 46 percent of the controls attend church weekly, with only 5.2 percent reporting that they never attend church at all. The remaining 49 percent indicate that they attend church once a month or whenever they can. This finding emphasizes that religious commitment to Catholicism is a significant determinant of whether or not one becomes a Spiritualist patient and adherent.

The final point of comparison, which bears on visitation patterns, reveals that the controls tend to interact more with neighbors than do adherents.

This is not surprising; as I pointed out earlier, Spiritualists tend to be viewed negatively by society generally. In response to the question "Whom do you visit most?" 22.2 percent of the regulars but only 12.5 percent of the controls reported, "Nobody." But whereas 19.1 percent of the controls indicated that they visited most with neighbors, only 2.8 percent of the regulars gave a similar response (significant at .05 level).

The results bearing on relational networks raise an intriguing question: Are these differential patterns a result of affiliation with Spiritualism or are persons who tend to interact with "nobody" other than their immediate families more prone to experience biomedically untreatable afflictions, which in turn lead to Spiritualist treatment and a diagnosis of being "troubled spiritually"?

In the words of one man, a regular, "I feel most alone when I am with people." Although I could not assess the regulars' behavior in dealing with others before they became Spiritualists, my observations of them suggest that they interact relatively infrequently even among themselves outside the temple. The fact that regulars reside in numerous villages dispersed over a thirty mile radius is no doubt a contributing factor, but there are other reasons for the lack of close interactions among regulars, which I will discuss later.

To conclude the comparison between regulars and the control group, a profile of a regular, using standard sociological variables, suggests that regulars tend to be persons who have had lengthy experience with wage-labor migration, limited interaction with immediate neighbors, and are probably not integrated into the national political structure through the land reform program.

HEALERS SOCIAL AND ECONOMIC STATUS

For those who become leaders of Spiritualist temples, membership in the movement opens the way for personal economic enhancement. In contrast for the majority of regulars, especially the healers, temple participation adversely affects both individual economic mobility and aggregate social change. Unlike physicians, Spiritualist healers are not accorded special privileges, prestige or status within Mexican society at large, within the communities in which they reside, or even within the temple hierarchy, despite their superior knowledge of healing and botanicals.[2]

That Spiritualist healers and other adherents lack social status in the society at large is, of course, not surprising. As we have seen from the sociological profile, by and large Spiritualists form part of Mexico's lower and marginal socioeconomic sector.

Moreover, as is noted by Lewis (1971) regarding similar types of groups elsewhere, Spiritualists' power to manipulate the spirits is considered threatening to the society at large, since those who can control the spirits for benevolent purposes might also do so for malevolent reasons. In light of Spiritualists' powers, physicians and clergy brand Spiritualist healers as sorcerers who must be avoided at all times.

With the exception of the temple head (Finkler 1981b), Spiritualist healers also fail to attain high status and prestige within the community of patients whom they serve and in the Spiritualists hierarchy itself. That they lack prestige and status within Spiritualism itself relates to Spiritualists' view of themselves: they regard the healing role as an adjunct to their religious role. Consequently, Spiritualism accords highest prestige to the functionaries who irradiate God's word, rather then to healers.

Curiously, Spiritualist healers fail to gain special status or prestige in their own communities or among their own clientele, as is frequently the case elsewhere (e.g., Fabrega & Silver 1973), because of a paradox intrinsic to Spiritualism. Ironically, in order to gain legitimacy, Spiritualist healers must disclaim their accomplishments as healers. As we saw earlier, their legitimacy emanates from their alleged abilities to summon spirit protectors during an altered state of consciousness. In order to reinforce this ideology, the healers incessantly stress to everyone that any healing powers they possess flow from their protectors, not from them. In fact, healers dissociate themselves completely from the spirit protectors during normal consciousness to the extent that some even repudiate any knowledge of curing or medicinal plants. To cite a significant example, I attempted to query four healers about specific medicinal properties, preparations, and uses of plants. During informal interactions, at meals, and on other occasions, healers delighted in instructing me about all aspects of illness and its remedies. But when I asked each individually for more formal instructions on these subjects, two healers, including Mariana, the temple head, disclaimed any knowledge of the materia medica or cures, on the grounds that their powers and knowledge stem from spirit protectors, they claimed total ignorance of such matters during a normal waking state. By so doing, these healers seem to strive to maintain a logical consistency but they also deny themselves any possibility of attaining prestige in their communities.

Nor is Spiritualism a vehicle for economic mobility for most regulars (Finkler 1981b). Healers are, in fact, even penalized economically more than other functionaries because they, unlike irradiators, must usually devote at least two days a week to treating patients at the temple. The frequency with which healers and regulars participate in temple rituals depends upon their home situation and on the temple head's talents for managing positive social relations with the membership. Some functionaries cease attending because of dissension with the temple head; others do so because of expanded obligations at home--such as a newborn child or increased economic pressure--which may leave them less time for temple rituals. As a matter of fact, healers are placed under extraordinary pressure at home because women healers must also fulfill their household chores, and by serving as healers in the temple both men and women are forclosed from engaging in economic activities.

Unlike curers elsewhere (e.g. Fabrega and Silver 1973; Metzger and Williams 1963), Spiritualist healers are permitted to work only at the temple; nonetheless, they are not remunerated for their services. The fact that participation in temple activities removes individuals from economic pursuits and even requires considerable expenditure of time and money for travel and incidental expenses away from home is especially significant within a theoretical context of social and economic change.

Scholars have proposed that membership in minority religious groups often abets economic mobility (e.g., Garrison 1974; Macklin 1974a; Roberts 1968). Spiritualism confronts us, however, with an intriguing paradox. While the role change restores patients to behavioral effectiveness and functioning to day-to-day routines, simultaneously it tends to inhibit their economic advancement owing to their dependence upon temple participation. Consider, for example, the case of Chucha and her husband, who neglected to attend to their market stall. The husband frequently remarked on how his income had decreased as a result of his and his wife's activities at the temple. Or Jaime, who remains in his village (which he had left at one time because of a lack of economic opportunities) in order to continue participating in the temple.

Some curers are supported by their husbands and are not engaged in financially remunerative enterprises. But others who must support themselves, women as well as men, lose potential income on the days they work as healers. While healers recognize the financial loss, they also acknowledge that by ministering to others they minister to themselves. In fact, many claim that when they are absent from the temple and fail to carry out their assigned tasks, they suffer from pain in the *cerebro* and feel anxious and distressed, consequences which, according to them, result from failure to fulfill their obligations to God. Not only does this serve as an example of a point made earlier, that temple healing techniques are inherently anxiety provoking, but it also demonstrates how by becoming a regular--i.e., by becoming riveted to the temple--the patient becomes anchored in a socioeconomic status quo. Thus, participation in Spiritualism limits rather than promotes socioeconomic mobility.

Moreover, maintenance of the status quo is reinforced by Spiritualist teachings during irradiations; e.g., God explains to His children that he chooses not to improve the lot of regulars because they would abandon Him. Hence, on the one hand, the movement is adaptive by assisting individuals to recuperate from their affliction, but, on the other hand, it tends to lock participants into their current social class. The exception to this is the regular who becomes a temple head; for her the movement affords a modicum of economic mobility.

Similarly paradoxical are the facts that on an individual level of experience Spiritualism restores one and gives one healing powers, whereas on the level of the society as a whole Spiritualism is maladaptive, in that it tends to lock in its participants economically and politically. Viewed within a societal framework, the social outcome of Spiritualist wellness is a social-structural status quo.[3]

I contend that the special emphasis placed by Spiritualists on individual interaction with the world of the spirits--an emphasis fostered by trancing--militates against any kind of social activism or or political mobilization. Owing to the very nature of its rituals, in fact, Spiritualism is not conducive to generating social interaction. In particular, trancing requires each individual to turn inward. Interaction is therefore vertical, between the human being and the supernatural, rather than horizontal, between person and person. This phenomenon accounts in large measure for the lack of communal cohesion among Spiritualists, which precludes any possibility of their becoming a political force (cf. Worsley 1968), which would enable them to act in unison on behalf of the extant social wrongs that they themselves perceive and suffer.

Secondarily, Spiritualism's nationalistic cast and the Spiritualist teachings included in the twenty-two commandments enjoin members from participating in civil wars. Injunctions against "brothers raising arms against brothers" promote the sociopolitical status quo. In sum, although regulars may attain power by transforming persons into God, they fail to attain political power or deal with class conflict on this earth.

Viewed clinically, regulars regain their abilities to function satisfactorily by rebuilding their lives after an episode of affliction. Spiritualist healing techniques and premises provide them with a sense of dignity they previously lacked. Regarded from a social-structural perspective, however, regulars have little to look forward to but the promise of a mansion in heaven made for them by their God during irradiations.

11. CONCLUSION

The two interrelated tasks of this book have been (1) to demonstrate the ways in which an alternative healing system succeeds and fails to heal, as perceived by its patients, and in which one rural segment of a complex society expresses and manages illness, and (2) to describe the interaction between a therapeutic regime and the historical, social, and economic forces of the larger society of which it is a part. I have identified the people's recovery requisites, explored the beliefs and practices of an important alternative health-care delivery system in contemporary Mexico, and have analyzed its impact on the clientele within a personal and societal framework. I have unveiled a folk Mexican cognitive model of recovery, which I postulate is rooted in the history of its bearers and is fostered by current ecological conditions.

In support of my first objective, I presented a corpus of empirical data, the kind still lacking in the medical anthropological literature, that identifies Spiritualist therapeutic results as perceived by the patients. Here we saw that religious healing is not a miraculous cure, as it is regarded by believers, nor is it a hoax or sham as it is viewed by many medical practitioners. We witness instead its limitations and its strengths. It is limited in much the same way as prescientific medicine was limited prior to the discovery of pharmaceutical agents capable of radically eradicating the causes of a series of diseases, and as medicine still is limited vis-a-vis numerous dysfunctions.

Spiritualist healers' strengths lie in providing symbolic treatments. Patients respond differentially to these treatments, to be sure; but biomedicine fails altogether to offer them.

Biomedicine's symbols are not readily transferable to other cultures and so fail to meet recovery requisites cross-culturally.

Therapeutic regimes, including biomedicine, are products of a given cultural system (Kleinman 1980). They and their accompanying symbols are molded by the ecology and the sociocultural and historical forces in which they are embedded. Contemporary biomedicine with its scientific substrate is an outgrowth of Western culture and like science itself is a Western cultural phenomenon (Freidson 1970; cf. Ricther 1972). Yet despite its specific cultural underpinnings, it aims at universal applicability. Science, like biomedicine, purports to be inherently noncultural; its intrinsic validity rests upon its transcendence of spatial and temporal boundaries.

Paradoxically, however, owing to the cultural nature of both illness and recovery requisites, the intrinsic strength of biomedicine is also its weakness when it is applied clinically outside the cultural milieu from which it sprang. In much the same way that science cannot be changed without changing itself (Weinberg 1974), biomedicine cannot be changed to meet specific cultural requisites without changing itself.

Physicians everywhere are trained to share similar assumptions about disease and methods of treatment that support their claim to a universalistic science. As a result, physicians are expected to follow the same methods cross-culturally, but their patients' responses to treatment vary culturally and even within the same culture.

Radical biomedical cures using pharmaceutical agents that speedily mitigate diseases are accepted throughout the world, but when biomedical symbolic techniques are utilized in nontechnological sociocultural settings, they fail to produce the desired effects because they lack the appropriate cultural therapeutic recovery symbols. As I noted earlier, modern technology serves as a healing symbol for patients reared in industrial societies where life is governed and managed by technology. In fact, the task still remains to identify the numerous symbolic aspects of biomedical practice. But, patients from developing societies such as Mexico are not accustomed to these technologies nor to the institutional structures and cognitive orientations which flow from them and by which they are confronted in the biomedical system. The exceptions in Mexico, as elsewhere, are those in the upper classes who have been enculturated into the industrialized cognitive orientation (cf. Berger, et al. 1974) and to which members of industrialized societies are heir. It is therefore not surprising that medicine based upon modern technology is, generally speaking, widely accepted in industrialized societies and the industrial sectors of developing nations irrespective of its intrinsic efficacy; the same technology may lack symbolic meaning for people who have not been exposed to machines of any kind. In contrast, pills and injections are not threatening and when they produce a speedy recovery they are accepted by patients.

As I noted by and large, Mexicans seek treatment from Spiritualist healers in prolonged illness episodes that biomedicine has failed to cure. Then they attempt to do something about the condition, unmanageable by physicians, by seeking healing symbols meaningful to them.

In the rural region of Mexico prolonged illness is perpetuated to a great extent by exogenous circumstances including adverse ecological and socioeconomic conditions. The ecological environment fosters an overall poor state of health and a high rate of infant mortality which in turn may contribute to depressive disorders and somatized conditions. Along with the adverse ecological and socioeconomic environment found in most third world countries, modern medicine also contributes to prolonged illness states. Rural Mexicans are cognizant of this; they always say that physicians give them only palliatives and do not cure their conditions. Hence, I contend that, along with exogenous circumstances, paradoxically, continuous expansion of biomedicine serves to promote nonbiomedical therapeutics of the Spiritualist kind which deals symbolically with their disease.

In sum, I argue that in an alien setting medicine's symbolic cures applied to patients with syndromes not readily amenable to speedy recovery are frequently rejected in favor of culturally specific recovery symbols and hence traditional healers flourish. Biomedical symbols lack efficacy outside their own environment--Western industrial society--because illness must be resolved by culturally significant symbols, which flow from common historically shared cultural experiences. Thus, if a real cure cannot be effected by removing the cause of the illness then symbolic cures spawned in one's own cultural milieu are preferred.

Based upon this type of analysis, I predict that Spiritualist healing will continue to grow, contingent upon adverse exogenous conditions and biomedicine's success in sustaining people's lives without curing them, that is, without eliminating the causes of their dysfunctions.

This, of course, suggests that nonbiomedical systems of the Spiritualist variety complement rather than compete with biomedicine. In point of fact, the type of data I present enables us to begin to identify specific symptoms and syndromes most amenable to biomedical technological management, to symbolic ministration, or to both. With these sorts of findings, medical anthropology can address theoretical and clinically applied issues. To illustrate, my findings lead me to contend that the complementary relationship between the two modalities could be institutionalized to the benefit of both patients and health practitioners. Both physicians and Spiritualist healers could as a matter of course refer a patient for appropriate treatment, depending on the syndrome and based on an understanding of the patient's cultural requisites for recovery. While some have advocated that nonbiomedical practitioners should be brought into a medical setting, I argue, as other have done (Kleinman 1980; Leininger 1979; Lock 1980), that physicians and nurses must learn the cultural realities of health and illness, rather than attempt to bring in nonbiomedical healers under the medical canopy. In much the same way that scientific medicine is difficult to transplant to alien environments, nonbiomedical systems brought under the aegis of biomedicine would be faced with the same difficulties. As Lock (1980) astutely points out, when acupuncture is practiced in the West, it fails to possess the same meaning and effect as it enjoys in Asia.

It is, therefore, important for physicians and nurses to realize the limitations of biomedicine and to refer patients to appropriate nonbiomedical practitioners when biomedicine fails to meet culturally specific cognitive models of illness resolution. By the same token, Spiritualist healers need to recognize, as some already do, the limitations of their healing techniques and ministrations and to refer patients to physicians accordingly.

It has frequently been asserted that folk practitioners are patronized because physicians lack compassion, understanding, or an appropriate healing personality. Although these attributes are, no doubt, important for therapy, they may have been overstated with reference to nonbiomedical practitioners. The Spiritualist materials suggest that Spiritualist techniques coupled with patients' capacities to respond to Spiritualist symbols, influence treatment outcomes more than do healers' personal styles.

The emphasis placed on the role of the health practitioner's personality and expressions of concern for patients may reflect the modern industrial person's yearning for personalistic affective ties (cf. Berger et al. 1974) and for compassion for suffering in an impersonal industrial world. Consider, for example, Horton's (1973) suggestion that the scientific world view gave rise to the conviction "... that science and technology are destroying the fabric of society..." and "With this have come various movements assuming an antagonism between reason and feeling, and vociferously exalting the latter at the expense of the former" (p. 298). concomitantly "... the romantic search for a 'lost world' has given rise to an image of traditional culture which can be understood entirely as a reaction to the stresses and strains in the modern West" (ibid p. 293). Perhaps members of traditional and modernizing societies are more pragmatic in this regard when they must spend their meager means for health maintenance. I was struck by the fact that the sole criterion for judging a health practitioner in rural Mexico was whether he dispensed "good medicine." Be they physicians or medicine hucksters, both were judged by the same yardstick: whether they provided treatment instrumental in the patient's recovery.

In the last analysis, I am convinced that the significance of Spiritualist healers, like that of practitioners elsewhere,[1] rests on their success in ministering to patients with chronic pain in a way that biomedicine cannot match because the latter lacks emotionally charged symbols derived from the sufferers' collective experience. Symbols of this sort attenuate, if they do not eliminate, sufferers' pain and help to make their lives tolerable in a meaningful way within the context of the culture.

Research has just begun to demonstrate the ways in which culturally meaningful symbolic ministrations may alleviate pain physiologically and biochemically, opening new approaches in medical anthropology (cf. Prince 1982). Within a wider perspective, I conclude, therefore, that illness resolution requires not only technical but also symbolic regulation. In fact, I would assert that symbolically mediated recovery requisites belong to a category of invariant human universals (cf. Berger & Luckmann 1967) fundamentally embedded in the human evolutionary adaptive strategy. The symbolic content for managing illness remains, however, an empirical question. We have seen that purification procedures are meaningful to Mexican patients, although I suspect that purification is equally important in healing in other cultures.

Purification procedures symbolize a renewal of order. Relevant to the Mexican context, I postulate that the symbolic concern nurtures a cultural imperative for the restoration of order created by the inherent disorder of an illness experience. The cultural imperatives on a personal level of experience interlock with the societal experience. In the Mexican case a societal disorder dates back to the Conquest period.

I have dealt with two other important issues relevant to the role of symbols as they relate to affliction. First, I raised the question of the proportionate power of symbols by exploring whether all members of a given social segment share the same symbols equally. As we have seen, not all healing symbols are shared until human beings become exposed to similar serious or chronic illness states. In the region of Mexico under study, such states are often promoted by adverse ecological conditions and other exogenous factors. This brings into view the ways in which ecological factors contribute to shaping shared symbolic requisites for recovery.

While anthropologists have long recognized the interaction between ecology and the symbolic universe (cf. Rappaport 1979), this paradigm has not been sufficiently explored in relation to health-care phenomena. We saw how the ecology and life circumstances in the region promote ongoing illness states that biomedicine fails to alleviate.

Second, in the same way as symbols are not always shared, we have seen that not all persons have an equal capacity to respond to culturally produced symbols. Patients lacking this capability are unresponsive to Spiritualist cures. Hence we encounter cases of persons who fail to respond to cultural symbols, suggesting that recovery is as much dependent on the patient and the individual syndrome as on the therapeutic regime used. Scholars have observed that successful illness resolution by psychotherapy similarly depends on patients' personality more than on the specific psychotherapeutic techniques. A similar conclusion must be reached when we compare psychotherapy with Spiritualist healing.

Moving to my second objective, studies of biomedicine usually lack a historical or societal framework. Yet health delivery must be examined from this broader perspective as well. Historical paradigms must be brought to bear on health-care delivery systems because they illuminate the sociocultural factors that bring about a given health-care delivery establishment. For instance, we have seen that an exploration of Spiritualist history reveals that Spiritualist temples in their role as health providers owe their presence in Mexico to the development of Spiritualism as a dissident religious movement. Spiritualism emerged in Mexico in response to the development of industrialization accompanied by a more fluid social structure than before, one that brought together in church individuals who otherwise would have been kept apart in sacred places. In addition, viewed from a diachronic perspective, we saw how historical phenomena became transferred and encoded into symbolic requisites relevant to recovery as they do in other forms of cultural expression.[2]

I also examined the social aspects of wellness, the resultant effects of therapeutic practices on the larger social structure. I conclude that, from the perspective of the society at large, restoring patients to health by Spiritualist techniques removes people from active social participation. In fact, it anchors them in an organization that fosters perpetuation of social arrangements that circumscribe rather than open avenues for social mobility.

The social consequences of a therapeutic regime take on various expressions and are not confined, of course, to the Spiritualist mode alone. These are observable in other societies as well. Consider, for example, psychotherapy and its attendant goals. As we have seen, the latter aims at promoting individual autonomy in its clients, its major goal being to foster patients' autonomy and independence of family and groups and thereby to enable them to make more rational choices. With this program the patient is in fact being better prepared to behave rationally, conforming to the demands of a modern society. Psychotherapy aims also to help the individual but lays stress on the patient's achieving self-control at all times. By emphasizing self-control, psychotherapy advances the interests of a democratic government by relieving the state of having to impose physical coercion on its citizens, who can just as well control themselves.[3]

Spiritualism controls its adherents on behalf of the wider society by emphasizing an inward perspective through trance and ritual (a personally pleasurable state), leaving the important social issues to be managed by politicians who do not always act in the interests of the social segments from which Spiritualists largely emerge. With few exceptions (e.g., Laurell et al. 1977; Navarro 1976; Taussig 1980), broader considerations of this type are not addressed by social scientists concerned with medical phenomena. Yet it is only by taking a multifaceted approach to therapeutic regimes and their attendant techniques, as I have done, that we will comprehend the numerous components that comprise illness, health, and health restoration.

One final point: indirectly, I have called attention to the fundamental question whether human illness lends itself to scientific analyses using quantitative methodologies. My research strategy encompassed quantitative methods in an attempt to identify behavioral regularities, but the limitations of this methodology quickly became apparent. In fact, quantification proved to be inadequate when dealing with basic existential dilemmas relating to affliction and its resolution. Experiential phenomena related to illness are not readily measurable or quantifiable; they can only be identified and assessed by probing into subjective perceptions of the human condition. Paradoxically, then, use of quantitative methodology in this study has led me to advance a phenomenological perspective in order that we may attain a multidimensional understanding of human health and illness. It is to this end that this study contributes.

APPENDICES

APPENDIX A METHODOLOGIES USED IN THE STUDY

I gathered the data using several techniques including participant observation, directed and open-ended interviews, life histories, the 82-item socioeconomic interview schedule, and the CMI questionnaire in consultation with local physicians. In addition, I made use of the last available census data (1970) and epidemiological materials for the region made available to me by the Ministry of Health in Mexico City. For comparative purposes I collected materials at the various sites cited earlier. The quantitative results reported here are based upon all these sources with the exception of four government health centers. The procedure for data collection in the temple involved myself as participant and observer and two interviewers who were instructed to interview every fifth person entering the temple to see a curer. Individuals who came to the temple for consultation or advice about a problem of living were not included in this phase of the study.

DATA COLLECTION TECHNIQUES

Interviews were conducted on Tuesdays and Fridays, the two principal curing days in Spiritualist temples. While the interviewers were administering the questionnaires at the entrance of the temple, I sat in the curing room recording the number of patients that arrived there on any given curing day, and in my role as apprentice I assisted the curers in the various ways I noted in Chapter 1. As I wrote prescriptions, I also timed and recorded the verbal exchanges between patients and healer, including the patients' complaints and the healer's prescription. During the interview phase of the study, I recorded 1212 complaints and prescriptions and the interviewers interviewed 410 patients.

Of those 410 subjects interviewed, 125 were selected for follow-up study. Selection was done on a geographic basis: all subjects who resided within a twenty-five mile radius of Juarez were chosen for follow-up visits in their homes (this area encompassed forty separate village communities). Two home visits were made to every subject thus selected, once 7-13 days after the initial interview at the temple, and again 30-45 days after the first follow-up home visit. However, if two attempts to contact the patient failed, that patient was dropped from the roster of individuals selected for intensive study. Measures of successful outcome along with attribution for recovery were established by using the CMI and patients' verbatim reports of beneficial effects with respect to the alleviation of specific symptoms for which treatment was sought and patients' expressed satisfaction with the treatment. Treatment outcome was assessed in two ways during two separate follow-up visits to the patient's home: by readministering the CMI questionnaire and by directed interviews and open-ended discussion.

The first follow-up home visit, which lasted on the average 2 1/2 to 3 hours, usually began with my assistant reading to the subject those CMI questions to which the subject had responded with a "yes" at the initial interview at the temple. The purpose of this procedure was twofold: (1) to establish whether there had been any change in symptoms since the initial interview at the temple; (2) to explore in detail how the subject dealt with a given symptom reported on the CMI both in the past and in the present. The CMI proved to be a useful tool for eliciting illness histories and the ways in which subjects managed separate illness episodes. Subjects who indicated that they had sought medical treatment for a particular symptom or condition were asked about the medical diagnosis. In addition, patients were asked what types of treatments they had sought or administered during the period between the initial interview and the first follow-up; in the event that there was a change in response between the first and second CMI, patients were asked how they explained the changes as well as to what they attributed the disappearance of the particular symptom. Patients were also questioned about any new symptoms or behavioral changes they had been experiencing since the initial interview. Other areas were covered as well, including the onset and course of the disorder, length of illness, and the patient's life history with focus on marriage, children, economic circumstances, work, and migration.

The second follow-up home visit consisted of open-ended exploration with the patient of his or her current condition and the type of treatment, if any, that the patient had sought between the first and second interview. With the permission of subjects, all follow-up interviews and discussion were tape-recorded. The tapes were transcribed verbatim. The data presented in Tables 8.2 and 8.4 represent verbatim translations of patients' reports. Because of missing data on some of the questionnaires 389 cases out of the 410 were used in the quantitative analyses.

Interviews at the doctor's office were done by a personally trained doctor's lay assistant. Patients were usually interviewed prior to consultation with the doctor. After the consultation, the doctor provided his diagnosis on the CMI protocol for each patient who had been interviewed (displayed in Table 6.4). One hundred and ninety patients were interviewed at the physician's office, but because of missing data on some of the questionnaires the computer analysis is based upon 156 subjects.

The control group (N = 372) was geographically matched with subjects interviewed in the temple corresponding to the villages from which patients interviewed at the temple originated. Interviewers were instructed to select every tenth household in a village. Before the interview was initiated, respondents were screened on the basis of prior contact with a Spiritualist temple and current health state. Nineteen subjects' households from the control group were then selected for more intensive studies. I visited these famillies in their homes and obtained life histories including past illness experiences for purposes of comparison with twenty-one similar histories of Spiritualist adherents. In addition, as I noted earlier, I participated in all religious and healing rituals, including healer training sessions. The latter experience called my attention to the possible physiological underpinnings of trance induction during training and irradiation sessions, presented in Chapter 9.

To test my hypothesis regarding male adherents whom I perceived as being less "macho" than nonadherents, I selected nonadherent informants--five men and five women--and asked them to list at least five characteristics identifying a "macho" male. Using these characteristics, I attempted to match them with what I knew about male adherents, as well as to question Spiritualist adherents about their perceptions of "macho" males. These findings are discussed in Chapter 10.

THE QUANTITATIVE ANALYSES

The socioeconomic schedule solicited a wide variety of data bearing on family structure, household composition, occupation, social networks, religious affiliation, nature of previous illness episodes and related treatment-seeking behavior, decision-making process in the household bearing on illness management, and other variables.

The Cornell Medical Index necessitates some discussion. While other instruments were also considered, the CMI has considerable advantages, as has been noted by others (Ness 1980), including the fact that it is relatively brief and easy to administer in comparison with other instruments. It is a questionnaire containing 195 items. Subjects are required to supply a "yes-or-no" answer to a broad range of questions related to all body organ systems as well as to emotional difficulties; but the CMI has its difficulties as an objective measure of illness, especially in a foreign setting.

By and large, there are extensive problems related to using questionnaires cross-culturally (see Brislin et al. 1973). Perhaps their greatest limitation is due to the fact that the target subjects are not accustomed to responding to questionnaires even when the questionnaires are administered orally, as was done in this study. Some (e.g., Gostkowski 1964) have rightly argued that questionnaires are a cultural product of industrially developed nations where populations are constantly exposed to them, unlike in the nonindustrialized or developing countries. Despite such reservations, the questionnaire has been widely used not only in the United States but also cross-culturally (Abramson 1966; Cassel & Tyroler 1961; Chance 1962; Croog 1961; Garrison 1977; Kalimo et al. 1970; Morsy 1978; Ness 1977, 1980; Scotch & Geiger 1963; Suchman & Phillips 1958). It has been found valid for measuring perceived health status (Garrison 1977; Suchman & Phillips 1958) and as a good indicator of emotional disturbance (Kalimo et al. 1970). Significantly, Scotch and Geiger (1963) also found it a valid predictor of morbidity among Zulus, and others have established a positive correlation between the medical and psychiatric symptoms queried on the CMI (Matarazzo et al. 1961).

The questionnaire is divided into two sections related to physical and emotional symptoms. The physical section is comprised of 12 subsections totaling 145 questions. The remaining 50 questions are divided into six subsections relating to emotional disturbance. According to Brodman et al. (1952), when more than 25 items on the entire questionnaire are answered "yes" it suggests some overall serious disorders. Emotional disturbances are suspected when 30 or more "yes" responses are given on the entire questionnaire. Inasmuch as 25 and 30 item baselines were established for an American sample population, it cannot be readily applied to the Mexican case. In the absence of an available baseline for the Mexican population, I used the mean item baseline obtained from the control group of 51 "yes" responses as equivalent to the 30 item baseline established by Brodman, et al. (1952).

The CMI as well as the specially designed socioeconomic schedule containing a section on the individual's illness history and type of health care sought for each illness episode were pretested on ten individuals and then administered verbally to the subjects, taking approximately two hours. As a result of the pretests, the Spanish version of the CMI was altered to conform to

Mexican standard usage and eight of the 195 CMI questions were eliminated because they were deemed inappropriate. For example, question 151 "Do you have difficulty doing exercise every day?" Inasmuch as the population studied is predominantly rural, and given the living conditions under which most subjects exist, the pretest group considered that people's daily tasks were sufficiently arduous; or question 143: "Do you drink more than six cups of coffee or tea a day?" In this region coffee is drunk only in the mornings and rarely, if ever, at any other times. Teas are usually drunk as remedies rather than as table beverages. Questions 001, 002, 140, 170, 171 were similarly judged inappropriate.

When the subject selected for interview turned out to be an infant or a child under 12 years of age, only 35 out of the 187 CMI questions and the socioeconomic schedule were asked of the child's mother. The 35 CMI questions were selected on the basis of which questions the mother could answer for her child. A zero order correlation coefficient was computed between the adult scores for 152 questions and the children's scores for the 35 questions and was found to be .87. In view of the high correlation between the adults' and children's scores, it can be concluded that the 35 questions asked of the children were in fact a representative subsample from the total CMI. Therefore, for purposes of analysis of the data displayed in Table 8.3 and, where both children and adults were included, each question asked of the children was weighted by 5.3 points, the ratio of 187/35.

For purposes of assessing the CMI's validity as a research instrument in Mexico, several types of analyses were done using the two data sets: (1) the entire sample of sick individuals, including those who were interviewed at the two temples, at the physician's office, and at four health centers (n = 768); (2) the control group of ostensibly healthy individuals who were interviewed at home.

Turning to the computed results yielded by the CMI: first, based upon these sample populations, the CMI discriminates between the sick population and the control group at the .001 level of significance, using analysis of variance, with individuals at the various health delivery sites yielding a mean CMI score of 61 as compared with the control group's mean score of 51.

Second, the physical and psychological sections of the CMI correlate positively (significant at .001 level), supporting the findings by others (Hinkle et al. 1957; Matarazzo et al. 1961; Ness 1980) that physical and psychological disorders are highly intercorrelated. This is important within the context of this study because the subject population tended to yield high scores on both the psychological and physiological sections of the questionnaire, supporting the assumption that we are dealing with a population suffering from overall bodily malfunctions owing to the various extant ecological and social conditions.

Third, the mean scores on individual subsections of the CMI correspond significantly with patients' stated complaints. In our sample, the most commonly stated complaints involve the digestive tract and respiratory, cardiovascular, and musculoskeletal systems.

Analysis of variance was employed to relate respondents' stated complaints and mean scores for each of the eighteen subsections on the CMI. Those subjects who stated they had come to treat a cardiovascular impairment also scored highest (significant at the .001 level) on Section C of the questionnaire, which corresponds to the cardiovascular system. Similar analyses were performed for the other three categories and the findings were equally significant at the .001 level for patients reporting gastrointestinal dysfunctions and their CMI scores on Section D, the digestive tract; and patients complaining of respiratory-related malfunctions also scored highest on Section B pertaining to the respiratory organ system. However, CMI scores on Section E, musculoskeletal system failed to correspond at a statistically significant level to respondents' stated complaints of musculoskeletal disorders. This may be due to the diffuse nature of mus-culoskeletal dysfunctions, in contrast to the greater symptom specificity associated with the other three types of impairments. These data tend to reveal a consistency (Ness 1977) between patients' stated complaints and systematized symptom inventory elicited by the instrument (Kalimo et al. 1970), thereby adding a degree of confidence in the ability of the CMI to yield a systematic measure of self-perceived symptoms within the Mexican setting.

It is noteworthy that comparison between the physician's diagnosis and CMI scores failed to render any meaningful correspondence between the two. This result substantiates the well-established fact that the biomedical model of pathology usually fails to correspond to patients' self-perceived illness (Fabrega 1974; Freidson 1970; Kleinman 1980; Trussel et al. 1956). For this reason too, the CMI protocols fail to reveal the severity of a given disease (Abramson 1966; Scotch & Geiger 1963) in biomedical terms. For further discussion of CMI, see Finkler (1981B).

But while the instrument may fail to pinpoint patients' diseases, it does call attention to the prevalence of self-perceived symptoms within a given region and as such is of epidemiological import (cf. Abramson 1966; Fabrega 1974). Moreover, the highest frequencies of symptoms reported on the CMI (i.e. digestive, respiratory, cardiovascular) tend to correspond to the available epidemiological data reported in Appendix D.

Elsewhere (Finkler 1981B) I explore in great detail the association between socio-economic variables and the CMI in the two sample groups using analysis of variance and regressions. Briefly summarizing the results, analysis of variance calls attention to the following variables influencing significantly CMI scores; years of schooling, age, sex, relational networks, occupation, type of land holding (*ejido* (public) or private), place of residence (village, municipal town, or urban center), and family structure. The variables that do not affect significantly CMI scores are literacy, marriage, number of children in school, land ownership of any kind, migration, number of adults - male or female - in the household, length of employment, length of absence from natal town, religious preference and several variables linked to illness behavior. But while the analysis of variance points to several important variables affecting CMI scores, multiple regression analysis computed for the sick and for the control groups indicate that years of schooling followed by age of subjects affect the sick population's CMI scores on the physical sections, whereas years of schooling alone influence their emotional disturbance scores. The multiple regression results for the control sample reveals that education alone influences responses on the physical section, and both years of schooling and sex influence the emotional disturbance scores. Not unexpectedly, whereas in the sick population age overrides sex, in the healthy group sex predominates over age.

Importantly, the Multiple R's for the two groups are relatively low (0.407 sick group; 0.300 control group) and thereby explain in all cases less than 20 percent of the variation in the CMI scores. This implies that factors other than the postulated standard socioeconomic variables are at play, possibly attributable to experiential, endogenous and exogenous factors, including, of course, the ecological conditions discussed in Chapter 3.

Nevertheless, the fact that the Multiple R is greater for the sick group than for the controls indicates that exogenous factors such as education also play a role in promoting symptomatic expression (see Finkler 1981b).

Tentatively, then, we may conclude (1) that the CMI tends to furnish a relatively accurate profile of the predominate health problems in a Mexican rural setting; (2) that it is a valuable tool for pinpointing the expression of self-perceived symptoms in a given ecological and cultural enclave; and (3) that it tends to identify exogenous variables that may influence illness states.

APPENDIX B

Regional Plants Used by Spiritualist Healers

BOTANICAL NAME	FAMILY	SPANISH NAME	ENGLISH NAME	LOCAL USAGE	CHEMICAL ANALYSIS*	USAGES IN OTHER CULTURES
Acacia shaffneri	Leguminosae	Huizache	Acacia	Diabetes; hydropsy		
Acalypha langiana	Euphorbiaceae	Yerba de cancer	Copperleaf	Incipient cancer; cancer; internal hemorrhage; wounds fever		
Agastache mexicana	Labiatae	Toronjil	Balm	Susto		
Agave sp.	Agavaceae	Maguey pinto	Agave	Sprains; bronchitis; tumors; inflammation of kidneys		Aztecs dissolved leaves in water, used as enema against dysentery (Vogel, p. 185)
Aloe vera L.	Liliaceae	Savila	Aloe	Fever; hemorrhoids; ulcers; kidneys and liver pain; internal wound; kidney inflammation	Anthraquinones, anthranols, anthrones, and their glycosides (beneficial for healing of skin) chrysophanic acid (beneficial for healing of skin) (Lewis, p. 337)	Purgative (Lewis, p. 283)
Aloysia triphylla	Verbenaceae	Cedron	Lemon verbena	Stomach pain; para-		
Ambrosia artemisiaefolia L.	Asteraceae	Caballo	Ragweed	Kidney pain; massage; rheumatism; bilis	Lactones (many sesquiterpenes); causes contact dermatitis (Lewis, p. 84); most allergenic pollen in N.A. (Lewis, p. 68)	

BOTANICAL NAME	FAMILY	SPANISH NAME	ENGLISH NAME	LOCAL USAGE	CHEMICAL ANALYSIS	USAGES IN OTHER CULTURES
Apium graveolens L.	Umbelliferae	Apio	Celery	Embolism; liver pain; varicose veins	Terpenes, limonene-causing contact dermatitis (Lewis, p. 82); experimental hypoglycemic activity (Lewis, p. 218)	Insulin substitute (Lewis, p. 218)
Aporocactus flagelliformis L.	Lem.	Flor de junco	Rattail cactus	Heart problems; cough; susto (flower)		
Argemone ochroleuca	Papaveraceae	Chicalote (vindri)	Prickly poppy	Cataracts; gall-bladder pain; cough; liver pain; eye irritation	Argemone mexicana toxic alkaloids; sanguinarine; berberine; protopine (Lewis, pp. 31-32)	Comanches used a decoction for the treatment of sore eyes (Lewis, p. 224)
Artemisia af. absinthium L.	Compositae	Ajenjo	Wormwood	Diarrhea; bilis; stomach pain; high blood pressure; diabetes	Artemisia mexicana (deMontellano, 1976, Table V) santonin	Aztecs vomit (deMontellano) (Table V, 1976)
Bougainvillia spectabilis	Nyctaginaceae	Bugambilia	Bougainvillaea	Cough		
Bouvardia ternifolia	Rubiaceae	Trompetilla		Susto; tranquilizer; heart pain	Family - glycosides (some toxic); sinigrin[+][o]	
Brassica campestris L.	Brassicaceae	Nabo	Mustard	Blurred vision; liver dysfunction; bilis	Glycosides (some toxic) (Lewis, p. 20); sinigrin-harmless if dried, but can be converted into an irritant mustard oil in the presence of water (Lewis, p. 79)	
Brickellia veronicaefolia	Asteraceae	Pesto	Brickellia	Wounds; stomach pain; bilis; children's diarrhea and stomach problems		Family-some plant parts chewed and act as local anesthetic (Lewis, p. 248)[+]

BOTANICAL NAME	FAMILY	SPANISH NAME	ENGLISH NAME	LOCAL USAGE	CHEMICAL ANALYSIS	USAGES IN OTHER CULTURES
Buddleia cordata	Loganiaceae	Tepozan		Wounds; chills; for the mother during child-birth		Diuretic (Lewis, p. 313) healing agent for wounds (Lewis, p. 342)
Buddleia marrubiifolia	Loganiaceae	Escobilla		Stomach pain		
Calendula officinalis L.	Asteraceae	Mercadela	Calendula	Washing inside of cheeks; throat infec-tion; tonsillitis	NN-dimethylhista-mine°	
Casimiroa edulis	Rutaceae	Zapote blanco	Kel apple	High blood pressure; nerves; to become stronger		
Chenopodium album L.	Chenopodiaceae	Ediondia	Lamb's quarters	Skin eruptions	Family-angiosperm (Lewis, p. 69); one of the most impor-tant causes of allergy of weeds (Lewis, p. 71)†	Chenopodium graveolens; help asthmatics breathe, dysentery, anthel-mintic; (deMontellano, 1975, p. 215)
Chenopodium foetidum	Chenopodiaceae	Hipazote de zorlilo	Goose foot	Stomach pain; men-strual pain; colic; pain in joints	Chenopodium graveolens-ascaridole; p-cymene; l-limonene; mentha-diene†	
Chrysanthemum parthenium L.	Asteraceae	Santa Maria (artemisa)	Fever few	Baths; massages; cleansing; stomach pain		Dried flowers have been used in home remedies in Europe to induce abortion and to promote menstrua-tion (Lewis. p. 323)
Chicus rhaphilepsis	Asteraceae	Cardo santo	Blessed thistle	Cough, bronchitis; kid-neys and liver pain dysentery; diabetes; difficulty in urination		

BOTANICAL NAME	FAMILY	SPANISH NAME	ENGLISH NAME	LOCAL USAGE	CHEMICAL ANALYSIS	USAGES IN OTHER CULTURES
Commelina sp.	Commelinaceae	Pollo	Blue day flower	Diuretic		
Cuscuta sp.	Convolvulaceae	Fideo cimarron	Dodder	Children's difficulty in urination		
Cydonia oblonga	Rosaceae	Membrillo	Quince	Internal infection in children with suspicion of cancer (leaves)		
Datura metel L.	Solanaceae	Florifundio	Downy thorn apple	itch	Toxic: scopolamine, L-hyoscyamine (leaves, unripe capsules, and especially seeds) (Lewis, p. 54)	India-leaves smoked to relieve asthma (Lewis, p. 395)
Datura stramonium L.	Solanaceae	Toloache	Jimson weed	Sore throat; tonsillitis; itchy arms; hydropsy; hemorrhoids; inflammation of liver; massages; rheumatism; inflammations (leaves)	Toxic: atropine alkaloids; scopolamine, 0.3-0.6% atropine, L-hyoscine (Diaz, p. 84); small amounts of leaves and seeds can be fatal (Lewis, p. 54); lectins (including nitrogens) can induce killing of tumor cells (Lewis, p. 96); can modify a variety of physiological processes of lymphocytes in such a way that cytotoxicity is induced (Lewis, p. 99)	Leaves at one time widely smoked to relieve respiratory complaints (Lewis, p. 395); Aztecs-gout, chest pain, fever (deMontellano, 1975, p. 256)
Dichondra argenta	Convolvulaceae	Oreja de raton (colico)	Morning glory	Refreshment drink; hearing loss; kidney pain; children's colic		Purgative (Lewis, p. 281); hallucinogenic (Lewis, p. 397)†
Echeveria sp.	Crassulaceae	Oreja de burro		Massage for lungs; respiratory ailments		

BOTANICAL NAME	FAMILY	SPANISH NAME	ENGLISH NAME	LOCAL USAGE	CHEMICAL ANALYSIS	USAGES IN OTHER CULTURES
Eryobotrya japonica	Rosaceaea	Mispero	Loquat	Inflammation of liver; kidney pain	Toxic plant having cyanogenic glycosides (Lewis, p. 18)[†]	
Eucalyptus globulus	Myrtaceae	Alcanfor, eucalipto	Eucalyptus	Cough; bronchitis; low blood pressure; vapor for the house during a sore throat; cough, bronchitis (branch); cough, bronchitis; lung problems; kidney pain (leaves)	Oxide-cineole (eucalyptol) causes contact dermatitis (Lewis, p. 84)	Oxide volatile oils used for toothpaste flavoring (Lewis, p. 246)
Euphorbia prostrata	Euphorbiaceae	Golondrina	Spurges; Snow-on-the mountains	Kidney pain; colic	Complex esters (toxic) (Lewis, p. 37)	
Ficus carica L.	Moraceae	Higo	Fig	High blood pressure; nerves; to increase lactation; cough; stomach pain, diarrhea (leaves)	Provokes photodermatitis in man (Lewis, p. 81)[‡]	Ficus continifolia used by Indians of Mexico for treating wounds and bruises (Lewis, p. 342)[†]
Fraxinus udhei	Oleaceae	Fresno	Ash	Typhoid; fever; brushing teeth; purgative; pain in feet; bilis; susto; hearing loss	Aeroallergen-causes allergic rhinitis, bronchial asthma, and/or hypersensitivity pneumonitis (Lewis, p. 69)[†]	Bark used to treat hemorrhoids in 19th century (Lewis, p. 294); Fraxinus albus used by the Meskwakis for sores and itch (Lewis, p. 352)[†]
Gnaphalium sp.	Asteraceae	Estafiate	Larkspur	Stomach pain	Family-sesquiterpene lactones (cytotoxic) (Lewis, p. 56)[†]	Mexican-American empacho (Geffner & Sandler, 1980, p. 436)
Gnaphalium viscosum	Compositae	Gordolobo	Everlasting	Cough; lung impairment; kidney pain		

BOTANICAL NAME	FAMILY	SPANISH NAME	ENGLISH NAME	LOCAL USAGE	CHEMICAL ANALYSIS	USAGES IN OTHER CULTURES
Jacaranda cuspidifolia	Bignoniaceae	Jacaranda	Cancerbush	Intestinal parasites; diarrhea with blood; diarrhea with parasites	Jacaranda filicifolia-contains lapachol as a deterrent to insects (Lewis, p. 368)†	Jacaranda oxyphylla-used to treat syphilis in Brazil (Lewis, p. 334)†
Jacobinia spicigera	Acanthaceae	Muicle		Blood fattener; anemia; to make more and redder red blood cells; to purify the blood when it has white points; nerves		
Jatropha dioica	Euphorbiaceae	Sangre de drago	Physic nut bush	dysentery; diarrhea; bleeding gums; loose teeth; skin eruptions; pain and inflammation of gall bladder; hair loss (root)		Periodontal disease; tea for tightening teeth (Lewis, p. 261) Jatropba curcas - stem used in India as purgative (Lewis, p. 234)†
Laelia speciosa	Orchidaceae	Flor de mayo		Cough; reduce swelling caused by a blow (flower)	Family-lactone (coumarin compound) anticoagulants that reduce the synthesis of prothrombin (Lewis, p. 192)†	
Lantana camara L.	Verbenaceae	Flor de 7 colores	Lantana	Susto; to bathe children; stomach ache in children; "evil eye" (flower)		Leaves used as a stimulant and tonic (Lewis, p. 376)
Lepidium intermedium	Brassicaceae	Chinda	Pepperbush	Children's diarrhea and colic; diarrhea; chills	Family-toxic (Lewis, p. 36); provokes photodermatitis in man (Lewis, p. 81)† Powdered seeds act as stimulant to gastris mucosa and increase pancreatic secretions (Lewis, p. 273)†	Family-used as an emetic for children; treating narcotic poisoning (Lewis, p. 278)

BOTANICAL NAME	FAMILY	SPANISH NAME	ENGLISH NAME	LOCAL USAGE	CHEMICAL ANALYSIS	USAGES IN OTHER CULTURES
Loeselia mexicana	Polemoniaceae	Espinosilla		Susto; massage; kidney dysfunction; insomnia in children; fever; headache		
Malva parviflora L.	Malvaceae	Malva	Mallow	Stomach inflammation; drooling in babies; skin eruptions; children's diarrhea; refreshment; inflamed liver; wounds; ear discharge; loss of appetite; purgative; stomach inflammation; kidney pain; skin eruptions, grippe (root).		Fever (Ford, p. 230); sores, purgative, enema (Ford, p. 371)
Marrubium vulgare L.	Labiatae	Manrrubio	Horehound	Diabetes; bilis; liver and gall bladder pain; children's diarrhea; stomach pain; diarrhea (root)		Coughs; sore throats; colds; expectorant (Lewis, p. 307)
Maurandia antirrhiniflora	Scrophulariaceae	Juanimipil		Refresher; wash for babies; purgative; intestinal infection; skin eruptions; fever	Family - same as digitalis (cardiac glycoside) (Lewis, p. 13)†	
Medicago sativa L.	Leguminosae	Alfalfa	Alfalfa	Skin eruptions; kidney pain; cough; massage; sore muscles; inflammation; kidney dysfunction; improve memory; cough·(root)	Triterpene saponins and/or sapogenins (toxic) (Lewis, pp. 19-20); causes photosensitive reactions in animals (Lewis, p. 81)	

BOTANICAL NAME	FAMILY	SPANISH NAME	ENGLISH NAME	LOCAL USAGE	CHEMICAL ANALYSIS	USAGES IN OTHER CULTURES
Mentha	Labiatae	Mastranto	Mint	Children's diarrhea; massage; baths; cleansing	Mentha spicata (spearmint) - volatile oils; hydrocarbons; primary component; phellandrene; also limonene, pinene, ketone, and alcohols (Lewis, p. 82)† causes contact dermatitis (Lewis, p. 82)	Pliny the Elder (A.D. 23-79) prescribed infusion of peony (Paeonia officinalis), mint (Mentha), and chick pea (Cicer arientenum) to dissolve stones in the bladder and kidney (Lewis, p. 314)
Mirabilis jalapa L.	Myctaginaceae	Maravilla	Four o'clock	Skin eruptions; wounds; susto; pus	Angiosperm; causes gastroenteritis in children when roots or seeds are eaten (Lewis, p. 33)‡	
Montanoa tomentosa	Asteraceae	Yerba de to		Increase contractions during childbirth	Montanol zoapatanol°	Aztecs: diuretic; okytoxic; hydropesia (deMontellano, 1975, p. 218)
Nerium oleander L.	Apocynaceae	Laurel	Oleander	Cough (leaves)	Cardiac glycoside (Lewis, p. 18); oleandrin from leaves used to treat cardiac insufficiency (Lewis, p. 51)	
Ocimum basilicum L.	Labiatae	Albacar	Basil	Tranquilizer for sleeping problems; stomach pain; high blood pressure; massages		
Oenothera rosea	Onagraceae	Golpe	Pink evening primrose	Physical blow; hemorrhage	Tannin; βSitosterol qurcetin°	

BOTANICAL NAME	FAMILY	SPANISH NAME	ENGLISH NAME	LOCAL USAGE	CHEMICAL ANALYSIS	USAGE IN OTHER CULTURES
Physalis (angulata L.; peruviana; pubescens L.)	Solanaceae	Tomate	Winter cherry	Headache; teething and diarrhea in children (leaves)	Family - alkaloids, tropane (toxic) atropine (±) (hyoscyamine) and scopolamine (hyosine) (Lewis, pp. 14, 18, 164)†	Antispasmodic (Lewis, p. 164)
Plumbago (capensis) auriculata	Plumbaginaceae	Plumbago	Blister leaf	Children's diarrhea; kidney pain; problems with urination		Plumbago zeylamica used to control weight gain (Lewis, p. 212)†
Plumbago pulchella	Plumbaginaceae	Tianguiz	Leadwort	Enema for children to lower temperature; skin eruptions; empacho infections (root)		
Portulaca aff. oleracea L.	Portulacaceae	Verdolaguilla	Purslane	Itch; skin eruptions	Oxalates - organic acids of plants toxic to animals (Lewis, p. 20)	
Punica granatum	Punicaceae	Granada	Pomegranate	Cough; children's diarrhea (flower)	Alkaloid - isopelletierine (toxic); (Lewis, p. 15); tannin°	
Ricinus communis L.	Euphorbiaceae	Higueria	Castor bean (castor oil plant)	Measles (leaves)	Angiosperm (toxic) (Lewis, p. 28); tannin and resins - potential protection of teeth (Lewis, p. 243)†	Arthritis and pinched nerves (Orellana, p. 124) leaves applied for pain (earache and deafness) (Orellana, p. 130) S. Africa - root paste into carious teeth (Lewis, p. 253)†

BOTANICAL NAME	FAMILY	SPANISH NAME	ENGLISH NAME	LOCAL USAGE	CHEMICAL ANALYSIS	USAGES IN OTHER CULTURES
Rosa	Rosaceae	Rosa o te de Castilla	Rose	Purgative; eye irritation; children's diarrhea and colic; insomnia in children (petals)	Tannins - causing astringent properties (Lewis, p. 285); amygdalin - a glycoside yielding hydrocyanic acid is one product of hydrolysis (cyanogenic) (Lewis, p. 14)*	Antidiarrheal (Lewis, p. 285)
Rosmarinus officinalis L.	Labiatae	Romero	Rosemary	Cerebro; cleansings; baths; massages for rheumatism		
Ruta chalepensis L.	Rutaceae	Ruda	Rue	High blood pressure; nerves; pain in stomach; bilis; massages; with artichoke for liver pain		
Salix bonplandiana	Salicaceae	Flor de sauco	Willow	Cough (flower)	Glycoside (salicin); antirheumatic drug (Lewis, p. 151)	N.A. Indians - pain and fever (Lewis, p. 150); Greeks (B.C. 500) - pain and gout (Lewis, p. 150); antirheumatic drug (Lewis, p. 151)
Salvia microphylla	Labiatae	Flor de mirto		Nerves; insomnia; diarrhea	Tannin°	
Salvia sp.	Labiatae	Chupona (chilla)	Sage	Surface eruptions; headache		
Scabiosa atropurpurea L.	Dipsaceae	Ambar		Stomach pain; colic; headache; nerves; massages		

BOTANICAL NAME	FAMILY	SPANISH NAME	ENGLISH NAME	LOCAL USAGE	CHEMICAL ANALYSIS	USAGES IN OTHER CULTURES
Schinus molle L.	Anacardiaceae	Arbol de pirul (Arbol macho)	California pepper tree	Cold body; pain in feet; molar toothache; stomach pain; massage; dysentery; measles; cleansing; low blood pressure; back pain	Oleoresins (urushiol containing 3-penta-decylcate-chol); produces contact dermatitis (Lewis, pp. 83, 85, 86)	Brazil - chewing gum (Lewis, p. 266)
Sedum dendroideum	Crassulaceae	Flor de siempre viva	Stone crop	Cough; fever; kidney pain; inflammation; (flower)	Pyridine, piperidine (deMontellano, 1976, Table V)	Aztecs - vomit; diuretic (deMontellano, 1975)
Selaginella sp.	Selaginellaceae	Flor de pena	Gray lichen or moss	Kidney pain; heart problems; cerebro; low blood pressure; children who think falsely; help children learn to read (flower)		Pyorrhea; sores or injuries (Ford, p. 350)
Solanum nigrum L. or Solanum cervantesil	Solanaceae	Yerba mora	Black night-shade	Diarrhea; distended stomach in children; skin eruptions on children	Solanine and related alkaloids (Lewis, p. 17)	Sedative; stimulant; local analgesic, anti-parkinsonian, antiepileptic (Diaz, p. 85)
Solanum rostratum	Solanaceae	Duraznillo	Buffalo burr	Skin eruptions; liver pain; cough; susto (root)	Several distinct glycoalkaloids responsible for poisoning in solanum and on hydrolysis these compounds yield either di- or tri- saccharides and one of several alkamine aglycones that are steroidal (Lewis, p. 55)#	
Sonchus deraceu L.	Asteraceae	Endivia	Sow thistle	Liver pain; inflammed stomach; gall bladder pain; kidney pain; liver inflammation; bilis; nerves; skin eruptions (root)		

BOTANICAL NAME	FAMILY	SPANISH NAME	ENGLISH NAME	LOCAL USAGE	CHEMICAL ANALYSIS	USAGES IN OTHER CULTURES
Sphaeralcea angustifolia	Malvaceae	Yerba del negro or vara de San Jose	Stone crop	Loss of appetite; kidney pain; cleansing womb; diarrhea; children's teeth		
Tagetes erecta	Compositae	Flor de simpasuchil	Marigold	Diarrhea; eye irritation (flower)	Lactones (many sesquiterpenes) causing contact dermatitis (Lewis, p. 84)	
Taraxacum officinale	Asteraceae	Pata de leon (chicoria)	Dandelion	Skin eruptions; irritation of urinary tract; inflammations; surface eruptions in children (root)	Experimental hypoglycemic activity (Lewis, p. 218)	Roasted dandelion root used as a coffee substitute (Lewis, p. 387); used to treat chronic diseases of the liver in 19th century (Lewis, p. 289)
Taxodium mucronatum	Taxodiaceae	Sabino	Bald cypress	Burns		
Tecoma stans L.	Bignoniaceae	Catade	Ginger Thomas	Nerves; children's diarrhea, diabetes (leaves)	Alkaloids (tecomine and tecostanine) could serve as models for new prototypes of hypoglycemic agents (Lewis, p. 219)	
Tillandsia	Bromeliaceae	Corteza de encino	Spanish moss	Ulcers; teeth, gums		
Tillandsia recurvata L.	Bromeliaceae	Pasle de mezquite		Skin eruptions		
Tropaeolum majus L.	Tropaeolaceae	Mastuerzo	Nasturtium	Depigmentation of skin in children		

BOTANICAL NAME	FAMILY	SPANISH NAME	ENGLISH NAME	LOCAL USAGE	CHEMICAL ANALYSIS	USAGES IN OTHER CULTURES
Urtica dioica L. var. angustifolia	Urticaceae	Ortiga	Nettle	To avoid hemorrhages; cleansing; baths; susto; vaginal discharge; nosebleed; cough	Aeroallergen (Lewis, p. 70)[†] produces irritant dermatitis; contains histamine-like substances (Lewis, p. 78)	Diuretic (Lewis, p. 313); as a nettle hair rinse in Europe (Lewis, p. 340); generalized skin disease (Lewis, p. 354)
Unidentified	Convolvulaceau	Yerba marota		Pain in head; external wounds		
Verbena carolina L.	Verbenaceae	Verbena	Verbena	Bathing children (branch); kidney pain; nosebleed; burns; ear pain (leaves); urinary tract irritation		Family – used for teas (Lewis, p. 391)[†]
Zaluzania robinsonil	Asteraceae	Limpia tuna		Overeating; susto; ulcers; diarrhea; vomiting		
Zea mays L.	Poaceae	Cabellos de maiz	Indian corn	Poor circulation; urinary tract irritation; kidney pain; colic; cough	Toxic plant having cyanogen glycosides (Lewis, p. 18);[‡] Aeroallergen causing allergic rhinitis, bronchial asthma, and/or hypersensitivity pneumonitis (Lewis, p. 70);[†] undefined antibiotic active against fungi (Lewis, p. 364)	Traditional tobacco substitute in the New World (Lewis, p. 395)

*Pertains to medicinal and toxic properties.

[†]No data for specific genus and/or species; family and/or alternate species data offered instead.

[‡]Chemical analysis not known; some chemical constituents and/or reactions offered.

[°]Ortiz deMontellano, Personal Communication.

APPENDIX C

Miscellaneous Botanicals Used by Spiritualist Healers
(Obtained by purchase or grown at home)

Spanish Name	English Name	Botanical Name	Local Usage
Aguachalalate			Kidney pain; ulcers; liver pain
Ajo	Garlic	Allium sativum L.	Cough; rheumatism
Alcachofa	Artichoke	Cynara scolymus L.	Liver pain
Alucema	Lavender	Lavandula spica	Asthma; cerebro; head pain; for vaporizing
Anis de estrella	Star anise	Illicium verum or Illicium anisatum	Children's colic
Anis del chiquito	Anise	Pimpinella anisum L.	Diarrhea with stomach pain; children's colic; susto
Aranto			Liver pain; wounds
Artemisa	Sagebrush	Artemisia sp.	Aid in childbirth; muscle pain
Azares (flor de)	Orange flower	Citrus	Heart problems; nerves; susto; bilis
Barba de cebolla	Onion skin		Diarrhea in teething children
Barba de coco	Hair on coconut shell	Cocos nucifera L.	Menstrual pain; children's diarrhea; dysentery
Berro	Watercress	Nasturtium officinale L.	Liver inflammation; bilis; liver pain (leaves)
Bola de fuego			Cleansings; bringing out measle spots; back pain; nerves
Boldo		Peumus boldus	Liver dysfunction; lung problems; kidney dysfunction; bilis
Borraja	Borage	Borago officinalis L.	Children with fever; internal infection

Spanish Name	English Name	Botanical Name	Local Usage
Camote de pega ropa		Mentzelia aspera	Wash for wounds; stomach pain; vaginal discharge
Cancerina	Milkwood	Asclepias sp.	Cancer; douche; wash for wounds and to dissolve tumors (root)
Cascara de chirimolla		Annona squamosa	Severe bronchitis; cough, children's diarrhea; vomiting; increase lactation
Cascara de nuez	Nutshell		Diarrhea; vaginal hemorrhage
Cebolla (azada)	Onion (singed; burned)	Allium cepa L.	Muscular inflammation; inflammation; sprain; pain in lungs; itch; hernia
Cimonillo			Bilis; nervous breakdown; gall bladder dysfunction
Ciruelas pasas	Raisins		Constipation; cough
Clameria		Potentilla thurbin	Dysentery; children's diarrhea; diarrhea with blood
			Dysentery (root)
Cuacia	Surinam quassia	Quassia amara L. or Picrasma excelsa	Nerves; bilis; liver; gastritis
Flor de tilia		Taeonaba sp. or Ternstroemia pringlei	Nervous breakdown; heart problems; bilis; susto; high blood pressure
Flor de magnolia		Magnolia grandiflora	Cerebro; nerves; heart problems
Flor de arnica		Mentzelia conzattii; Zexmenia pringlei	Ulcer; wounds; internal infection; appendix; liver pain; stomach inflammation; a blow; nosebleed
Flor de nochebuena		Euphorbia pulcherrima	Swellings
Guayaba	Guava	Psidium gyauyaba	Diarrhea; stomach ache; children's cough (leaves)
Inojo			Anger; nerves; children's colic; stomach ache; children's diarrhea

Spanish Name	English Name	Botanical Name	Local Usage
Itamo real		Pedilanthus tithymaloides	Cough
Jarilla		Dodonaea sp.	Baths; wounds and skin eruptions; pain in feet; cleansing; massage
Lantel	Greater plantain	Plantago major	Liver dysfunction; children's diarrhea (leaves)
Lechuga	Lettuce	Lacheca sp.	Insomnia in children; nerves; throat irritation
Lentejuela		Lepidium virginicum	Fever; children's diarrhea; sprains
Magnolia		Magnolia grandiflora	Cerebro; nerves; heart problems (flower)
Manita			Heart problems; high blood pressure; nerves (flower)
Mandarina	Tangerine	Citrus reticulata	Nerves; heart problems; low blood pressure (leaves)
Manzanilla	Camomile	Matricaria chamomilla L.	Nerves; pain in head; stomach ache
Naranjo	Orange	Citrus sp.	Tea; nerves; purgative (tree leaves)
Nejayo	Water in which corn is soaked		Throat; tonsillitis; chills
Nici			Purgative; empacho
Nuez noscada	Nutmeg		General body pain; stomach ache; vomiting; throbbing in head; headache with influenza
Ocote	Pine	Pinus sp.	Cough; bronchitis; lung pain
Ojasen		Flourensia cernua	Children's enema for stomach ache and infection with fever
Oregano chico	Oregano		Stomach ache; menstrual pain; children's stomach ache
Oregano grande	Marjoram	Origanum sp.	Children's stomach ache; empacho in children; children's colic

Spanish Name	English Name	Botanical Name	Local Usage
Palo de orozus		Lippia dulcis	Cough; asthma; nerves; bilis
Panal de abeja	Honeycomb		Chills; fever; general body pain; bronchitis; children's vomiting; children's suto; children's rashes; when a child is uncomfortable and cries a lot; children's empacho
Pericon	African marigold	Tagetes florida	Low blood pressure; children's diarrhea, and stomach ache; liver pain
Perejil	Parsley	Petroselinum sativum	Hysteria; depression; to control blood pressure; liver dysfunction (root)
Pimpinella	Anise	Pimpinella anisum	Fever; children with measles
Pinguica	Bearberry	Arctostaphylos tomentosa	Kidney dysfunction (leaves)
Pollito			Kidney dysfunction; measles
Prodigiosa		Calea zacatechichi or Coleosanthus sp.	Anger; bilis
Santo domingo			Children's diarrhea; vomiting; stomach ache
Shite			Children's susto
Semilla de aguacate	Avocado pit	Persea sp.	A blow; internal hemorrhage; to stop drooling of teething babies
Tabachin		Caesalpina pulcherrima	Cough; bronchitis; lung problems (flower)
Tamarindo	Tamarind	Tamarindus indica	Wounds; cough
Tejocote	Pear thorn	Crataegus mexicana	Wounds; cough
Tequesquite blanco	Pumice stone		Cold feet; empacho; lung dysfunction
Tomillo	Thyme	Thymus sp.	Cough; diarrhea of teething children
Yerba blanca			Diarrhea; fever; hangover; grippe; influenza

Spanish Name	English Name	Botanical Name	Local Usage
Yerba buena	Spearmint	<u>Mentha spicata</u>	Children's diarrhea; hookworm; children's stomach ache
Zanahorias	Carrots	<u>Daucus carota</u>	Improvement of vision; to fortify oneself

<u>NOTE</u>: Unless otherwise specified, the botanical names are taken from Ford 1975.

APPENDIX D

Principal Causes of Morbidity...State of Hidalgo

1973 - 1975

Enteritis and diarrheas

Influenza and pneumonia

Dysenteries of all kinds

Mange

Whooping cough

Measles

Common cold

Typhoid and other salmonelosis

Chicken Pox

Mumps (parotitis)

Blennorrhea

Ascariasis

Source: Estadisticas Vitales de los Estados Unidos Mexicanas
        1974.   Secreatria de Salubridad y Asistencia 1976.

NOTES

1 / INTRODUCTION

1. See Colson 1971; Fabrega 1971; Fabrega & Manning 1973; Fabrega & Silver 1973; Garrison 1977; Gonzalez 1966; Gould 1965; Harwood 1977a; Ingham 1970; Jilek 1974; Kleinman 1980; Lebra 1976; Maclean 1971; Nash 1967; Press 1969; Rubel 1960, 1964; Romanucci-Schwartz 1969; and many others.

2. The basic literature includes Bourguignon 1976; Crapanzano 1973; Garrison 1977; Kennedy 1967; Kleinman 1980; Kleinman & Sung 1979; Koss 1975; Maduro 1975. Adequate follow-up over a long term is a feature of only several studies, notably Garrison 1977; Jilek 1974; Jilek & Todd 1974; Kleinman 1980; Kleinman and Sung 1979.

3. Yet even disease as a biological entity subject to medical assessment is a Western cultural category based upon Western epistemology supported by definitions determined by the medical profession (cf. Freidson 1970).

4. While I recognize that from a medical perspective it is desirable to evaluate treatment efficacy using objective measures, from a practical vantage point it is important to establish patients' perceived criteria of treatment outcomes, because normally patients relinquish the sick role on the basis of their self-perceived health state rather than objective medical standards.

5. Bonilla 1969; Colson 1971, Fabrega 1971; Gonzalez 1966; Gould 1965; Maclean 1971; Nash 1967; Roger & Hollinghead 1961; Romanucci-Schwartz 1969.

6. Based upon figures of a random and partial count furnished me by the Mexican government there wete 115 temples in central Mexico alone. Based upon my calculations this figure is but one-fifth of the number of temples dispersed throughout Mexico. Some estimate a following of as many as five million. (Lagarriga 1978).

2 / SPIRITUALISM AS A RELIGION

1. Flowers are important in Spiritualist religious rituals. Interestingly, flowers were also ritually important in the pre-Conquest period (Duran 1971) (orig. circa 1590). Like Spiritualist mobilization of Aztec and other Indian spirits as spirit protectors, their emphasis on ritual use of flowers suggests perhaps their recognition of ties with their pre-Conquest past.

2. Interestingly, the founder seems to have been an innovator in the sphere of sex roles. Presumably he allocated twelve sacerdotal positions to men and twelve to women when he charted the movement. Of these twenty-four positions, seven were granted seals to establish churches, two of which were granted to women. In fact, the head temple in Mexico City claims direct descent from the woman who was awarded the sixth seal. The head temple continues to be headed by a woman and thus far the headship has been transmitted matrilineally. For further discussion of the women's role in Mexican Spiritualism, see Finkler (1981a).

3. These numbers, and especially the numbers "three" and "seven are important in Spiritualism, as they are in other systems rooted in early Christianity. See Sharon (1978) for a discussion of their meanings.

4. This has led to some confusion because different irradiators had issued conflicting orders. Consequently, an order was given that only one designated irradiator issues new orders pertaining to structural or other important changes in Spiritualist practices.

3 / ECOLOGICAL CONSIDERATIONS

1. For the entire country, see Laurell 1979.

2. This may explain the statistically significant difference in self-perceived health status as measured by the Cornell Medical Index health questionnaire between ejido and non-ejido holders (Finkler 1981b).

3. For a discussion of differential migration patterns in the region, see Finkler (1974, 1980b).

4. Nader (1963) provides a similar explanation why persons in urban centers, where nuclear families are more prevalent, tend to resort more frequently to local courts to settle interpersonal conflicts as compared with individuals from rural areas, where extended families still prevail.

4 / THERAPEUTIC OPTIONS

1. This phenomenon is related to increased wage labor in the region, resulting in increased spending on consumption goods rather than capital investment on improving the homestead and the family farm.

2. In 1979 1 peso equaled 4.5 U.S. cents.

3. These figures are based upon the 1970 census. I expect that in actuality the population has perhaps doubled, considering that Mexico has one of the highest birthrates in the world.

4. The interviewers at the health center complained to me that they lacked patients to interview during the course of a working day.

5 / ILLNESS ETIOLOGIES

1. These particular symptoms are espcially interesting in light of the Mexican saying, *"Ojala que la boca se te haga chicharron"* ("Oh, that your mouth might become like a crackling"--meaning wrinkled or squashed). This suggests an example of the way in which symptomatic expression concretize linguistic and cultural symbolisms and analogously, cultural symbolism represents concrete experience, as I show in Chapters 9 and 11.

6 / PATIENTS AND THEIR PATTERNS OF RESORT

1. The subject population originates from rural villages (approximate population 200-3,000), municipal towns (approximate population 4,000-15,000), and three urban centers in the region (approximate population 25,000-50,000).

2. As elsewhere, speedy recovery is associated cognitively with injection. According to one physician, his patients insist on injections or intravenous procedures, otherwise they fail to believe that his therapeutics are effective.

3. Regulars are not included because, unlike the other two groups in the temple, they had not come specifically to seek treatment at the time of the interview.

7 / SPIRITUALIST HEALING TECHNIQUES

1. Healers usually recognize regulars, I assume by the unhesitating manner in which they salute the healers and by the linguistic mode which they share with the healers.

8 / SPIRITUALIST THERAPEUTIC OUTCOMES

1. For example see Donabedian 1978; Fabrega 1974; Fiske et al. 1970; Kane et al. 1977; Lindsay et al. 1976; Luborsky et al. 1975; Malan 1973; McAuliffe 1978; McDermott 1977; Mechanic 1968; Mitchell 1978; Morrell 1978; Rutstein et al. 1976; Starfield and Scheff 1972.

2. CMI scores displayed in the figures represent the mean number of "yes" answers per number of questions on the subscale. Thus ($EX/N)/n$, where n = number of items per CMI subscale and N = sample size.

3. In this region corpulence tends to represent health and slenderness ill health. This sign of illness was also prevalent in Europe not so long ago (See Sontag 1978).

9 / HOW SPIRITUALIST HEALERS HEAL

1. I am dealing with both biomedicine and psychotherapy because while

Spiritualists have been likened to psychotherapists, they deal with physiological and psychological disorders.

2. Nalaxone is an opiate antagonist and as such it blocks opiate receptors. On this basis researchers have used nalaxone to demonstrate the presence of endogenous opiates. The effect of enkephalin and endorphins (Beta EP) "is prevented by the administration of the opiate antagonist nalaxone, an important criterior for implicating the opiate receptor" (Akil & Watson 1980, p. 203).

3. Significantly, the largest amount of binding sites for opiates is found in the limbic system of the brain, the region of the brain involved in emotional arousal (Snyder 1977a and 1977b). The same area of the brain is also involved in the ergotropic-trophotropic system involved in trancing. To what degree the biochemical and neurophysiological systems work in tandem on a physiological level in Spiritualist healing is an important research question, one that is, however, beyond the scope of this investigation.

4. This is not an inaccurate evaluation of Mariana, the temple head.

5. I wish to acknowledge my special thanks to Dr. Claudio Cepeda for suggesting that I explore Petra's case along this diagnostic line. I, however am responsible for the final evaluation.

10 / SOCIAL CONSEQUENCES OF WELLNESS

1. Part of Mariana's economic success, however, is due to her extraordinary efforts to put two daughters through normal school, one of whom lives with her and assists her financially to maintain her large household.

2. It is beyond the scope of this book to demonstrate, as my data suggest, that Spiritualist healers tend to possess knowledge of botanicals that is superior to their patients. My data, based upon systematic questioning of patients and healers, suggest that by the time a person becomes a Spiritualist healer he or she has accumulated extensive experience with afflictions. Healers' past experience, coupled with their intense interest in medicinal plants, gives them a broader understanding of medical phenomena and botanicals than their patients.

3. The social consequences of medical and psychiatric therapy are not usually explored. However, the wide use of drugs in maintaining patients in psychiatric hospitals may render similar patients docile. Such patients also become locked into the sociostructural status quo.

11 / CONCLUSION

1. For example, the Campo of Japan, who have been studied by Lock (1980), and the Puerto Rican Spiritists, studied by Garrison (1977).

2. Witness, for example, Hunt's (1977) brilliant analysis of the Hummingbird myth.

3. With some modification, this line of argument follows along Berger and Luckmann's (1967) discussion of modernization.

BIBLIOGRAPHY

Abramson, J.H. 1966. "The Cornell Medical Index as an Epidemiological Tool." American Journal of Public Health, 56:287-298.

Adams, Richard N. 1967. The Second Sowing. San Francisco: Chandler Publications.

Adams, Richard N., and Rubel, Arthur J. 1967. "Sickness and Social Relations." In Robert Wauchope, ed., Handbook of Middle American Indians, vol. 6. Austin: University of Texas Press, pp. 333-56.

Akil, H., and Watson, S.J. 1980. "The Role of Endogenous Opiates in Pain Control." In H. W. Kosterlitz and L. Y. Terenius, eds., Pain and Society: Report of the Dahlem Workshop on Pain and Society, Berlin, Nov. 26-30 1979. Life Sciences Research Report 17. Weinheim: Verlag Chemie, pp. 201-21.

Alba, Francisco 1982 The Population of Mexico, New Brunswick: Transaction Books.

Amkraut, Alfred, and Solomon, George F. 1975. "From the Symbolic Stimulus to the Pathophysiologic Response: Immune Mechanisms." International Journal of Psychiatry in Medicine, 5:541-63.

Anderson, W. Timothy, and Helm, David T. 1979. "The Physician-Patient Encounter: A Process of Reality Negotiation." In E. Jaco, ed., Patients, Physicians, and Illness. New York: Free Press, pp. 259-71.

Antonovsky, Aaron. 1980. Health, Stress and Coping. San Francisco: Jossey-Bass Publishers.

Bahr, Donald M. et al. 1974. Piman Shamanism and Staying Sickness. Tuscon: University of Arizona Press.

Battle, C., et al. 1966. "Target Complaints as Criteria for Improvement." American Journal of Psychotherapy, 20: 184-92.

Bazant, Jan 1972. "Desamortización y Nacionalización de los Bienes de la Iglesia." In La Economía Mexicana en la Epoca de Juárez. Mexico City: Secretaria de Industria y Comercio, pp. 189-221

Beecher, Henry K. 1962. "Pain, Placebos and Physicians." Practitioner, 189:141-55.

Benfari, Robert, et al. 1976. "The Measurement of Health in Populations." In B. Kaplan, R. Wilson, and A. Leighton, eds., Further Explorations of Social Psychiatry. New York: Basic Books, pp. 290-307.

Ben-Sira, Zeev. 1976. "The Function of the Professional's Affective Behavior in Client Satisfaction: A Revised Approach to Social Interaction Theory." Journal of Health and Social Behavior, 17:3-11.

Benson, Herbert. 1974. "Your Innate Asset for Combating Stress." Harvard Business Review, July-Aug., pp. 49-60.

Benson, H., and Epstein, M. D. 1975. "The Placebo Effect: A Neglected Asset in the Care of Patients." Journal of the American Medical Association 232:1225-27.

Benson, Herbert, and McCallie, David. 1979. "Angina Pectoris and the Placebo Effect." New England Journal of Medicine, 300-1424-29.

Benson, Herbert, et al. 1976. "Historical and Clinical Considerations of the Relaxation Response." American Scientist, 65:441-45.

Berger, Peter L. 1969. "The Sacred Canopy. Elements of a Sociological Theory of Religion." Garden City: Anchor Books.

Berger, Peter L., and Luckman, Thomas 1967. The Social Construction of Reality. Garden City: Anchor Books.

Berger, Peter, et al. 1974. The Homeless Mind. New York: Vintage Books.

Bergin, Allen E. 1971. "The Evaluation of Therapeutic Outcomes." In Allen E. Bergin and Sol L. Gardield, eds., Handbook of Psychotherapy and Behavior Change. New York: John Wiley & Sons. 217-270.

Bloom, Samuel W. 1963. The Doctor and His Patient. New York: Russell Sage Foundation.

Blumer, Dietrich, et al. 1980. "Systematic Treatment of Chronic Pain with Antidepressants." Henry Ford Hospital Medical Journal (Detroit), 28:15-21.

Bonilla, E. 1969. "Spiritualism, Psychoanalysis and Psychodrama." American Anthropologist, 71:493-97.

Bourguignon, Erica. 1976. "The Effectiveness of Religious Healing Movements: A Review of Recent Literature." Transcultural Psychiatric Research Review, 8:5-21.

Breuer, J., and Freud, S. 1966. "On the Psychical Mechanism of Hysterical Phenomena" (pub. 1893). In James Strach, ed., S. Freud and J. Breuer Studies on Hysteria, trans. New York: Avon Books.

Brislin, Richard W., et al. 1973. Cross-Cultural Research Methods. New York: John Wiley & Sons.

Brodman, Keeve, et al. 1952. "The Cornell Medical Index-Health Questionnaire. III. The Evaluation of Emotional Disturbances." Journal of Clinical Psychiatry, 8:119-24.

Brody, Howard. 1977. Placebos and the Philosophy of Medicine. Chicago: University of Chicago Press.

Brown, R. E. 1966. "Medical Problems of the Developing Countries." Science, 153:271-75.

Burridge, Kenelm. 1969. New Heaven, New Earth. New York: Schocken Books.

Butler Flora, Cornelia. 1976. Pentecostalism in Columbia, Baptism by Fire and Spirit. Associated University Press. East Brunswick, N. J.

Casper, E. G., and Philippus, M. J. 1975. "Fifteen Cases of Embrujada: Combining Medication and Suggestion in Treatment." Hospital and Community Psychiatry, 26:271, 274.

Cassell, Eric J. 1976. The Healer's Art. Philadelphia: J. B. Lippincott.

Cassel, John, and Tyroler, Herman. 1961. "Epidemiological Studies of Culture Change." Archives of Environmental Health, 3:25-33.

Cay, Elizabeth L., et al. 1975. "Patient's Assessment of the Result of Surgery for Peptic Ulcer." Lancet, 1:29-31.

Chance, N. 1962. "Conceptual and Methodological Problems in Cross-Cultural Health Survey Research." American Journal of Public Health, 52:410-17.

Chapple, Eliot D. 1970. Culture and Biological Man. New York: Holt, Rinehart & Winston.

Clark, Margaret. 1959. Health in the Mexican-American Culture. Berkeley: University of California Press.

Cohen, Yehudi. 1968. "Culture as Adaptation." In Yehudi Cohen, ed., Man in Adaptation: The Cultural Present. Chicago: Aldine, pp. 40-60.

Colson, Anthony C. 1971. "The Differential Use of Medical Resources in Developing Countries." Journal of Health and Social Behavior, 12: 226-37.

Comaroff, J. 1978. "Medicine and Culture: Some Anthropological Perspectives." Social Science and Medicine, 12B: 247-54.

Cosio Villegas, Daniel 1956. Historia Moderna de Mexico Vol. 3. La Republica Restaurada, la Vida Politica. Mexico City: Hermes.

Craine, Jay B. 1975. In Thomas R. Williams, ed., Psychological Anthropology, 9th ed. The Hague: Mouton, pp. 487-500. "Understanding Ritual Process in the Medical Setting in International Congress of Anthropological and Ethnological Sciences."

Crapanzano, Vencent. 1973. The Hamadsha. Berkeley: University of California Press.

Croog, Sydney H. 1961. "Ethnic Origins, Educational Level and Responses to a Health Questionnaire." Human Organization, 20:65-69.

Currier, Richard L. 1966. "The Hot-Cold Syndrome and Symbolic Balance in Mexico." Ethnology, 5:251-63.

Davis, John, and Cole, Jonathan O. 1975. "Antipsychotic Drugs." In Aflred M. Freedman, Harold I. Kaplan, and B. Sadock, eds., Comprehensive Textbook of Psychiatry II. Baltimore: Williams & Wilkins, pp. 1921-41.

Davis Tzu, Vivien. 1980. "Underutilization of Health Centers in Rural Mexico: A Qualitative Approach to Evaluation and Planning." Studies of Family Planning, 11:145-77.

DeMontellano, Bernard Ortiz. 1974/5. "Aztec Medicine: Empirical Drug Use," Ethnornedizin, 3/4: 249-71.

———— 1975. "Empirical Aztec Medicine," Science, 188: 215-20.

———— 1976. "The Rational Causes of Illnesses Among the Aztecs," International Congress of Americaniots, Paris, France, Sept. 23-24.

Diaz, Jose Luis. 1979. "Ethnopharmacology and Taxonomy of Mexican Psychodysleptic Plants." Journal of Psychedelic Drugs, 11:71-101.

DiTella, Torcuato. 1973. "The Dangerous Classes in Early Nineteenth Century Mexico." Latin American Studies, 5:79-105.

Dohrenwend, Bruce P., and Dohrenwend, Barbara Snell. 1965. "The Problem of Validity in field Studies of Psychological Disorder." Journal of Abnormal Psychology, 70:52-69.

Donabedian, Avedis. 1972. "Models for Organizing the Delivery of Personal Health Services and Criteria for Evaluating Them." The Milbank Memorial Fund Quarterly. Medical Cure and Medical Care 50:103-54.

Donabedian Avedis. 1978. "The Quality of Medical Care." Science, 200:856-64.

Douglas, Mary. 1966. Purity and Danger. London: Routledge & Kegan Paul.

Duran, Fray Diego. 1971. Book of the Gods and Rites and the Ancient Calendar, trans. and ed. Fernando Horcasitas and Doris Heyden. Norman: University of Oklahoma Press.

Egbert, Lawrence, et al. 1964. "Reduction of Post-Operative Pain by Encouragement and Instruction of Patient." New England Journal of Medicine, 270:825--827.

Eisenberg, Leon. 1977. "Disease and Illness: Distinctions between Professional and Popular Ideas of Sickness." Culture, Medicine and Psychiatry, 1:9-23.

Eister, Allan W. 1974. "Culture Crises and New Religious Movements: A Paradigmatic Statement of a Theory of Cults." In Irving I. Zaretsky and Mark P. Leone, eds., Religious Movements in Contemporary America. Princeton, N.J.: Princeton University Press, pp. 612-27.

Engel, George L. 1973. "Personal Theories of Disease as Determinants of Patient-Physician Relationships." Psychsomatic Medicine, 35:184--86.

———— 1977 "The Need for a New Medical Model: A Challenge for Biomedicine." Science, 196:129-36.

Escudero, Jose Carlos. 1980. "On Lies and Health Statistics: Some Latin American Examples." International Journal of Health Services, 10:421-34.

Fabrega, Horacio, Jr. 1970. "On the Specificity of Folk Illnesses." Southwestern Journal of Anthropology, 26:305-14.

_____ 1971 "The Study of Medical Problems in Preliterate Settings." Yale Journal of Biology and Medicine, 43:385-407.

_____ 1974 Disease and Social Behavior. Cambridge, Mass.: M.I.T. Press.

_____ 1977 "Group Differences in the Structure of Illness." Culture, Medicine and Psychiatry, 1:379-94.

Fabrega, Horacio, Jr., and Manning, Peter K. 1973. "An Integrated Theory of Disease: Ladino-Mestizo Views of Disease in the Chiapas Highlands." Psychosomatic Medicine, 35:223-39.

_____ 1979 Illness Episodes, Illness Severity and Treatment Options in a Pluralistic Setting. Social Science and Medicine 13B:41-52.

Fabrega, Horacio, Jr., and Silvler, Daniel. 1973. Illness and Shamanistic Curing in Zinacantan. Stanford: Stanford University Press.

Fabrega, Horacio, Jr., et. al. 1967. "Working Class Mexican Psychiatric Outpatients." Archives of General Psychiatry, 16:704-12.

Fernandez, James W. 1965. "Symbolic Consensus in a Fang Reformative Cult." American Anthropologist, 67:902-28.

Finkler, Kaja. 1974. Estudio Comparative de la Economia de dos Comunidades de Mexico. Mexico City: Sep INI series, Institute Nacional Indigenista.

_____ 1977 "El Cuidado de la Salud: un Problema de Relaciones de Poder." American Indigena, 37:435-56.

_____ 1978 "From Sharecroppers to Entrepreneurs: Peasant Household Production Strategies under the Ejido System of Mexico." Economic Development and Cultural Change, 27:103-20.

_____ 1980a "Land Scarcity and Economic Development: When is a Landlord a Client and a Sharecropper His Patron?" In Peggy F. Bartlett, eds., Agricultural Decision Making. New York: Academic Press, pp. 265-86.

_____ 1980b "The Effects of Differential Policies on Social Integration in One Region of Mexico, a Historical Perspective." Central Issues in Anthropology, 2:51-68.

_____ 1981a "Dissident Religious Movements in the Service of Women's Power." Sex Roles A Journal of Research, 7:481-95.

_____ 1981b "A Comparative Study of Health Seekers: or, Why Do Some People Go to Doctors Rather than to Spiritualist Healers?" Medical Anthropology, 5:383-424.

_____ In Press "Symptomatological Differences between the Sexes in Rural Mexico." Culture, Medicine and Psychiatry.

Firth, Raymond. 1967. "Ritual and Drama in Malay Spirit Mediumship." Comparative Studies in Society and History, 9:190-207.

Fiske, Donald W., et. al. 1970. "Planning of Research on Effectiveness of Psychotherapy." Archives of General Psychiatry, 22:22-32.

Flores, Caballero, Romeo. 1972. "Etapas del Desarrollo Industrial." In La Economía Mexicana en la Epoca de Juárez. Mexico City: Secretaria de Industria y Comercio, pp. 105-125.

Florescano, Enrique, and Maria del Rosano Lanzagarta. 1972. "Politica Economica." In La Economía Mexicana en la Epoca de Juárez. Mexico City: Secretaria de Industria y Comercio. 57-102.

Ford, Daren Cowan. 1975. Las Yerbas De La Gente: A Study of Hispano-American Medicinal Plants, Ann Arbor: The University of Michigan.

Foster, George M. 1953. "Relationships between Spanish and Spanish-American Folk Medicine." Journal of American Folklore, 66:201-17.

_____ 1963 "The Dyadic Contract in Tzintzuntzan, II: Patron-Client Relationships." American Anthropologist, 65:1280-94.

_____ 1976 "Disease Etiologies in Non-Western Medical Systems." American Anthropologist, 78:773-82.

Foster, G. M., and Anderson, B. G. 1978. Medical Anthropology. New York: John Wiley & Sons.

Fox, J. Robin. 1974. "Witchcraft and Clanship in Cochiti Therapy." In Ari Kiev, ed., Magic, Faith and Healing. New York: Free press, pp. 174-200.

Frank, Jerome D. 1974. Persuasion and Healing. New York: Schocken Books.

n.d. Holistic Medicine - A View from the Fence. (Manuscript) Jerome D. Frank, Phipps Clinic, John Hopkins Hospital, Baltimore, MD.

Freedman, Alfred M., and Kaplan, Harold I. 1972. Diagnosing Mental Illness. New York: Atheneum.

Freidson, Eliot. 1970. Profession of Medicine. New York: Harper & Row.

Garrison, Vivian. 1974. "Sectarianism and Psychosocial Adjustment: A Controlled Comparison of Puerto Rican Pentecostals and Catholics." In Irving J. Zaretsky and Mark P. Leone, eds., Religious Movements in Contemporary America. Princeton N.J.: Princeton University Press, pp. 298-329.

_____ 1977 "Doctors, Espiritista or Psychiatrist: Health-Seeking Behavior in a Puerto Rican Neighborhood of New York City." Medical Anthropology, 1:65-180.

Geffner, Mitchell E., and Sandler, Alan. 1980. "Oral Metallic Mercury: A Folk Remedy for Gastroenteritis," Clinical Pediatrics, 19:435-43.

Gellhorn, Ernst. 1967. Autonomic-Somatic Integrations. Minneapolis: University of Minnesota Press.

Gellhorn, Ernst, and Kiely, William F. 1972. "Mystical States of Consciousness: Neurophysiological and Clinical Aspects." Journal of Nervous and Mental Disease, 154:399-405.

Gill, Derek G. 1976. "Limitations upon Choice and Constraints over Decision-Making in Doctor-Patient Exchanges." In Eugene B. Gallagher, ed., The Doctor-Patient Relationship in the Changing Health Scene. Washington, D.C. U.S. Department of Health, Education, and Welfare; Public Health Service, National Institutes of Health, DHEW Publication No. (NIH) 78-183, pp. 141-54.

Gillin, John. 1965. "Magical Fright." In William A. Lessa and Evon Z. Vogt, eds., Reader in Comparative Religion., 2nd ed. pp. 402-410.

Glade, William P., Jr. 1968. "Revolution and Economic Development." In William P. Glade, Jr., and Charles W. Anderson, The Political Economy of Mexico. Madison: University of Wisconsin Press.

Glasser, Morton. 1977. "Psychiatric Cases in a Family Practice: Analysis of Outcomes." Medical Anthropology, 1:55-73 .

Glick, Leonard B. 1967. "Medicine as an Ethnographic Category: The Gimi of the New Guinea Highlands." Ethnology, 6:31-55.

Glueck, Bernard and Charles F. Stroebel. 1978. "Psychophysiological Correlates of Relaxation." In A. Arthur Sugerman and Ralph E. Tarter, eds. Expanding Dimensions of Consciousness, New York: Springer, pp. 99-129.

Goldkind, Victor. 1965. "Social Stratification in the Peasant Community: Redfield's Chankom Reinterpreted." American Anthropologist, 67:863-84.

Gonzalez, Luis. 1972. "La era de Juárez." In La Economia Mexicana en la Epoca de Juárez. Mexico City: Secretaria de Industria y Comercio, pp. 13-56.

Gonzalez, Nancy. 1966. "Health Behavior in Cross-Cultural Perspective." Human Organization, 25:122-125.

Gonzalez Navarro, Moises et al. 1954. "Instituciones Indigenas en Mexico Independiente". In Memorias del Instituto Nacional Indigenista, Mexico City: Insituto Nacional Indigenista, 6: pp 115-69.

Goode, William J. 1963. World Revolution and Family Patterns. New York: Free Press.

Gostkowski, Zygmunt. 1964. "Algunas Consideraciones en Torno a la Validez de las Tecnicas de Investigacion Utiliza en los Paises en Vias de Desarrollo." Ciencias Politicas y Sociales, 10:441-51.

Gould H. 1965. "Modern Medicine and Folk Congition in Rural India." Human Organization, 24:201-8.

Hahn, Robert A. 1978. "Is Mental Illness Cured in Traditional Societies?" Transcultural Psychiatric Research Review, 15:157-63.

Hahn, Robert A., and Kleinman, Arthur. 1981." Belief as Pathogen, Belief as Medicine: VooDoo Death and the Placebo Phenomenon in Anthropological Perspective." Paper presented at a conference on Symbols, Meaning ana Efficacy in the Healing Process, held by the Society for Applied Anthropology, Edinburg, Scotland, 12-17 April, 1981.

Harwood, Alan. 1977a. RX: Spiritists as Needed. New York: John Wiley & Sons.

_____ 1977b "Puerto Rican Spiritism (Part I)." Culture, Medicine and Psychiatry, 1:69-96.

Haynes, Alfred M. 1976. "Medical Care and the Doctor-Patient Relationship." In Eugene Gallagher, ed., The Doctor-Patient Relationship in the Changing Health Scene. Washington, D.C.: U.S. Department of Health, Education and Welfare; Public Health Service, National Institutes of Health, DHEW Publication No. (NIH) 78-183.

Heukelekian, H. 1962. "Informe Sobre el Use do las Aguas Negras y las Superficiales en el Valle de México y la Región de el Mezquital, Hgo." Secretaría de Recursos Hidráulicos, Comision Hidrológica de la Cuenca del Valle de Mexico.

Hinkle, Lawrence E., et. al. 1957. "Studies in Human Ecology." American Journal of Psychiatry, 114:212-20.

_____ 1960 "II. An Examination of the Relation between Symptoms, Disability and Serious Illness, in Two Homogeneous Groups of Men and Women." American Journal of Public Health, 50:1327-41.

Hogarty, Gerard E., and Goldberg, Solomon C. 1973. "Drug and Sociotherapy in the Aftercare of Schizophrenic Patients." Archives of General Psychiatry, 28:54-64.

Holden, Constance. 1973. "Chiropractic: Healing or Hokum? HEW Is Looking for Answers." Science, 185:922-25.

Holmes, T., and Masuda, M. 1974. "Life change and Illness Susceptibility." In B. S. Dohrenwend and B. P. Dohrenwend, eds., Stressful Life Events. New York: John Wiley & Sons, pp. 45-72.

Horton, Robin, 1973. "Levy-Bruhl, Durkheim and the Scientific Revolution." In Robin Horton and Ruth Finnegan, ed., Modes of Thought. London: Faber & Faber, pp. 249-305.

Hudson, Charles. 1975. "Vomiting for Purity: Ritual Emesis in the Aboriginal Southeastern United States." In Carole E. Hill, ed., Symbols and Society. Athens, Ga.: Southern Anthropological Society.

Hughes, Charles C. 1976. "Of Wine and bottles, Old and New: An Anthropological perspective on the 'New' Family Physician." In Madelaine Leininger, ed., Transcultural Health Care Issues and Conditions--Health Care Dimensions. Philadelphia: F. A. Davis, pp. 37-49.

Hunt, Eva. 1977. The Transformation of the Hummingbird: Cultural Roots of a Zinacantecan Mythical Poem. Ithaca, N.Y.: Cornell University Press.

Idler, Ellen L. 1979. "Definitions of Health and Illness and Medical Sociology." Social Science and Medicine, 13A:723-31.

Ingham, J. M. 1970. "On Mexican Folk Medicine." American Anthropologist, 72:76-87.

Inui, T., et al. 1976. "Improved Outcomes in Hypertensions after Physician Tutorials." Annals of Internal Medicine, 84:646-51.

Jacobs, Selby, and Ostfeld, Adrian. 1977. "An Epidemiological Review of the Mortality of Bereavement." Psychosomatic Medicine, 39:344-57.

Janzen, John M. 1978. The Quest for Therapy in Lower Zaire. Berkeley: University of California Press.

Jilek, Wolfgang G. 1974. Salish Indian Mental Health and Culture Change. Toronto: Holt, Rinehart & Winston of Canada.

Jilek, Wolfgang G., and Todd, Norman. 1974. "Witchdoctors Succeed Where

Doctors Fail: Psychotherapy among Coast Salish Indians." Canadian Psychiatric Association Journal, 19:351-56 (reprinted in Anthropology Full Circle, ed. Ino Rossi, John Buettner-Janusch, and Dorian Coppenhaver. New York: Praeger, 1977, pp. 400-403.

Jones, Judith K. 1980. "Do Over-the-Counter Drugs Act Mainly as Placebos? Yes." In Louis Lasagna, ed., Controversies in Therapeutics. Philadelphia: W. B. Saunders.

Jospe, Michael. 1978. The Placebo Effect in Healing. Lexington: D. C. Heath.

Kalimo, Esko, et al. 1970. "Cross-Cultural Analysis of Selected Emotional Questions from the Cornell Medical Index." British Journal of Preventive Social Medicine, 24:229-40.

Kane, R. L., et al. 1977. "Relationship between Process and Outcome in Ambulatory Care." Medical Care, 15:961.

Katon, Wayne, et al. 1982a. Depression and Somatization: a Review. Part I The American Journal of Medicine, 72:127-35.

_____ 1982b Depression and Somatization: a Review. Part II The American Journal of Medicine, 72:241-47.

Kearney, Michael, 1978a. "Spiritualist Healing in Mexico." In Peter Morley and Roy Wallis, ed., Culture and Curing. London: Peter Owen, pp. 19--39.

Kearney, Michael. 1978. "Espiritualismo as an Alternative Medical Tradition in the Border Area." In Boris Velimirovic. ed., Modern Medicine and Medical Anthropology in the United States-Mexico Border Population. Scientific Publication no. 359. Pan American Health Organization, pp. 67--72.

Kelly, Isabelle. 1965. Folk Practices in North Mexico. Austin: University of Texas Press.

Kennedy, Donald A. 1973. "Perceptions of Illness and Healing." Social Science and Medicine, 7:787-805.

Kennedy, John G. 1967. "Nubian Zar Ceremonies as Psychotherapy." Human Organization, 26:185-94.

Kernberg, Otto. 1975. Borderline Conditions and Pathological Narcissism. New York: Jason Aronson.

Kiev, Ari. 1973. "Magic, Faith, and Healing in Modern Psychiatry." In Richard H. Cox, ed., Religious Systems and Psychotherapy. Springfield: Charles C. Thomas, pp. 225-35.

Kleinman, Arthur M. 1974. "Cognitive Structures of Traditional Medical Systems: Ordering, Explaining, and Interpreting the Human Experience of Illness." Ethnomedizin, 3:27-49.

_____ 1977 "Explaining the Efficacy of Indigenous Therapies: The Need for Interdisciplinary Research." Culture, Medicine and Psychiatry, 2:133-34.

_____ 1980 Patients and Healers in the Context of Culture. Berkeley: University of California Press.

Kleinman, A., and Sung, L. H. 1979. "Why Do Indigenous Practitioners Successfully Heal?" Social Science and Medicine, 13B:7-26.

Kleinman, Arthur M., et al. 1978. "Culture, Illness and Care: Clinical Lessons from Anthropological and Cross-Cultural Research." Annals of Internal Medicine, 88:251-58.

Korsch, Barbara, and Negrete, Vida. 1972. "Doctor-Patient Communication." Scientific American, 227:66-74.

Koss, Joan D. 1975. "Therapeutic Apsects of Puerto Rican Cult Practices." Psychiatry, 38:160-71.

Kosterlitz, H. W., and Terenius, L. Y., eds. 1979. Pain and Society (Report of the Dahlem Workshop on Pain and Society, 26-30 Nov., Berlin). Life Sciences Research Report 17. Weinheim: Verlag Chemie.

Krieger, Dolores, et al. n.d. "Physiological Indices of Therapeutic Touch." Mimeo. Dolores Krieger, New York University Division of Nursing, New York, N.Y.

Krippner, Stanley. 1978. "Psychic Healing: A Multidimensional View." In James

L. Fossage and Paul Olsen, eds., Healing. New York: Human Sciences Press, pp. 48-83.

Kunkel, John H. 1961. "Economic Autonomy and Social Change in Mexican Villages." Economic Development and Cultural Change, 10:51-63.

Kuknstadter, Peter. 1978. "The Comparative Anthropological Study of Medical Systems and Society." In Arthur Kleinman, Peter Kunstadter, E. Russell Alexander, and James L. Gale, eds., Culture and Healing in Asian Societies. Cambridge, Mass.: Schenkman, pp. 393-406.

LaBarre, Weston. 1971. "Materials for the History of Studies of Crisis Cults: A Bibliographic Essay." Current Anthropology, 12:3-44.

Lafaye, Jacques. 1974. Quetzalcóatl and Guadalupe: The Formation of Mexican National Consciousness 1531-1813, trans. Benjamin Keen. Chicago: University of Chicago Press.

Lagarriga Attias, Isabel. 1975. Medicina Tradicional y Espiritismo. Mexico City: Sepsetenta.

Lagarriga Attias, Isabel. 1978. "Tecnicas Catarticas en los Templos Espiritualistas Trinitarios Marianos". In Carlos Viesca Treviño Estudios Sobre Etnobotanica y Antropologia Medica, No. 3. Mexico City: Instituto Mexicano para el Estudio de las Plantas Medicinales, p. 115-26.

Landy, David. 1977. Role Adaptation. Traditional Curers Under the Impact of Western Medicine. In David Landy Culture, Disease, and Healing. New York: Macmillan Publishing pp. 468-80.

Lanternari, Vittorio. 1963. The Religions of the Oppressed: A Study of Modern Messianic Cults. New York: Mentor Books.

_____ 1974 "Nativistic and Socio-Religious Movements: A Reconsideration." Comparative Studies in Society and History, 16:483-503.

Laurell Asa, Cristina. 1979. "Work and Health in Mexico." International Journal of Health Services, 9:543-68.

Laurell Asa, Cristina, et al. 1977. "Disease and Rural Development: A Sociological Analysis of Morbidity in Two Mexican Villages." International Journal of Health Services, 7:401-23.

Leach, Edmund. 1976. Culture and Communication. Cambridge: Cambridge University Press.

Lebra, William P., ed. 1976. Culture-Bound Syndromes, Ethnopsychiatry, and Alternate Therapies. Honolulu: University Press of Hawaii.

Leighton, Alexander H., et al. 1968. "The Therapeutic Process in Cross-Cultural Perspectives; A Symposium." Journal of Psychiatry, 124:1171-83.

Leininger, Madelaine. 1979. Transcultural Nursing. New York: Masson International Nursing Publications.

Leslie, Charles, ed. 1976. "Introduction." Asian Medical Systems: A Comparative Study. Berkeley: University of California, pp. 1-17.

Levine, J. D., et al. 1978. "The Mechanism of Placebo Analgesia." Lancet (8091), 2:654-57.

Levine, J. D. et al., 1979. "Naloxone Dose Dependently Produces Analgesia and Hyperalgesia in Postoperative Pain." Nature 278:740-41.

Levi-Strauss, Claude. 1967. "The Effectiveness of Symbols." In Structural Anthropology. Garden City: Anchor Books, pp. 181-201.

Lewis, I. M. 1971. Ecstatic Religion. Middlesex: Penguin Books.

Lewis, Walter H. 1977. Medical Botany: Plants Affecting Man's Health. New York: John Wiley & Sons, Inc.

Lex, Barbara W. 1976. "Physiological Aspects of Ritual Trance." Journal of Altered States of Consciousness, 2:109-22.

_____ 1978 "Neurological Bases of Revitalization." ·Zygon, 13:276-312.

Lieban, R. W. 1973. "Medical Anthropology." In J. J. Honigmann, ed., Handbook of Social and Cultural Anthropology. Chicago: Rand McNally, pp. 1031-72.

_____ 1976 "Traditional Medical Beliefs and the Choice of Practitioners in a Philippine City." Social Science and Medicine, 10:289-96.

_____ 1978 "Symbols, Signs and Success: Healers and Power in a Philippine City." In R. D. Fogelson and R. Adams, eds., The Anthropology of Power. New York: Academic Press.

_____ 1978 "Sex Differences and Cultural Dimensions of Medical Phenomena in a Philippine Setting." In Peter Morley and Ray Wallis, eds., Culture and Curing. London: Peter Owen, pp. 99-114.

Lindsay, Malcolm I., et al. 1976. "Quality-of-Care Assessment. I.: Out-Patient Management of Acute Bacterial Cystitis as the Model." Mayo Clinic Proc., 51:307-12.

Lloyd, Camille. 1980. "Life Events and Depressive Disorder Reviewed." Archives of General Psychiatry, 37:541-48.

Lock, Margaret M. 1980. East Asian Medicine in Urban Japan. Berkeley: University of California Press.

Lopez Acuña, Daniel. 1976. La Crisis de la Medicina Mexicana. Puebla: Mexico Universidad autonoma de Puebla.

Low, Setha M. 1981. "The Meaning of Nervios: A Sociocultural Analysis of Symptom Presentaton in San Jose, Costa Rica." Culture, Medicine and Psychiatry, 5:25-48.

Luborsky, Lester, et al. 1975. "Comparative Studies of Psychotherapies." Archives of General Psychiatry, 32:995-1008.

_____ 1980 "Predicting the Outcome of Psychotherapy." Archives of General Psychiatry, 37:471-81.

Ludwig, Arnold M. 1968. "Altered States of Consciousness." In Raymond Prince, ed., Trance and Possession States. Montreal: R.M. Bucke Memorial Society, pp. 69-96.

Macklin, June. 1974a. "Belief, Ritual and Healing: New England Spiritualism and Mexican-American Spiritualism Compared." In Irving I Zazretsky and Mark P. Leone, eds., Religious Movements in Contemporary America. Princeton, N.J.: Princeton University Press, pp. 383-417.

_____ 1974b "Folk Saints, Healers and Spiritist Cults in Northern Mexico" Revista/Review Interamericana, 3: 351-67.

_____ 1978 "Curanderismo and Espiritismo: Complementary Traditional Approaches to Mental Health Services." In Boris Velimirovic, ed., Modern Medicine and Medical Anthropology in the U.S.-Mexico Border Population. Washington, D.C. Pan American Health Organization Scientific Publication no. 359.

Maclean, Una. 1971. Magical Medicine. Middlesex: Penguin Books.

Madsen, Claudia. 1968. "A Study of Change in Mexican Folk Medicine." Middle America Research Institute Publication, 25:89-138.

Madsen, William. 1955. Shamanism in Mexico. Southwestern Journal of Anthropology, 11:48-57.

_____ 1967 "Religious Syncretism.: In Manning Nash, eds., Handbook of Middle American Indians, vol. 6. Austin: University of Texas Press, pp. 361-91.

_____ 1974 Value Conflict and Folk Psychiatry in South Texas. In Ari Kiev Magic, Faith and Healing. New York: The Free Press.

Maduro, Renaldo. 1975. "Voodoo Possession in San Francisco." Ethos, 3:425-47.

Malan, David H. 1973. "The Outcome Problem in Psychotherapy Research." Archives of General Psychiatry, 29:719-29.

Marshall, Eliot. 1980a. "Psychotherapy Faces Test of Worth." Science, 207:35-36.

_____ 1980b "Psychotherapy Works, But for Whom?" Science, 207:506-8.

Matarazzo, Ruth G., et al. 1961. "The Relationship between Medical and Psychiatric Symptoms." Journal of Abnormal and Social Psychology, 62:55-61.

Maupin, Edward W. 1969. "On Meditation." In Charles T. Tart, ed., Altered States of Consciousness. New York: John Wiley & Sons, pp. 177-86.

May, Philip R. A. 1976. "Rational Treatment for an Irrational Disorder: What

Does the Schizophrenic Patient Need?" American Journal of Psychiatry, 133:1008-12.

McAuliffe, William E. 1978. "Studies of Process-Outcome Correlations in Medical Care Evaluations: A Critique." Medical Care, 16:907-30.

_____ 1979 "Measuring the Quality of Medical Care: Process versus Outcome." Milbank Memorial Fund Quarterly (Health and Society), 57:118-52.

McCreery, John L. 1979. "Potential and Effective Meaning in Therapeutic Ritual." Culture, Medicine and Psychiatry, 3:53-72.

McDermott, Walsh. 1977. "Evaluating the Physician and His Technology." Daedalus, 106:135-58.

Mechanic, David. 1968. Medical Sociology. New York: Free Press.

_____ 1972 "Response Factors in Illness; The Study of Illness Behavior." In E. Jaco, ed., Patients, Physicians and Illness. New York: Free Press, pp. 141-54.

_____ 1976 "Sex, Illness, Illness Behavior and the Use of Health Service." Research and Analytic Report Series, no. 2-76. Madison: University of Wisconsin, Center for Medical Sociology and Health Services Research.

Melzack, R. 1976. "Pain: Past, Present, and Future." In Matisyohu Weisenberg and Bernard Tursky, eds., Pain. New York: Plenum Press, pp. 135-46.

Melzack, Ronald, and Campbell, Perry. 1975. "Self-Regulation of Pain: The Use of Alpha-Feedback and Hypnotic Training for the Control of Chronic Pain." Experimental Neurology, 46:452-69.

Melzack, R., and Wall P.D. 1975. "Psychophysiology of Pain." In Matisyohu Weisenberg, ed., Pain, Clinical and Experimental Perspectives. Saint Louis: C. V. Mosby, pp. 8-23.

Meneses Adalberto, Cravioto. 1979. "Recent Progress in the Program for Extending Health Service Coverage to Rural Mexico." Bulletin of the Pan-American Health Organization, 13:244-48.

Metzger, Duane, and Williams, Gerald. 1963. "Tenejapa Medicine: The Curer." Southwestern Journal of Anthropology, 19:216-34.

Mitchell, Janet B. 1978. "Patient Outcomes in Alternative Long Term Care Settings." Medical Care, 16:439-52.

Moerman, Daniel E. 1979. "Anthropology of Symbolic Healing." Current Anthropology, 20:59-80.

Moore, R. Lawrence. 1977. In Search of White Crows. New York: Oxford University Press.

Morrell, David C. 1978. "The Epidemiological Imperative for Primary Care." Annals of the New York Academy of Sciences, 310:2-10.

Morsy, Soheir. 1978. "Sex Roles, Power and Illness in an Egyptian village." American Ethnologist, 5:137-50.

Nader, Laura, and Metzger, Duane. 1963. "Conflict Resolution in Two Mexican Communities." American Anthropologist, 65:584-92.

Nash, June. 1967. "The Logic of Behavior: Curing in a Maya Indian Town." Human Organization, 26:132-40.

Nathanson, Constance. 1979. "Sex, Illness and Medical Care." In Gary L. Albrecht and Paul C. Higgins, eds., Health, Illness and Medicine. Chicago: Rand McNally.

Navarro, Vincente. 1976. "Social Class, Political Power and the State and Their Implications in Medicine." Social Science and Medicine, 10:43757.

Nelson, G. K. 1969. Spiritualism and Society. New York: Schocken Books.

Ness, Robert C. 1977. "Modernization and Illness in a Newfoundland Community." Medical Anthropology, 1:25-53.

_____ 1980 "The Impact of Indigenous Healing Activity: An Empirical Study of Two Fundamentalist Churches." Social Science and Medicine, 14B:147-80.

Nobrega, Fred T., et al. 1977. "Quality Assessment in Hypertension: Analysis of Process and outcome Methods." New England Journal of Medicine, pp.145-48.

Obeyesekere, Gananath. 1976. "The Impact of Ayurvedic Ideas on the Culture and the Individual in Sri Lanka." In Charles Leslie, ed., Asian Medical Systems: A Comparative Study. Berkeley: University of California Press, pp. 201-26.

_____ 1977 "Psychological Medicine in Ayurvedic Tradition." Culture, Medicine and Psychiatry, 1:155-81.

Ocampo, Javier. 1969. Las Ideas de un Dia. Mexico: El Colegio de Mexico.

O'Nell, C. W., and Selby, H. A. 1968. "Sex Differences in the Incidence of Susto in Two Zapotec Pueblos: An Analysis of the Relationships between Sex Role Expectations and a Folk Illness." Ethnology, 7:95-105.

Orellana, Sandra L. 1977. "Aboriginal Medicine in Highland Guatemala." Medical Anthropology, 1:113-56.

Ortiz, Sylvia. 1977. Espiritualismo en Mexico. INAH: Cuadernos de Trabajo, no. 20.

Parsons, Talcott. 1975. "The Sick Role and the Role of the Physician Reconsidered." Health and Society, Summer:257-78.

Parsons, Talcott, and Fox, Renee. 1952. "Illness, Therapy and the Modern Urban American Family." Journal of Social Issues, 8:31-44.

Paz, Octavio. 1961. The Labyrinth of Solitude. New York: Grove Press.

Pellegrino, Edmund D. 1979. "The Sociocultural Impact of Twentieth-Century Therapeutics." In Morris Vogel and Charles E. Rosenberg, eds., The Therapeutic Revolution. Philadelphia: University of Pennsylvania Press, pp.245-66.

Pelletier, Kenneth R. 1979. "Mind as Healer, Mind as Slayer." New York: Dell.

Pomerleau, Ovide, and Brady, John Paul, eds. 1979. Behavioral Medicine: Theory and Practice. Baltimore: Williams & Wilkins.

Pratt, Lois V. 1976. "Reshaping the Consumer's Posture in Health Care." In Eugene B. Gallagher, ed., The Doctor-Patient Relationship in the Changing Health Scene. Washington, D.C. U.S. Department of Health, Education and Welfare; Public Health Service, National Institutes of Health, DHEW Publication no. (NIH) 78-183, pp. 197-214.

Press, Irving. 1969. "Urban Illness: Physicians, Cures and Dual use in Bogota." Journal of Health and Social Behavior, 10:209-18.

_____ 1971 "The Urban Curandero." American Anthropologist, 73:714-50.

_____ 1978 "Bureaucracy versus Folk Medicine: Implications from Seville, Spain." In M. H. Logan and Ed E. Hunt, eds., Health and the Human Condition: Persepctives on Medical Anthropology. North Scituate, Mass.: Duxbury Press, pp. 376-87.

Prince, Raymond. 1968. "Can the EEG Be Used in the Study of Possession States?" In R. Prince, ed., Trance and Possession States. Montreal: R.M. Bucke Memorial Society, pp. 121-37.

_____ 1973 "Mystical Experience and the Certainty of Belonging: An Alternative to Insight and Suggestion in Psychotherapy." In Richard H. Cox, ed., Religious Systems and Psychotherapy. Springfield: Charles C. Thomas, pp. 307-18.

Prince, Raymond, ed., 1982. "Shamans and Endorphins." Ethos, 10:299-423.

Rappaport, Roy A. 1979. Ecology, Meaning and Religion. Richmond, Va.: North Atlantic Books.

Rhein, Reginald W., Jr. 1980. "Placebo: Deception or Potent Therapy?" Medical World News, 21 4 Feb.:37-47.

Richter, Maurice N., Jr. 1972. Science as a Cultural Process. Cambridge: Schenkman.

Roberts, Bryan. 1968. "Protestant Groups and Coping with Urban Life in Guatemala City." American Journal of Sociology, 73:753-67.

Rogler, L., and Hollinghead, A. B. 1961. "The Puerto Rican Spiritualist as a Psychiatrist." American Journal of Sociology, 67:17-21.

Romanell, Patrik. 1952. The Making of the Mexican Mind. Lincoln: University of Nebraska Press.

Romanucci-Ross, Lola. (a.k.a. L.R. Schwartz). 1969. "The Hierarchy of Resort in Curative Practices: The Admiralty Islands, Melanesia." Journal of Health and Social Behavior, 10:201-9.
_____ 1973 Conflict, Violence, and Morality in a Mexican Village. Palo Alto: National Press Books.
Romm, F. J., et al. 1976. "Correlates of Outcomes in Patients with Congestive Heart Failure." Medical Care, 14:765.
Rosenberg, Charles E. 1979. "The Therapeutic Revolution: Medicine, Meaning and Social Change in Nineteenth-Century America." In M. J. Vogel and Charles E. Rosenberg, eds., The Therapeutic Revolution. Philadelphia: University of Pennsylvania Press, ppo. 3-25.
Rosenfield, Sarah, 1980. "Sex Differences in Depression. Do Women Always Have Higher Rates? Journal of Health and Social Behavior, 21:33-42.
Rubel, Arthur. 1960. "Concepts of Disease in Mexican American Culture." American Anthropologist, 62:795-814.
_____ 1964 "The Epidemiology of a Folk Illness: Susto in Hispanic America." Ethnology, 3:268-83.
_____ 1971 Across the Tracks: Mexican-Americans in a Texas City. Austin: University of Texas Press.
Rutstein, D. D., et al. 1976. "Measuring the Quality of Medical Care." New England Journal of Medicine, 294:582-88.
Schwartz, L. R. See Romanucci-Ross, Lola.
Scotch, N.A., and Geiger, H. Jack. 1963. "An Index of Symptom and Disease in Zulu Culture." Human Organization, 22:304-11.
Scrimshaw, Nevin S., et al. 1969. " Nutrition and Infection Field Study in Guatemalan Villages, 1959-1964: An Evaluation of Medical, Social, and Public Health Benefits, with Suggestions for Further Field Study." Archives of Environmental Health, 18:51-62.
Selby, Henry A. 1974. Zapotec Deviance. Austin and London: University of Texas Press.
Shapiro, Arthur K. 1959. "The Placebo Effect in the History of Medical Treatment: Implications for Psychiatry." American Journal of Psychiatry, 116:298-304.
_____ 1971 "Placebo Effects in Medicine, Psychotherapy and Psychoanalysis." In Allen E. Bergin and Sol L. Garfield, eds., Handbook of Psychotherapy and Behavior Change. New York: John Wiley & Sons, pp. 439-73.
Shapiro, Edward. 1978. "The Psychodynamics and Developmental Psychology of the Borderline Patient: A Review of the Literature." The American Journal of Psychiatry, Nov. 135:11.
Sharon, Douglas. 1978. Wizard of the Four Winds; A Shaman's Story. New York: Free Press.
Siegler, Miriam, and Osmond, Humphrey. 1974. Models of Madness, Models of Medicine. New York: MacMillan.
Sigerist, Henry E. 1977. "The Special Position of the Sick." In David Landy, eds., Culture, Disease and Healing. New York: MacMillan, pp. 388-94.
Silverman, J. 1967. "Shamans and Acute Schizophrenia." American Anthropologist, 69:21-31.
Simoni, Joseph J., and Ball, Richard A. 1978. "Institutionalized Exploitation: The Case of the Mexican Medicine Huckster." Sociological Symposium, 23:27-40.
Simpson, Lesley Byrd. 1967. Many Mexicos, 4th ed. Berkeley: University of California Press.
Skultans, Vieda. 1974. Intimacy and Ritual. London: Routledge & Kegan Paul.
Smith, Mary Lee, and Glass, Gene V. 1977. "Meta-Analysis of Psychotherapy Outcome Studies." American Psychologist, 32:752-60.
Snyder, Solomon H. 1977a. "Opiate Receptors and Internal Opiates." Scientific American, March:44-56.

_____ 1971b "The Brain's Own Opiates." Chemical and Engineering News, 28 Nov.

Solomons, Noel W. and Gerald T. Keusch, 1981. "Nutritional Implications of Parasite Infections." Nutrition Reviews, 30:149-81.

Sontag, Susan, 1979. Illness as Metaphor, New York: Vintage Books.

Starfield, Barbara, and Scheff, David. 1972. "Effectiveness of Pediatric Care: The Relationship between Processes and Outcome." Pediatrics, 49:547-52.

Stavenhagen, Rodolfo, 1967. "Las Relaciones Entre la Estratificacion Social y la Dinámica de Classes." In Anthony Leeds, ed., Social Structure, Stratification and Mobility. Washingtn, D.C.: Pan American Union.

_____ 1970 "Social Aspects of Agrarian Structure in Mexico." In Rodolfo Stavenhagen, ed., Agrarian Problems and Peasant Movements in Latin America. Garden City, N.Y.: Anchor Books, pp. 225-70.

Sternbach, Richard A. 1974. Pain Patients. New York: Academic Press.

Strupp, Hans H. 1980a. "Success and Failure in Time-Limited Psychotherapy." Archives of General Psychiatry, 37:595-603.

_____ 1980b "Success and Failure in Time-Limited Psychotherapy." Archives of General Psychiatry, 37:708-16.

_____ 1980c "Success and Failure in Time-Limited Psychotherapy." Archives of General Psychiatry, 37:831-41.

_____ 1980d "Success and Failure in Time-Limited Psychotherapy." Archives of General Psychiatry, 37:947-54.

_____ 1980e "Psychotherapy: Assessing Methods." Science, 207:590.

Suchman, Edward A. 1965. "Social Factors in Medical Deprivation." American Journal of Public Health, 13:1725-33.

_____ 1966 "Health Orientation and Medical Care." American Journal of Public Health, 1:97-105.

_____ 1972 "Social Patterns of Illness and Medical Care." In E. G. Jaco, ed., Patients, Physicians and Illness, 2nd ed. New York: Free Press, pp. 262-79.

Suchman, Edward, and Phillips, Bernard S. 1958. "An Analysis of the Validity of Health Questionnaires." Social Forces, 36:223-32.

Susser, Mervy. 1974. "Ethical Components in the Definition of Health." International Journal of Health Services, 4:539-48.

Swanson, Guy E. 1974. The Birth of the Gods. Ann Arbor: University of Michigan Press.

Szasz, Thomas S., and Hollender, Marc H. 1956. "A Contribution to the Philosophy of Medicine." Archives of International Medicine, 97:585-592.

Tambiah, S. J. 1977. "The Cosmological and Performative Significance of a Thai Cult of Healing through Meditation." Culture, Medicine and Psychiatry, 1:97-132.

Taussig, Michael T. 1980. "Reification and the Consciousness of the Patient." Social Science and Medicine, 14B:3-14.

Thomas, Lewis. 1974. The Medusa and the Snail. Toronto: Bantam Books.

_____ 1977 "On the Science and Technology of Medicine." Daedalus, 106:35-46.

Torrey, E. Fuller, 1972. The Mind Game: Witchdoctors and Psychiatrists. New York: Emerson Hall.

Truax, Charles B., and Mitchell, Kevin M. 1971. "Research on Certain Therapist Interpersonal Skills in Relation to Process and Outcome." In Allen E. Bergin and Sol L. Garfield, eds., Handbook of Psychotherapy and Behavior Change. New York: John Wiley & Sons, pp. 299-344.

Trussell, Raye E., et al. 1956. "Comparison of Various Methods of Estimating the Prevalence of Chronic Disease in a Community: The Hunterdon County Study." American Journal of Public Health and the Nation's Health, 46:173-82.

Turner, Victor W. 1967. The Forest of Symbols. Ithaca: Cornell University Press.

_____ 1968 The Drums of Affliction: A Study of Religious Process among the Ndembu of Zambia. Oxford: Clarendon Press and the International African Institute.

_____ 1969 The Ritual Process: Structure and Anti-Structure. Chicago: Aldine.

_____ 1974 "An Ndembu Doctor in Practice." In Ari Kiev, ed., Magic, Faith and Healing. New York: Free Press, pp. 230-63.

Tursky, B., and Sternbach, R. A. 1975. "Further Physiological Correlates of Ethnic Differences in Response to Shock." In Matisyohu Weisenberg, ed., Pain: Clinical and Experimental Perspectives. Saint Louis: C. V. Mosby, pp. 152-157.

Uzzell, Douglas. 1974. "Susto Revisited: Illness as Strategic Role." American Ethnologist, 1:369-78.

Villoro, Luis. 1967. El Proceso Ideológico de la Revolución de Independecia. Mexico City: Universidad Nacional Autonoma de Mexico.

Wallace, Anthony. 1960 "The Institutionalization of Cathartic and Control Strategies in Iroquois Religious Psychotherapy." In Marvin Opler Culture and Mental Health, pp. 3-98.

_____ 1966 Religion. New York: Random House.

_____ 1970 Culture and Personality, 2nd ed. New York: Random House.

Wallace, Robert. 1972. "The Physiology of Meditation." Scientific American, 226:34-90.

Wallace, Robert, and Benson, Herbert. 1970. "Psychological Effects of Transcendental Meditation." Science, 167:1751-54.

Waxler, Nancy E. 1976. "Social Change and Psychiatric Illness in Ceylon: Traditional and Modern Conceptions of Disease and Treatment." In William P. Lebra, ed., Culture-Bound Syndromes, Ethnopsychiatry, and Alternate Therapies, pp. 222-40. Honolulu: The University Press of Hawaii.

Weinberg, Steven. 1974. "Reflections of a Working Scientist." Daedalus, 103(3):33-46.

Weisenberg, Matisyohu. 1977. "Pain and Pain Control." Psychological Bulletin, 84:1008-44.

_____ 1978 "The Regulation of Pain." Annals of the New York Academy of Sciences, 340:102-14.

Weissman, Myrna M. and G. L. Klerman. 1977. "Sex Differences and the Epidemiology of Depression." Archives of General Psychiatry, 34:98-112.

Weissman, Myrna et al. 1979. "The Efficacy of Drugs and Psychotherapy." American Journal of Psychotherapy, 136(4B):555-58.

Werner, Richard. 1980. "Deception and Self-Deception in Shamanism and Psychiatry." International Journal of Social Psychiatry, 26:41-52.

White, Kerr L. 1973. Life and Death and Medicine. San Francisco: W. H. Freemen, pp. 3-16.

Whitehurst, Carol A., and Jaco, E. Gartly. 1979. "Hospital Utilization before Medicare-Medicaid: A Baseline Study." In E. Gartly Jaco, ed., Patients, Physicians and Illness, 3rd ed. New York: Free press, pp. 53-68.

Willems, Emilio. 1967. Followers of the New Faith: Cultural Change and the Rise of Protestantism in Brazil and Chile. Nashville: Vanderbilt University Press.

_____ 1974 "Religious Mass Movements and Social Change in Brazil." In Dwight B. Heath, ed., Contemporary Cultures and Societies of Latin America. New York: Random House, pp. 452-68.

Willis, W. D., et al. 1979. "Central Mechanisms of Pain Control." In Kosterlitz and Terenius, eds., 239-62.

Wilson, Bryan. 1963. "Millennialism in Comparative Perspective." Comparative Studies in Society and History, 6:93-114.

Wolf, Eric R. 1956. "Aspects of Group Relations in a Complex Society: Mexico." American Anthropologist, 58:1065-78.

_____ 1959 Sons of the Shaking Earth. Chicago: University of Chicago Press.

Wolf, Eric, and Hansen, Edward. 1972. The Human Condition in Latin America. New York: Oxford University Press.

Wolff, Berthold B. 1980. "Perceptions of Pain." Sciences, 20(6):10-29.

Wolff, B. B., and Langley, S. 1975. "Cultural Factors and the Response to Pain: A Review." In Matisyohu Weisenberg, ed., Pain, Clinical and Experimental Perspectives. Saint Louis: C. V. Mosby, pp. 144-51.

Wolff, B. B., et al. 1979. "Evolution of Expression of Pain (Acute and Chronic)." Kosterlitz and Terenius, eds. (80-91).

Worsley, Peter. 1968. The Trumpet Shall Sound. New York: Schocken.

Young, Allan. 1976. "Some Implications of Medical Beliefs and Practices for Social Anthropology." American Anthropologist, 78:5-24.

_____ 1977 "Order, Analogy and Efficacy in Ethiopian Medical Divination." Culture, Medicine, and Psychiatry, 1:183-99.

Young, James C. 1978a. Health Care in Pichataro: Medical Decision Making in a Tarascan Town of Michoacan, Mexico. Ph.D. diss. University of California, Riverside.

_____ 1978b "Illness Categories and Action Strategies in a Tarascan Town." American Ethnologist, 5:81-97.

Zales, Michael R. 1978. "Mysticism: Psychodynamics and Relationship to Psychopathology." In Arthur Sugerman and Ralph E. Tarter, eds., Expanding Dimensions of Consciousness. New York: Springer.

Zborowski, Mark. 1952. "Cultural Components in Response to Pain." Journal of Social Issues, 8:16-30.

_____ 1968 People in Pain. San Francisco: Jossey Bass.

Zea, Leopoldo. 1968. El Positivismo en Mexico. Nacimiento, Apogeo y Decadencia. Mexico City: Fondo de Cultural Economica.

Ziegler, Frederick, et al. 1960. "Contemporary Conversion Reactions: A Clinical Study." American Journal of Psychiatry, 116:901-10.

Zimmermann, Manfred, et al. 1979. "Recurrent Persistent Pain: Mechanisms and Models." In Kosterlitz and Terenius, eds. (367-82).

Zinberg, Norman E., ed. 1977. Altered States of Consciousness. New York: Free Press.

Zola, I. K. 1966. "Culture and Symptoms: An Analysis of Patients' Presenting Complaints." American Sociological Review, 31:615-30.

_____ 1973 "Pathways to the Doctor: From Person to Patient." Social Science and Medicine, 7:677-89.

Zoraida, Vazquez, Josefina. 1976. "Los Primeros Tropiezos." Historia General de Mexico, vol. 3. Mexico City: Colegio de Mexico, vol. 3, pp. 1-84.

GLOSSARY

Aire	traditionally an illness produced by a tormented spirit possessing the body. The predominant symptom is a crooked mouth.
Bilis	the expression of extreme anger traditionally believed instrumental in producing a variety of illness states.
Bruja (f)	a sorcerer or witch.
Cabeza	pertains to the forehead area and around the temples.
Cantina	a local bar or liquor serving place.
Cerebro	pertains to the occipital-medula region of the head—down to the nuchal muscle.
Cintura	refers to pain in waist as well as lower back. Women may also associate the pain in the waist with pain in the ovaries.
Compadrazgo	ritual kinship ties established between individuals through religious (e.g. baptism, marriage) or secular (e.g. graduation) rituals.
Coraje	the expression of anger (less intense than *bilis*), traditionally believed instrumental in producing illness.
Cuajo	a cultural illness of children associated with symptoms such as intestinal dysfunction and loss of body symmetry.
Curandera (f) *curandero* (m)	a folk curer. (Spiritualists do not like to be called *curanderos;* or *curanderas,* because they usually associate its designation with witchcraft.)
Desalojo	a term Spiritualists use to refer to a cleansing of the body which they provide in the temple.
Ejido system	Mexico's land reform program under which land was redistributed to the peasants following the Mexican Revolution of 1910.
Ejidatario	a holder of *ejido* land.

243

Empacho	bolus attached to the stomach, traditionally believed to be experienced by children.
Limpia	traditionally referred to a cleansing of the body using special branches. (Spiritualists mock the use of this term.)
Limpio	(literally meaning clean) A concept in Spiritualism referring to one's carrying out ritual activities properly "as it ought to be done."
Loco	crazy, characterizing persons "who don't know what they are doing," and "who have lost their five senses."
Material	Spiritualist's designation, to physical aspects of a human being. Spiritualists also use *material* when speaking of physicians.
Muina	expression of anger, believed instrumental in producing illness.
Nervios	nerves, refers to an illness etiology or an illness associated with a nervous state and physical impairment.
Pasante	medical students who have completed all their requirements except a one-year mandatory social service.
Promesa	in traditional Catholicism a vow made to the saints. Spiritualists scoff at this practice.
Pulque	undistilled alcoholic beverage extracted from *Agave* widely used in rural Mexico and especially in central Mexico where it had its origins in Pre-Conquest times.
Reumatismo bilioso	an extreme rheumatic condition.
Susto	an illness state traditionally associated with an unexpected startle or fright.

INDEX

Acute pain, distinguished from chronic, 166–167
Adams, R., 18, 19, 43, 51, 171
Aire: belief in and social order, 51–52; control group's lack of experience with, 72; and somatization, 124–126; supernatural traditional Mexican etiological belief in, 51, 56, 185, and compared with Spiritualist etiological beliefs, 52, 185; symptoms of, 51, 124–126. *See also* Cultural illness; Etiological beliefs; Perturbed spirits
Agrarian Reform in Mexico. *See Ejido* lands; *Ejido* system; *Ejido* holders
Akil, H., 167
Alcohol use in Mexico, 31; prohibited by Spiritualists, 21, 31, 165, 186–187
Altered States of Consciousness. *See* "Development"; Spiritualist rituals; Trance; Trance States
Amkraut, A., 50
Anderson, W., 160
Anger, types of, 49–50. *See also* Etiological beliefs, Traditional Mexican
Antonovsky, A., 5, 50, 167
Autonomic nervous system, and Spiritualist healing, 164–165. *See also* Spiritualist therapeutic techniques; Physiological analysis of nonbiomedical therapeutics

Bahr, D., 161, 174
Battle, C., 4
Bazant, J., 17, 18
Beecher, H., 168
Benfari, R., 120
Ben-Sira, Z., 162
Benson, H., 109, 160, 164, 168, 169
Bereavement, and traditional Mexican etiological beliefs, 49. *See also* Etiological beliefs, Traditional Mexican, Spiritualist.
Berger, P., 18, 160, 170, 174, 182, 194, 196, 197, 227n3
Bergin, A., 4, 161, 180

Biomedicine: and chronic illness, 8, 173, 195; components of, 158–159; in Hidalgo State, 44–46; and doctor-patient relationship model of 85–86; limitations of, 158–159, 194–196; in Mexico, 41, 49; patients' perception of, 65–66; rejection of 8; scientific aspects of 3, 192; in synbiosis with nonbiomedical therapeutics, 8, 51, 54, 60, 62, 77, 78, 195–196; symbolic aspects of, 7–8, 159–160, 194, 197; and technology, 8, 159–160, 194–195; as a therapeutic option, 42, 44–45, 49, 63–64, 75, 76, 78; as a Western cultural phenomenon, 194. *See also* Physicians; *Pasante*
Blumer, D., 63, 129, 167
Bone-setters, 10, 43, 47; patient seeking treatment from, 131
Borderline personality, defined, 178–179, example of (case vignette), 175–179. *See also* Symbols
Bourguignon, E., 163
Breuer, J., 125
Brody, H., 8, 168, 169
Brown, R., 37
Burridge, K., 33
Butler Flora, C., 25

Case vignettes: examples of recruitment into Spiritualism, 29–30, 30–31; patients' complaints, 72–74, 92–108, 109–111, 111–116; of successfully treated patients, 124–126, 126–128, 131–132, 132–134, 134–135, 135–137; failed patients, 175–179, 179–180
Cassell, E., 170, 173
Casper, E., 168
Catholic church: in conflict with Spiritualist ideology, examples of, 113–114, 132–134; in Mexico, 17–18; and social conflict, 34; and therapeutic choice, 70, 173, 188; vs Spiritualism, 31–32, 33
Cay, E., 118
Chapple, E., 171

245

Children: effects of Spiritualist
therapeutics on, 123; not recruited
as regulars, 128; patients of
Spiritualist healers, 67, 94, 98, 103;
proportion of, 58, 123; and response
to Spiritualist healing, 126;
treatment of at home, 67
Clark, M., 6
Chronic illness: and biomedicine, 8,
195; failure of biomedicine to deal
with, 158–159; perpetuated in
rural Mexico, 8, 195; presented to
healers, 63–64, 65; and regulars
(adherents of Spiritualism), 129;
and study of therapeutic
outcomes, 118–119; and symbolic
cures, 8
Chronic pain: and biomedicine, 8,
195; distinguished from acute pain,
166–167; and placebo effect, 168;
and psychological states, 166–167;
treated by Spiritualist healing, 197.
See also Spiritualist healing.
Cintura: See Cultural illnesses.
Cleansing: effect on patients, 125,
126, 127, 137–138, 162–163;
meaning to patients, 91; and
Spiritualists, 108; performance of,
86–87, 89, 108; and variation in,
90; and restoration of order,
170–171; as rite of purification,
170–171, 197; sought by patients,
60–61, 62, 77; symbolic
significance of, 163, 170–172,
terminates the sick role, 162;
traditional practice in Mexico,
171
Cohen, Y., 181, 187
Comaroff, J., 159
Control group (healthy individuals,
non-Spiritualists): compared with
Spiritualist adherents (regulars)
along socioeconomic and
sociocultural dimensions, 187–189,
and life histories compared, 72,
173; distinguished by their
professed Catholicism, 188, and by
absence of past illness, 72, 173
Cornell Medical Index (CMI):
described, 202–204; how baseline
established for Mexican
population, 123–124; physician and
temple patients' scores compared,
63–64, 78; scores of successfully
and unsuccessfully treated patients
145; scoring of, 127, 129–130; used

in study to measure therapeutic
outcome, 120, 121
Cosio Villegas, D. 17, 19
Craine, J. 159
Crapanzano, V., 163
Cultural analysis: of nonbiomedical
therapeutics, 170–172; and
purification, 171–172; and symbolic
aspects of, 171–172
Cultural illnesses: *aire,* 51–52, 56,
124–126, 185; *cintura,* 55, 56, 132,
134; *cuajo,* 43; *empacho,* 60; *susto,*
49, 60, 126–128. *See also Aire;*
Etiological beliefs
Curanderas/Curanderos:
nonbiomedical type healer, 10, 43,
47; being replaced by Spiritualist
healers, 43; patients seeking
treatment from, 73, 132, 179;
Spiritualist healers similar to urban
type, 6. *See also* Nonbiomedical
healers.
Currier, R., 171

Davis Tzu, V., 45
Davis, J., 129
Depressive disorders: in adherents
(regulars), 112–116, 129; and
chronic pain, 167; provoked by
Spiritualist therapeutics, 170;
somatization of, 115, 126, 163,
167; treated by Spiritualist
therapeutics, 174. *See also*
Patients, Temple (regulars);
Somatization
"Development": control of
adherents in, 27; described, 23,
25, 28; effects on patients, 30, 73,
74, 114, 132, 133, 134, 176; entry
into, 28, 29, 73; and indoctrination
of Spiritualist ideology, 172;
physiological effects of, 164–165;
and preparation for healing and
functionary roles, 29; as a
therapeutic procedure, 109. *See
also* Spiritualist therapeutic
techniques; Trance
Diaz, J., 171
Disease: biomedical model of,
53–54; and biomedial treatment
of, 7; curtailed symbolically, 8;
and ecological conditions, 36–37;
as diagnosed by physician, 62–63,
78; difficulties in assessing
outcomes of, 4; distinguished from
illness, 5; healing of, 66; in

Hidalgo State, causes of, 223
Disorders, untreatable by Spiritualist therapeutic techniques, 121, 122, 174–175, 175–179
Dissident religious movement, Spiritualism as a, 10, 11, 13, 32–34, 191, 198. *See also* Spiritualism, Mexican
DiTella, T., 17
Doctor-patient relationship: biomedical model of, 85–86; component of the therapeutic encounter, 7; emphasized in industrialized societies, 162; and the healing process, 6, 160–162; Spiritualism compared with psychotherapy, 161; and sharing of common beliefs, 161. *See also* Healer-patient relationship (Spiritualist)
Dohrenwend, B., 63
Donabedian, A., 118, 161
Douglas, M., 19, 171
Dual use, defined, 5: examples of, 60, 75–76. *See also* Therapeutic choice
Dysphonic affect. *See* Somatization; Depressive disorders

Ecology: Hidalgo State, of, 35–40; effects on population's health, 8, 36–37, 136–137; and healing symbols, 197
Education in Hidalgo State: expanded demand for, 39; effects on women, 39
EEG patterns and Spiritualist healing, 164–165
Efficacy. *See* Therapeutic outcomes of, Biomedicine; Spiritualist therapeutics
Egbert, L., 160, 168
Eisenberg, L., 54
Eister, A., 32
Ejido lands: disputes over and illness, 73; distribution of, 37, 38; and health status, 73; holdings of adherents, 188; size of holdings in region, 38; transmission of, 73
Ejido system, Mexico's, defined, 18
Ejido holders, integration into Mexican bureaucracy, 188
Endorphins/enkephalins. *See* Pain reduction
Engel, G., 3, 50, 54, 158, 159

Escudero, J., 40
Etiological beliefs: biomedical 53–54; and Mexican history, 19; and social institutions 19, 51–52
Etiological beliefs, traditional Mexican: *aire,* 51; altered by Spiritualists, 113, 114, 133; and anger, 49–50; categories of, 48–52, 55–56; compared with etic stress model, 50–51; and emotions, 49; holistic explanatory model, 50; and natural causes, 29, 48–51, 55–56; and nerves, 29, 50; and nutrition, 49; and psychological disturbances, 179–180; and supernatural causes, 51–52, 56; and *susto,* 49; and witchcraft, 51–52, 132
Etiological beliefs, Spiritualist: *aire,* 52; compared with biomedical etiologies, 53–54; compared with traditional etiologies, 11, 51–53; and natural causes, 52–54; and mind/body dualism, 52, 53; and social inequality, 53; and social organization, 52–53; and supernatural causes, 52, 54, 176; and witchcraft, 52, 59

Fabrega, H., Jr., 5, 9, 41, 49, 54, 63, 66, 84, 120, 160, 161, 166, 185, 190, 191, 204, 224n5, 226n1
Family structure: and change in rural Mexico, 40; and differential effect on men and women; and role of Spiritualist healers, 67
Family structure and therapeutic choice, 68–69
Fernandez, J., 173
Firth, R., 20
Fiske, D., 4, 119
Flores Caballero, R., 17
Florescano, R., 17
Folk healers. *See* Nonbiomedical healers; Spiritualist healers; Therapeutic options
Folk healing. *See* Nonbiomedical healing; Spiritualist healing
Foster, G., 4, 41, 43, 48, 51, 52, 54, 119, 182
Founder, of Mexican Spiritualism. *See* Spiritualism, Mexican
Fox, R., 82, 184
Frank, J., 159, 161, 180
Freedman, A., 126, 129, 181
Freidson, E., 41, 194, 204, 224n3

Functionaries, in Spiritualist temples: core membership, 28–29; duties of, 14; elite group, 27; hierarchy of, 15; interaction among, 16, 34; preparation of, 23; recruitment of, 28; relation with spirit protectors, 28; and with temple head, 16; tasks of, 15, 84. *See also* Recruitment into Spiritualism; Spiritualism, Mexican

Garrison, V., 5, 10, 25, 136, 180, 185, 191, 202, 224n1, 227n1
Gellhorn, E., 109, 164, 165
Gill, D., 160
Gillin, J., 165, 172
Glade, Wm., 18, 34
Glasser, M., 161, 180
Glick, L., 158
Glueck, B., 164
Goldkind, V., 18, 34
Gonzalez, L., 18
Gonzalez Navarro, M., 19
Goode, Wm., 39, 187

Hahn, R., 168
Harwood, A., 10, 13, 16, 25, 61, 163, 180
Haynes, A., 160
Head of Spiritualist temple: abilities of, 16, 186; characterized by a patient, 177, 227n4; controls spirit world, 26; description of, 1; economic mobility of, 186, 190; relation with Head temple in Mexico City, 15, 16, and with members and other functionaries, 16, and with spirit protectors, 85, and with temple healers, 85, 190; social status of, 190; and women, 10, 16, 186
Healer-patient relationship. *See* Doctor-patient relationship; Healer-patient relationship (Spiritualist)
Healer-patient relationship (Spiritualist): compared with physician, 85, 86, and with psychotherapy, 161–162; and differences in beliefs, 6, 11, 87, examples of exchanges with firstcomers and habitual users (nonregulars), 92–108, and with adherents (regulars), 109–111; nature of, 6, 84–85; impersonal nature of, 84–85; nonverbal

interaction of, 86; observations of, 200; phases of, 86–108; role in Spiritualist healing, 161–162; standard-interaction patterns of, 88–89; and time spent with firstcomers and habitual users (nonregulars), 84, with adherents (regulars), 108; variation in standard interaction patterns of, 89–91
Healing role, curative effect of on patients, 89–90, 109, 115; *See also* Therapeutic techniques, Spiritualist; Patients, Temple, (regulars)
Healing process; importance of understanding, 13; and doctor-patient relations, 7, 160–162; and recruitment into Spiritualism. *See also* Therapeutic outcomes; Therapeutic outcomes of Spiritualist healing
Healing techniques. *See* Spiritualist therapeutic techniques; Therapeutic techniques and procedures
Health: and ecological conditions; definition of, 5; and socio-economic conditions, 37–40; and therapeutic outcome, 120
Herbal medicines: patients' perception of, 66; popularity of, 44; usages of, 42–44, 205–222
Herbalists: popularity of, 44; as a therapeutic option, 44, 47
Heukelekian, H., 36
Hidalgo state: availability of physicians in, 44; industrialization in, 38; irrigation in, 35–36; socio-economic conditions in, 37–40 *See also* Education in
Hierarchical resort. *See* Dual use; Therapeutic options
Hinkle, L., 66, 70
Hogarty, G., 129, 181
Holden, C., 7
Holmes, T., 50
Homeopaths, 42
Horton, R., 196
Hudson, Ch., 174
Hughes, Ch., 161

Illness: Cultural nature of, 5, 72–74, 120, 194–195; distinguished from disease, 5; importance of studying, 9; lay models of, 60–64; compared with physician's model, 62–64, 78;

operational definition of, 120; prolonged by biomedical treatment, 158–159; and recruitment into Spiritualism, 28; reported to Spiritualist healers, 61–62, 77; and Spiritualist healing, 137, 161; unresponsive to therapy, 175–179; when not curable biomedically, 11

Illness attribution. *See* Etiological beliefs, traditional Mexican; Spiritualist

Illness networks and therapeutic choice, 70–71, and wage-labor migration 71, 173

Industrialization: in Mexico, 16–19; and education, 38–39; effects on Mexican society, 33; effects on region, 38; effects on women, 39; and emotional concerns, 62; and rise of Mexican Spiritualism, 16–18; 198; and social class, 33

Ingham, J., 51, 171

Intestinal parasites, in the rural region, 36

Intra-cultural diversity: anthropological study of, 5; in healing techniques and styles, 89–108; in response to Spiritualist treatments, 120–121, 122–123, 128; in response to symbols, 9; and therapeutic choice, 6, 57–60, 62–63, 172–174

Inui, T., 160

Irradiations, prescribed by healers as therapy, 93, 94, 102; and Spiritualist rituals, 21–23, 29. *See also* Spiritualist rituals

Jacobs, S., 50
Janzen, J., 174
Jilek, W., 120
Jones, J., 168
Jospe, M., 159, 168, 169, 175

Kalimo, E., 129
Kane, R., 119, 120
Kardec, Allan, unfamiliar to Spiritualists, 20
Katon, W., 163
Kearney, M., 6, 10, 54
Kelly, I., 10
Kennedy, D., 158
Kernberg, O., 178
Kiev, A., 180, 181
Kleinman, A., 4, 5, 41, 61, 65, 69, 70, 85, 86, 115, 117, 121, 136, 158, 159, 161, 185, 194, 196, 204

Korsch, B., 68
Koss, J., 16
Krieger, D., 87, 165
Krippner, S., 87, 165
Kunkel, J., 18, 34

La Barre, W., 32
Lafaye, J., 20
Lagarriga, I., 10, 40
Landy, D., 6
Lanternari, V., 32
Laurell, C., 169, 199
Leach, E., 174
Leighton, A., 129, 182
Leininger, M., 196
Leslie, Ch., 41
Levine, J., 168
Levi-Strauss, C., 168
Lewis, I., 27, 28, 52, 53, 164, 185, 189
Lex, B., 109, 164, 165
Liberal Reform, The, in Mexico, and Mexican Spiritualism, 17
Lieban, R., 6, 66, 161, 171
Limpio, concept in Mexican Spiritualism 26–27, and example of, 101
Lindsay, M., 118
Lloyd, C., 50
Lock, M., 41, 196
Lopez Acuña D., 44–45
Low, S., 50
Luborsky, L., 161, 181
Ludwig, A., 164

Macho males: definition of, 186; how ascertained, 202; and Spiritualism, 186–187
Macklin, J., 10, 13, 16, 20, 25, 42, 191
Madsen, Wm., 6, 10, 41, 51, 161, 171
Male-female: differential effects on, of Spiritualist healing, 165; differential effects of social change on, 39; differential patterns of therapeutic choice, 68–69; differentially dealt with by Spiritualists, 186; equality in Spiritualism, 10, 32, 225n2; interaction and illness, 61–64; reticence about relationships, 86; scores on Cornell Medical Index (CMI) compared, 64–65; tensions and illness, 40, 64

Malnutrition, effects on rural population of, 37
Marshall, E., 4, 181
Massages, effects of, 125, and Spiritualist healing techniques, 87. *See also* Spiritualist therapeutic techniques
Matarazzo, R., 66
Maupin, E., 164
May P., 175, 181
McAuliffe, Wm., 4, 118, 158
McCreery, J., 175
McDermott, W., 66, 118, 119, 158, 159
Mechanic, D., 6, 7, 66, 69, 129, 159, 161, 168
Medical technology. *See* Biomedicine
Medicine hucksters, 44, 47
Melzack, R., 165, 167
Meneses, C., 46
Methodology. *See* Research methodology
Metzger, D., 172, 191
Mexican government health programs, 45–46; temple and physician patients access to 67
Mexican society: and Catholicism, 17–18; and ideology of equality, 33; and industrialization, 11, 17–18, 19; and the Mexican Revolution, 18; in the Nineteenth Century, 11, 17, 19, 33; and social classes, 11, 18, 33
Mexican Spiritualist healers. *See* Healer-patient interaction; Spiritualist healers
Mind-body dualism. *See* Etiological beliefs
Mitchell, J., 119
Modern medicine. *See* Biomedicine
Moerman, D., 159, 168
Moore, R., 20
Multilevel analyses of nonbiomedical therapeutics: cultural 170–172; physiological, 163–165; psychological, 166–170; sociological, 162–163

Nash, J., 6, 20
Nathanson, C., 66, 69, 70
Navarro, V., 199
Nerves, etiology and illness, 50, 64, experienced by women, 64. *See also* Etiological beliefs; traditional Mexican; Spiritualist

Ness, R., 185, 202, 204
Nobrega, F., 82, 118
Nonbiomedical healers: anthropological study of, 4, 6; difficulties in studying therapeutic outcomes of, 119; types of in Mexico, 41–44, 47
Nonbiomedical therapeutics: characteristics of, 3; importance of studying, 2; and religious ideology, 7; significance of rituals in, 7; symbiosis with biomedicine, 8, 51, 54, 60, 62, 77, 78, 195–196

Obeyesekere, G., 41, 161, 170
Ocampo, J., 17
O'Nell, C., 49
Orellana, S., 171
Ortiz, S., 14, 20
Outcomes. *See* Therapeutic outcomes; Therapeutic outcomes of Spiritualist therapeutics

Pain: acute-chronic distinguished, 166–167; control of, 166–167; patients' perceptions of, 8
Pain prone disorders. *See* Somatization
Pain reduction, physiological correlates of, 167–168
Parasites, types of in region, 36
Parasitosis, in rural Mexico, 8; promoted by local ecological conditions, 36–37, 223
Parsons, T., 161, 162
Patient-Healer relationship. *See* Healer-Patient relationship (Spiritualist); Doctor-patient relationship
Patients: in conflict with Spiritualist beliefs, 114, 115, 132, 133–134; and characteristics of, significant in therapeutic encounter, 7, 180; focus of study on, 120; and experience of "catharsis," 87; how select healers, 83; and payment to healers, 88; and perception of Spiritualist vs biomedical treatment, 65–66; and response to symbols, 174–175; and symbolic requirements for recovery, 7, 8, 195; unresponsive to Spiritualist therapeutics, 121, 174–180
Patients, temple: compared with controls (healthy, nonSpiritualists), 72, 173;

complaints of, 60–62, 77; description of, 1, 2; effects on of noncompliance, 114; mothers of seeking reassurance, 67; numbers of seeking treatment, 2; and personal problems presented to healers, 77

Patients, temple, habitual users (nonregulars): described, 59–60; and illness networks, 71; therapeutic choice of, 60; and wage labor migration, 71

Patients, temple, first comers (nonregulars): described, 59; therapeutic choices of, 65

Patients, temple and physician compared: behavioral and demographic profiles, 66–71; complaints of, 63; education, 68; migration patterns, 71; religious beliefs, 70

Patients, physician's, compared with regulars, 130, complaints of, 62–65, 78

Patients, temple, regulars, (adherents): compared with controls (healthy non-Spiritualists), 186; compared with physician's patients, 130; complaints of, 129, 132; dependence on temple, 129, 170, 174, 182–183, 185, 191, and economic consequences on, 191; described, 58–59; more women than men; 128; life transformed, 184; and sick role converted to healing role, 89–90, 109, 115, 163; and somatization, 115–116, 129, 167

Pasantes, in rural Mexico, 45

Paz, O., 18, 86

Pellegrino, E., 3, 8, 82, 117, 157, 158, 159

Pelletier, K., 50, 164, 165

Perturbed spirits: effects on the living, 23, 26, 29; and spirit possession, 52–53, 87, 176; Spiritualist belief in 25, 29; traditional Mexican belief in, 51, 185. *See also Aire*; Etiological beliefs, Spiritualist

Physician, private: behavioral and demographic characteristics of patients seeking treatment from, 66–71; complaints about Spiritualist healers, 58; patients' expectations of 65–66; patients' mistrust of, 65; patients presenting complaints to, 62–65, 75–76, 133, 135–136; relations with Spiritualist healers, 46, 58, 91, 107; as a therapeutic option, 29, 44–45, 47

Pharmaceuticals, prescribed by Spiritualist healers, 88; used in psychotherapy, 129

Pharmacy attendants: as a therapeutic option, 45, 47; treating patients, 45

Physiological analysis: of nonbiomedical therapeutics, 163–165; and pain reduction, 168; and the role of trancing, 164–165; and the therapeutic touch, 165

Placebo effect: defined, 168–169; limits of, 175; linkage between culture and biology, 9; nonresponders to, 175–180; physiological effects of, 8, 168–169; and Spiritualist healing, 86; and symbolic healing, 8, 168, 175

Pomerleau, O., 119, 166, 168

Practitioner-patient relationship. *See* Doctor-patient relationship; Healer-patient relationship, Spiritualist

Pratt, L., 160

Press, I, 5, 6, 71

Prince, R., 164, 181, 197

Psychological analysis: of nonbiomedical therapeutics, 163–165; and affective correlates, 169–170; and the placebo effect, 168–169; and reduction of pain perception, 166–167

Psychotherapy: aims of, 180–183, 198; compared with Spiritualist therapeutics, 161, 180–182; and the doctor-patient relationship, 161–162

Purification: and renewal of order, 197; significance of in Spiritualism, 170–172, 173, and cross-culturally, 174; *See also* Therapeutic techniques, Spiritualist; Cleansing

Rappaport, R., 197

Recruitment into Spiritualism, 28–31; aspects of the healing process, 109; examples of (case vignettes), 29–31, 111–116; and the healing role, 109; and illness,

Recruitment into Spiritualism *Continued*
28, 29; of individuals with a
"gift," 28, 176
Regulars (adherents). *See* Patients,
temple, regulars
Religion, in Mexico. *See* Catholic
church; Spiritualism; Dissident
religious movement
Research methodology: data
collection techniques described,
200–202; discussion of, 9–10, 199,
200–204; and follow ups, 112; and
life histories, 72, 173; selection of
samples, 200–202
Rhein, R., 168, 175
Richter, M., 194
Roberts, B., 25, 191
Romanell, P., 19
Romanucci-Ross, L., (a.k.a.L.R.
Schwartz) 19, 60, 224n5
Romm, F., 82, 158
Rosenberg, Ch., 158, 160
Rosenfield, S., 70
Rubel, A., 49, 60
Rutstein, D., 118

Scrimshaw, N., 37
Selby, H., 19
Self (home) treatment: of children,
67, as a therapeutic option, 41–42,
47. *See also* Therapeutic options
Sewage waters: definition of, 36; and
disease, 36–37; effects of, 36, 137;
parasitic content of, 36
Shapiro, A., 168, 175
Shapiro, E., 178
Sick role: Spiritualist denial of, 6,
88, 162–163; symbolically
terminated, 8, 137, 162;
transformed into healing role, 109,
128, 184–185, 191
Siegler, M., 161, 181
Siegrist, H., 162
Silverman, J., 185
Simpson, L., 17
Simoni, J., 44
Skultans, V., 61
Smith, M., 161
Snyder, S., 167
Social classes in Mexico, 18, and
stress, 32
Social institutions, and illness
etiologies, 11, 19, 51–53, 137
Socio-economic conditions. *See*
Hidalgo State

Sociological analysis: of
nonbiomedical therapeutics,
162–163; and relational networks,
163; and the sick role, 162–163.
See also Sick role
Solomons, N., 37
Somatization: in adherents
(regulars), 115–116, 129; and
borderline disorder, 177–178,
defined, 61; of depressive
disorders, 61, 126, 167, 185,
an example of, 125; not reinforced
by Spiritualist healers, 163;
widespread cross-culturally, 61
Spirit possession: *See* Etiological
beliefs; Spiritualist; *Aire;*
Spiritualist beliefs
Spirit protectors: attacked by
patient's evil spirit, 87, 114; and
Catholic saints, 26; effect on
patients, 114, 176; fail to work
limpio, 26, 27, 101; function of,
23, 25; identify themselves during
development, 25, 29; patients'
relation with, 110, 133; possessed
by all humans, 28, 133;
provenance of, 25–26; Spiritualist
belief in, 23; summoned by
healers, 2, 83; types of, 25, 26
Spirit transferred from patient to
healer, 87, 89, 95, 106, 114
Spiritualist adherents (regulars):
compared with controls
(nonSpiritualists), 129–130, 152,
185–189, and with nonadherents,
129–130, 152, 185–186, and with
physicians's patients, 130, and with
professed Catholics, 130, 152;
psychological conflicts of, 113–114,
133–134; sociodemographic profile
of, 189; therapeutic choices of,
58–59; transform sick role to
healing role, 128, 184–185, 191
Spiritualists (Mexican): anti-macho
teachings, 186–187; beliefs and
ideology, 19–20; compared with
biomedicine, 53–54, and
psychotherapy 180–183; control of
spirit world, 26, 34; distinguished
from Spiritists, 42; emphasis on
submission and obedience 21;
24–26, 114; epistemology, 19,
24–27; etiological beliefs, 11,
51–54; hierarchical organization
of, 15; opposition to Catholic

Church, 21, 31–32; pantheon of, 20; relation with physicians, 58–59, 93; social organization of, 14–16; and status quo, 25; use of flowers, 14, 90, 225n1. *See also* Etiological beliefs, Patients, temple; Spiritualism (Mexican)

Spiritualist beliefs: and the Catholic Church, 21; in the Chosen People, 20, 21, 172; in perturbed spirits, 23, 26, 29, 53, 87; in spirit protectors, 23, 25, 28, and the status quo, 191; in three categories of spirits, 25; and witchcraft, 11, 26, 59. *See also* Etiological beliefs; Perturbed spirits; Spirit protectors; Witchcraft

Spiritualist healers: advice to patients, 90–91; assistants to, 2; as agents of cultural change, 10, 11; ages of, 1; complaints presented to, 60–62, 92–108, 108–112; description of, 1, 2; effects on of healing role, 89–90, 109, 115; initiation into healing role, 29, 114; lack of shared understandings with patients, 6, 11, 87; lack of opportunity for economic mobility, 190–197; neither charlatans, nor miracle workers, 6, 193; pharmaceuticals prescribed by, 88, 114; prepare for treating patients, 2; prescriptions to patients, 88, 92–108, 108–112; 205–222; props used in treating patients, 1, 89; possessed by patients' spirit, 87, 89, 95, 106, 114; replacing other type of nonbiomedical practitioners, 43; relation with biomedicine and physicians, 46, 58, 91, 107; recruitment of, 29–31; regarded as witches, 46, 113, 114; role in alleviating mothers' anxieties, 67; separate trance from waking state, 190; similar to urban *curanderos*, 6; socio-economic status of, 189–192; summoning spirit protectors, 83; supernatural powers of, 86; theoretical importance of studying, 2, 3; use of flowers, 90, 100, 127, 133, 225n1 and witchcraft, 11

Spiritualist rituals: and control of participants, 27; description of, 21–24; "development," 23; effects

on adherents, 23–24; and lack of social interaction, 34, 191–192; as therapy, 13, 23–28; 93, 102; when performed, 21. *See also* "Development," Irradiations

Spiritualism (Mexican): and alcohol use, 21, 31, 186–187; and Catholicism, 10, 13, 16, 20, 21, 27, 31–32, 113, 133; and children of Israel, 20; and communitas and structure, 14, 27, 172; description of, 10; dispersal of, 10, 28, 34, 224n6; a dissident religious movement, 10, 11, 13, 32, 198, and reason for joining, 32; and economic mobility 190–192; effect on individual, 11; effect on Mexican society, 11, 192; 198; and sexual equality, 10, 32, 225n2; founder of, 13–14, 20; growth of, 10, 16–17; Head temple of, in Mexico City, 14, 15; hierarchical organization of, 15; history of, 11, 13, 14, 16–19, 20; and industrialization, 11; in Latin America, 20; and Mexican society, 24–25; and nationalism, 14, 22, 24, 172, 192; nonbiomedical health care, 10, 11, 32, 34, 198; relation with Mexican government, 16; and requisites for order, 11, 25, 33; significance of, 10–12; and Spiritism, 10, 13, 25; and social class, 11, 18, 32–34; and social equality, 11; and status quo, 25, 198–199; in the United States, 15

Spiritualist temples: description of, 1, 2; headed by women, 10; healing room of, 1, 83; number of patients seeking treatment in, 2; physical layout of, 13–14; seating arrangement in, 14; reason for dispersion, 10, 34; affective correlates of, 169–170

Spiritualist therapeutics: aims of, 182–183; attenuates feelings of being sick, 8, 172; compared with psychotherapy, 161, 180–183; complementary with biomedicine, 46, 48, 51, 54, 60, 63, 77, 78, 195–196; cost of, 42; creates conflicts for patients, 112–114, 132–134, 169–170; cultural analysis of, 170–172; deals with illness, 137; effects of, on patients, 131–136; effects of, on society,

Spiritualist therapeutics:
aims of *Continued*
192; failure of 6, 121, 139, 193,
with psychoses, 179–180; historical
context of, 182, 197; limited
success with borderline and
psychotic disorders 175–180; neither
miraculous cure, nor hoax, 6, 193;
and patients' dependence on temple
participation, 129, 170, 174, 182–
183, 185, 191; and pain perception,
166–168; and placebo effect,
168–169; physiological analysis of,
163–165; psychological analysis of,
166–170; and ritual, 13; sociological
analysis of, 162–163; success of,
121–128, 139, 140–144, 193, with
chronic pain, 197; with mild
psychiatric disorders, 174; and
trancing, 164–165. *See also*
Therapeutic outcomes of Spiritualist
healing
Spiritualist therapeutic techniques:
affective correlates of, 169–170; as
applied to first comers and
habitual temple users
(nonregulars), 83–108, to
adherents (regulars), 108–116; and
the autonomic nervous system,
164; and chronic pain, 197;
compared with biomedical
treatments, 85–86, 129; and
continuity of care, 84; effects of,
on patients, 125, 131–136; effects
on Mexican society, 184–187; and
the healer-patient relationship,
161–162; and the healing role,
89–90, 109, 115; influence on
therapeutic outcome, 7;
importance of, 196–197; and
massage, 87, 92, 133; and pain
perception, 166–167; and pain
reduction, 167–168; and patient's
internalization of symbols, 170;
and patient's passive "catharsis,"
85–86; and patients' confidence in
supernatural power of healers, 86;
and the placebo effect, 168–169;
provokes distress in patients,
112–114, 169–170; purification
procedures of, 8, and spirit
possession, 87, 89, 95, 106, 114;
sociological aspects of, 162–163;
and tactile communication, 9,
86–87, 92, 165; and trancing, 7
Starfield, B., 118

Stavenbagen, R., 33, 188
Sternbach, R., 63, 129, 167
Stress, and traditional Mexican
etiological beliefs, 50–51. *See also*
Etiological beliefs, traditional
Mexican
Strupp, H., 161
Suchman, E., 6
Susser, M., 120
Susto: case vignette of 126–128;
cultural illness, 90; traditional
Mexican etiological belief, 49. *See
also* Etiological beliefs, traditional
Mexican
Swanson, G., 19
Symbolic healing: and intra-cultural
variability, 9; limits of, 9,
physiological transformation of, 7,
168–169; and placebo effect, 8, 168,
175; and the sharing of symbols, 9.
See also Biomedicine; Cleansing;
Symbols
Symbols: effects on patients, 197;
how become shared, 9; how
transmitted by Spiritualists, 171;
nonsharing of, 197; patients'
responses to, 175, 195–196;
patients' unresponsiveness to,
174–180; and placebo
nonresponders, 175–180;
significance of for therapy, 137–138;
the sharing of, 172–174, 197
Szasz, T., 85

Tactile communication, and
Spiritualist healing techniques, 7,
165. *See also* Spiritualist
therapeutic techniques
Taussig, M., 199
Temple patients. *See* Patients,
temple, regulars, nonregulars
Therapeutic choices: of attached and
unattached women compared, 69;
and Catholic orthodoxy, 70, 173;
and chronic illness, 195; difference
between men and women, 66,
68–69; and education 68; effects of
on patients, 65–66; existential
correlates of, 72–74; and illness
networks, 70–71; and patients'
sociological characteristics, 57; and
patterns of transmission from
generation to generation, 69; of
physician and Spiritualist patients
compared, 63, 75, 76, 77, 78; and

wage–labor migration, 71. *See also* Biomedicine; Spiritualist therapeutics
Therapeutic efficacy. *See* Therapeutic outcomes; Therapeutic outcomes of Spiritualist healing
Therapeutic encounter, components of, 7, 157–158
Therapeutic options: biomedical, 44–47; government subsidized, 45–46; gratis, 41–43, 47; nonbiomedical, 42–44, 47; nongratis, 41–46, 47; variety of in the region, 41–47
Therapeutic outcomes: of biomedicine, 117–118; and chronic disease, 119; cultural factors in, 170–172, definition of, 4, 120; differential effects, 137; and doctor-patient relationship, 160–162; influenced by healing techniques, 7, 161–162; holistic approach to, 5, 10; and follow-ups, 111–116; 124–128; measurement of, 4, 120, 200; need for studies of, 4–10; and patient characteristics, 179–180, 198; physiological factors in, 163–165; problems in assessing, 4, 5, 118–119, 120; and psychological factors, 163–165, 166–170; significance of studying, 6, 7; and sociological factors, 162–163; and studies done in the past, 4; subjective criteria of, 119–120; and the therapeutic touch, 165
Therapeutic outcomes of Spiritualist healing: compared with psychotherapy, 180–183; and chronic pain, 197; and first comers and habitual users (nonregulars), 121–128; demographic characteristics of patients with successful, 123, with failed, 6, 137, 193; depended on healing techniques, 161–162; and dependence on participation in temple, 129, 170, 174, 182–183, 185; diminish feelings of "being sick", 172; fail with psychosis, 179–180; holistic approach to, 10, 162–172; limited success with borderlines, 175–179; and limitation of patients, 180; percentage of failures, 139;

percentage of successes, 139; proportion of children successfully treated, 123; social consequences of, 198–199; and Spiritualist adherents (regulars), 128–138; and case vignettes of, 131–138; success of, 6, 193; success with mild psychiatric disorders, 174; symptoms successfully treated (nonregulars) described, 121–122, 140–144
Therapeutic techniques and procedures: of biomedicine 158–160, importance of studying, 82, of Spiritualist healing, 7, 82–89, 161, variation among Spiritualist healers, 89–92. *See also* Spiritualist therapeutic techniques
Therapeutic systems, and other aspects of culture, 9, within a societal context, 198
Thomas, L., 50, 66, 90, 111, 118, 158, 159
Torrey, E., 180
Traditional healers. *See* Nonbiomedical healers
Trance: behavior during rituals, 22, 27; effects on social interaction, 34, 192, on society, 199; healers in, 2, 84, 190; how persons feel after experience of, 73–74, 109; physiological effects of, 7, 164–165, 199; and Spiritualist therapeutic techniques, 7; and rituals, 22. *See also* Spiritualist therapeutic techniques
Traux, Ch., 180
Turner, V., 14, 34, 82, 170, 171, 172, 173, 174, 184
Tursky, B., 166

Uzzell, D., 6, 49

Villoro, L., 17

Wage labor migration and therapeutic choice, 71, 173
Wallace, A., 34, 82, 172, 173, 185
Wallace, R., 164
Weinberg, S., 194
Weisenberg, M., 167
Weissman, M., 70, 179, 181
Werner, R., 161
Western Medicine. *See* Biomedicine
White, K., 158
Whitehurst, C., 66

Willems, E., 10, 25, 31, 32, 34
Willis, W., 167
Wilson, B., 24
Witchcraft: patient suffering from, example of, 179–180; and social conflict, 9, 169; and societal institutions, 19; and Spiritualist beliefs, 26, 59; and Spiritualist healers, 11; and therapeutic choice, 43; traditional Mexican illness attribution, 132
Wolf, E., 18, 31, 33, 182, 188
Wolff, B., 166
Women: characteristics of as heads of temples, 10, 16, 186; effects of industrialization on rural Mexican, 39–40; experience symptoms more than men, 64, 128; and illness, 40; and infant mortality, 40; and patterns of therapeutic choice, 65, 66, 69; physical abuse of and health, 40, 112; and role of mothers, 116; seek treatment more than men, 66, 69; temple and physician's patients compared, 63–64; therapeutic choices of attached and unattached, 69. *See also* Male-female
Women's role and Spiritualist teachings, 91, 186
Waxler, N., 71
Worsley, P., 192

Young, A., 119, 159, 174
Young, J., 60

Zales, M., 164
Zborowski, M., 166
Zea, L., 19
Ziegler, F., 126
Zimmermann, M., 166, 168
Zinberg, N., 164
Zola, I., 166
Zoraida, J., 18